J
A

The Beasts of My Fields

The Beasts of My Fields

by

DAVID CREATON

ST. MARTIN'S PRESS   NEW YORK

Copyright © 1977 by David Creaton
All rights reserved. For information, write:
St. Martin's Press, Inc., 175 Fifth Ave., New York, N.Y. 10010.
Manufactured in the United States of America
Library of Congress Catalog Card Number: 76-62757

Library of Congress Cataloging in Publication Data

Creaton, David.
  The beasts of my fields.

1. Farm life—England.   2. Creaton, David.
3. Farmers—England—Biography.   I. Title.
S522.G7C73   636'.0092'4   [B]   76-62757
ISBN 0-312-07052-7

To My Mother

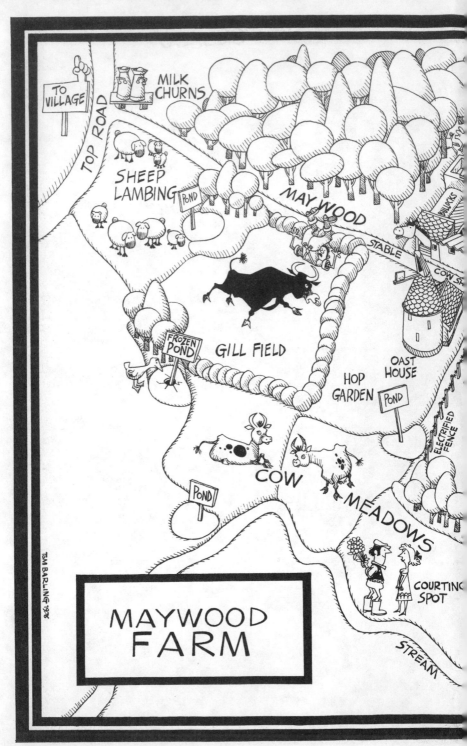

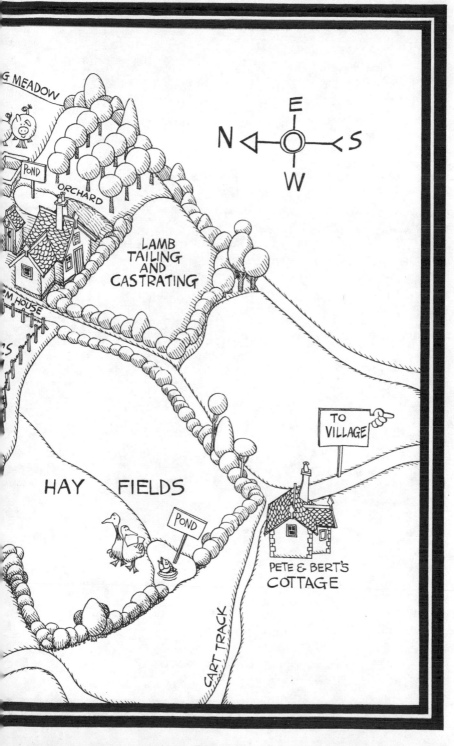

Contents

Autumn

1

SKINNY AND FATSO were two saddle-back sows. They were a gift from my last boss, Paddy Taylor, to start me off on my own farm at Maywood. He selected them from his hundred head herd of pedigree Essex pigs and brought them all the way down to Kent from Staffordshire in a trailer behind his car. He'd been a real friend, and when I said I was going to start farming on my own, he went out of his busy way to help and advise me over Maywood.

I think he was slightly horrified at how primitive it all was when he actually saw my farm. I'm sure he knew I hadn't a hope in hell of making more than a bare living there, particularly when he found out just how little I'd got in the way of capital. That was when he decided to give me the sows. His own farm was large, modern and very productive and he was one of those farmers who have the happy knack of being able to swan round from time to time, turning up at precisely the right place at the right time and never getting his own hands dirty. I don't think he had ever spent much time on a small, slog-it-out-yourself farm before. Neither had I. Perhaps that was why he kept on about admiring my enthusiasm and my willingness for work. He knew better than I how much I'd be needing them.

When Skinny and Fatso arrived they had grand long pedigree names, which were quite suitable for a huge hundred-pig breeding farm like Paddy's. But they were useless for an everyday farm like Maywood. Imagine shouting to a sow across a field when her name is Barton Ladybird Louise.

On a small farm each animal is an individual and is able to develop in its own way without having to follow the crowd. At least

Skinny and Fatso did and they earned their new names from the way their figures developed.

They were both very pregnant when they arrived and were quite content to lounge about in the sties we had prepared for them. They were still used to the artificial life at Paddy's and knew no more of the outside world than a warm straw bed in one corner, another corner to which they strolled to dung and a long trough where food arrived regularly twice a day. With all this and a good scratchy wall to rub against, what more could a pig want?

The pig sties were in the corner of the farmyard and each one had another door leading out to the back, into a small meadow. This meadow was the boundary of the farm on that side and beyond it stretched the May Wood, from which the farm took its name. But as yet Skinny and Fatso knew nothing of the earthy delights of the meadow and the delicious scrunch of the acorns showered from the oak trees into the long grass. First they had to concentrate on giving birth to their litters. Their introduction to the new world outside the sties could come later with their families.

As the days went by until they were due to farrow I spent many an odd moment hanging over each wall in turn, scratching first one back and then the other with the end of a stick. If I went into Fatso's sty she started talking with short, low grunts. When I walked towards her, holding out my hand and calling 'Pig, pig, pig,' in answer, she'd flop down on her belly and wait for me to rub her back. Slowly she'd roll over on to her side, close her eyes and smack her chops with huge delight as I ran my hand to and fro along her budding teats. The skin of her belly was soft and silky after the harsh stubble of her back, and as I massaged the rows of teats I could see the piglets heaving inside her. They seemed to be jockeying for position.

Sometimes Mother came and popped her head over the wall. 'You sure it's all right to be in there with her like that?' she asked. 'Mind she doesn't bite you. Urr! Look at those big teeth.'

'No. Of course not! They love having their tits rubbed.'

'Really, darling, *teats*. Tits are little blue birds.'

'Oh, you're hopeless, Mum. You never hear farm people call them teats. It's cow tits, pig tits as well as tom tits.'

We'd recently moved to Maywood and Mother escaped from the house whenever she got fed up with trying to sort the furniture out. There was far more than the house could comfortably hold and already some of it had been relegated to the oast house. Or sometimes she began to lose patience with the ancient kitchen stove – particularly when the wind was from the east and it had violent fits of billowing, filling the kitchen with black smoke. Then she had to escape for a breath of fresh air. But any excuse was better than none when she was as keen as I to keep an eye on the sows' progress.

Fatso was a glutton for her own comfort and she turned out to be a wretched mother. She gave uninterested birth to six bedraggled piglets, taking not the slightest notice as each one slid out and snuffled loose from its encasing membrane. Of course, she waited until it was dark to have them and she lay back in the comfortable glow of the hurricane lamp, a black, fat mound, which occasionally quivered with a begrudging grunt of welcome as she felt each new arrival clamber over her hind legs, to barge and squeak and scuffle as it laid claim to one of her teats.

I left her to sleep it off with her six piglets warm and dry against her belly. I robbed her of as much straw as I dared so that the litter wouldn't bury themselves in it. That way she would know where they all were when she came to change her position.

By the following morning she had lain on two and killed them. I cursed her roundly as I picked the bodies from the straw, their mouths fixed open in dying gasps. It was a miracle that the remaining four survived until they were agile enough to nip out of the way whenever she plonked herself down, oblivious of everything but her own comfort.

'Never mind,' Mother said, looking sadly at the casualties. Then she smiled. 'Cheer up! Better luck next time.' She stroked one of the dead piglets as though hushing it to sleep. 'I'm sure they didn't suffer.'

Fortunately it was altogether a different story with Skinny. Although I could never get on such intimate terms with her, I'm sure she appreciated a bit of fussing. Yet she never responded like the voluptuous Fatso. Life was a serious business for Skinny. Now she was coming close to her time there was a lot to be done. It was all very nice hanging around having your back scratched, but that didn't get the bed prepared. She would pick up a twist of straw in her mouth and pace around her sty, rump swaying, tail curling and grunting importantly.

Gradually she worried all the straw into a corner, rooting, turning, chewing until she had converted it into a pile of chaff. There was far more than was good for her, so I went in and carried out a couple of armfulls. She was indignant with peevish, high pitched grunts as she cleaned up behind me, rooting and blowing until she had swept up and made the bed again. I felt mean and wished I could explain.

Finally everything was to her liking and she settled herself down with her back firmly against the wall. And she treated me to a delightful running commentary throughout the birth of her twelve piglets.

As each one arrived she called to it with urgent, staccato grunts, her head raised slightly, black ear listening, beady eye a white edged marble revolving. She coaxed it to keep close to her, told it not to wander into the cold sty, urged it through the straw clinging to its wet back, tempted it to snuffle its pink snout against the milk weeping white from her black teats.

While she chatted to each new arrival so she prepared for the next birth. She lowered her head, silent for a moment, straining until it floundered out. In the sudden freedom the youngster shook its head, filled its lungs, clambered to free itself from its slimy coat and trailed its umbilical cord as it wobbled over the obstacles in its path.

Once I had to part the cocoon when a piglet failed to break through. It lay there limp. I picked it up, unwrapped it and blew sharply down its mouth. Suddenly it struggled, sturdy in my hands and I put it with the others to fight and find a teat to its liking.

The last arrival, the runt of the litter, took the wrong turning and wedged itself between Skinny's back and the wall. The more she called it, the harder it tried to scale her back, puzzled at the harsh hairs in its search for kindly teats. I picked it up and lifted it over. It squealed. Immediately Skinny reared up and wanted to know what the devil I was up to. Great grunts jerked out of her in quick succession as she swore at me and her litter tumbled about, feebly blaming each other because they had lost their places.

It was several minutes before she was sure all was well. She subsided and lay back, shuffling more on to her back so that her lower line of teats was accessible and each of her offspring had a place of its own.

She was a marvellous mother. Nearly everything she ate she converted into milk. Gradually even the fat on her back flowed away through her teats and she became gaunt, her backbone a row of notches, her ribs a cage and she had hollows below her hips like sucked-in cheeks. That's why she came to be called Skinny.

But beneath her haggard body she possessed two magnificent rows of teats. Each one was a bulging black bag of milk and they swayed from side to side as she walked, a swinging milk bar, a dangling delight which her large family followed and fought for.

Both she and Fatso soon had the run of the meadow. Just after the litters were born we had some golden days when the October sun shone like a thin echo of summer. They were days when the wood stood still, half gold, half green, caught in the autumn act and now lingering in case it was still summer. The long chestnut leaves were soft gold where they still clung to the slender poles, which rose in clusters from the old boles. The fallen leaves were already a crisp brown covering through which pert grey squirrels darted, searching for the prickly husks and breaking them open to pull out the shiny chestnuts. There were ash and beech in the wood as well, all underwood poles growing check by jowl with the leaves still clinging, the ash pale green and anaemic, the beech rough and going a rubious gold. Rising amongst them all were the oak trees, mostly tall and slender with heads bursting above the crowding underwood, but here and there a green cathedral, ancient, arching and flowing, its rafters the roost for owls and scurrying slopes for squirrels, its precinct a quiet glade holding back the thrusting undergrowth.

During these golden days there was no wind and the morning mist hung over the trees and dripped as it slowly shrank from the sun. It was quiet, still, and the trees seemed to be listening, almost as though they were straining to hear the first distant whisper of an autumn gale. But all they heard was the raucous cackle of the startled pheasant, echoing for only a moment.

But then Skinny and Fatso made their first foray with their families into the meadow. With a sniff and a grunt Fatso was off the moment I opened her door. She waddled into the morning, lowering her head and burying her snout in the wet grass as she went. She stopped and held her head high as she sniffed the dead-leaf tang in the air with growing excitement. This was new. This was the life. And away she went, cavorting and snorting, bundling along with abandon.

Halfway across the meadow she stopped. She was panting, unaccustomed to such exercise and her hot breath was steaming upwards. It was obvious she had quite forgotten her piglets and she started to graze, leaving them snuffling and squeaking in the doorway.

17

Pete and Bert were with me. They were two brothers, aged seventeen and fifteen, and they both sort of came with the farm. Together we drove Fatso's family across to her, clapping our hands, flapping our coats and tweaking their bums to keep them going in the right direction. When they spotted her and ran up to complain around her, she paid scant attention to them and continued to snuffle and tear at the grass.

'Go on, yer great Fatso, give 'em a drink,' Pete urged her.

'Aye,' Bert agreed, in his high pitched voice, "'tis opening time,' and he cackled at his own joke.

But Fatso was busy. The meadow claimed her undivided attention and she only half grunted in protest when Pete playfully kicked her on the backside in parting and called her a mean, fat sod.

Meanwhile Skinny was sharing the new adventure with her large family. Each step into the spreading meadow was a fuss. A snuffle and a bite of grass. A grunt of, 'Isn't this fun?' Another of, 'Mind I don't tread on you!' And she shepherded her litter across the meadow, delighting equally in their company and the soft surprise around her.

There was plenty of work to be done, but we stopped and watched this first excursion into the world beyond the sty. The piglets were too young to appreciate the meadow and soon it was time for one of the frequent feeds. In the early stages it seemed that the pressure of milk determined the frequency with which Skinny would lie back and offer it to her family. But soon they demanded it, nuzzling and shouting at her until they got their own way. They became bored with following her around the meadow. She kept talking to them but they began to wonder why she didn't stop to give them a drink. But she'd reached the fence by the wood and had discovered the acorns in the grass. For a while their savoury scrunch made her oblivious to the demands of her family. So they started to worry at her in earnest, some running under her belly and nipping at her teats, others deliberately barging in front of her and squeaking at her snout. One even poked his wet nose into her long, drooping ear: 'Listen! Listen! Give us a drink.'

Finally she lifted her head. She grunted, looking round at them as she champed through a last glorious mouthful, saliva and masticated acorns dripping from her chops. There was a sudden hush and the piglets stood stock still. They knew they had her attention

18

at last. Then there was pandemonium and a sudde
excited squeals as they milled around.

Skinny lowered herself slowly and carefully on to
teats. The piglets were beside themselves with anticipa
ning first one side and then the other in an urgent guessing
to which way she would roll, ramming their snouts into
When she did go over, the runt of the litter was among those
had guessed wrong. Little Willie we called him. He always seeme
to be in trouble and for a moment his leg was pinned beneath
Skinny's back. He squealed as though he'd been bitten. Immediately Skinny reared up with nervous grunts and he freed himself and hared round the other side to hurl himself into the
line-out.

Now each one had squabbling possession of a teat. And each one
worried, grumbled, shoved and swore in its own effort to persuade
its mother that it was ready. Skinny lay back grunting quietly:
'Are you all ready? Here it comes.'

Suddenly the milk flowed. The writhing line became rigid.
Ears went back, beady eyes half closed, pink tongues were quivering, squelching funnels for black teats, flowing faster than anxious
throats could swallow. Thick milk oozed and dribbled and a line of
sweet scented steam rose and disappeared. One little chap, bigger
than the others (and no wonder), had acquired the sole rights to
two adjoining teats. He played them like a man at a mouth-organ,
darting from one to the other in one glorious guzzle. His eyes were
wide, rolling white from side to side, anxious of the opposition,
afraid to believe his luck could last.

The milk stopped flowing as suddenly as it began. The tense
bodies relaxed, eyes closed and pink snouts nudged lazily against
the belly now sticky with spilt milk. Soon there was a heaving
tumble which grumbled and farted as it buried itself in slumber.

Skinny remembered the acorns. With a single movement she
reared herself up and walked off, leaving her family writhing and
swearing as they tried to cadge warmth from each other in the
wet grass. Sleep just wouldn't come. One by one they extricated
themselves and toddled off, stretching, curling their tails into tight
coils, determined to find out what was so marvellous about acorns.

A few days later all the piglets had learnt to forage. Their enthusiasm, and the lengths to which they would go to enjoy life, were
more than we had bargained for.

y between the meadow and the wood was but a
ge, all straggly and drawn up in pitiful competition
ood, a line of ragamuffins beside ranks of busbied
. As it was no match for foraging sows, we had rein-
with square-mesh pig netting, fastened to stout chestnut
driven into the hedge.
hat'll keep 'em,' Pete kept repeating as he drove the spiles into
ground.

'Aye, that'll keep 'em,' Bert repeated as he came along behind, fixing the netting with staples as I held it against the spiles. But chestnut spiles are hard and staples are wobbly, so every now and then Bert's rejoinder was varied to: 'That'll keep 'em, bugger 'em,' when he hit his thumb instead of the staple. Bert always managed to land himself with the lightest job and was at pains to make it out to be tough going, just in case either Pete or I were thinking of suggesting a change round. He was a short boy for his age, fair as a ferret and he'd inherited his father's cunning as well as his stature.

We were proud of the fence when we had finished it. It was tight, shining and formidable.

'That'll keep 'em,' Pete repeated, yet again. 'Them won't go through that in a hurry.' He laughed. 'Us be first-class fencers, yer know.' He was proud. He had never put up a fence before in his life. Pete was full of open laughter and was as different from his brother as was their father from their mother. Bert had the furtive look of old Jack, the bunched up wisp of a father, who scrounged a sort of a living from a few animals on a few acres at the top of the hill, and from this and that, and from a bit of poaching—nobody could be completely sure.

But Pete was dark haired, swarthy, full lipped and with a large-toothed, red-cheeked smile. He was jolly, like buxom Mildred, his mother, who was always busy, always singing. Whereas Bert had grey eyes, peering from beneath the brim of an over-large cap, Pete's eyes were dark brown and there was always a hank of black hair sprouting from the rim of his greasy beret. His beret was part of him. It became so greasy that cows' hairs and hay seeds embedded themselves in it, and so perfectly impregnated was it that raindrops slid off it as though it was duck feathers. He was never without it. He worked in it. He went courting in it. He went to the pub in it. I was beginning to think he slept in it until, one morning, he appeared in the cowshed with a wide, self-conscious grin and a new beret. It was untrained, virgin and puffed up like a soufflé on his head.

Both Skinny and Fatso made a careful inspection of our new fence. For the first few days they respected it. But the piglets soon found they could hop through the squares in the netting like poodles through a hoop. We'd not thought of this and presumed they would stay with their mothers. But now they had got the hang of foraging, they nipped through into the wood where acorns lay scattered like handfuls of sweets. And when they tired of eating, they soon discovered that a game of tag was much more fun through rustling leaves than through wet grass. They crouched in the leaves, ears back, eyes alert, still as sentries. One moved and away they all went, 'uff, uff, uff, uff', snorting, chasing, squealing, in and out and around the trees.

The two families had joined forces and for a day or so Skinny and Fatso were content to graze and forage on their own in the meadow. But gradually the games in the wood became more adventurous and the piglets roamed farther, returning less often for refreshment at the milk bars.

Fatso was indifferent. While her lot were in the wood, so much the better. They weren't bothering her. She could stretch out in the sun with nice cool grass against her hot belly. She could flick her ears, smack her chops and remember the acorns she had just eaten.

Skinny took a different view. She decided that something should be done about straying offspring and she began to patrol the fence, ordering them to return. She couldn't see them but she could still hear them. Her grunts became more impatient and her teats uncomfortable. Surely they were hungry?

One day fifteen-year-old Bert was watching from the door of the cowshed. We were busy laying concrete, trying to turn an old hovel of dung-filled cobbles and draughty walls into a parlour fit for the cows I was going to buy. From where Bert stood he could see across the yard and into the meadow. He paused, shovel over his shoulder, to give us a running commentary while we worked at tamping the wet concrete with a heavy board.

'Her ain't arf kickin' up a racket.' We could hear her grunts above the chugging of the concrete mixer.

'Now her's tryin' the fence!' He had taken a pace forward and was half out of the door.

Pete stopped pulling his end of the board. 'Come on here, Bert, fer Chrissake,' he grumbled. 'Don't think you'm going ter get out of mixin' the next barrow load. Get shovellin'. We ain't going ter do it all.'

'But ol' Skinny keeps tryin' the fence.'

'Sod her. That fence'll keep 'er. You come on 'ere and get cracking.' Pete had some courting lined up for that evening and was anxious to get off on time.

Bert banged his shovel on the floor and his voice rose to an excited squeak. 'Buggered if 'er ain't gettin' out! Her's rootin' the fence right up. Now 'er's gettin' *under* it.'

So began the first of many a chase after Skinny. Leaving a crumpled hole in our new fence she went huffling off into the wood like an express train. She was soon lost to view. Bert went scurrying after her, an eager volunteer, delighted that we should finish the work without him.

We could hear him still cursing and scrunching about in the wood when we finished and Pete said goodnight. I could manage with Bert, couldn't I? Pete was red faced, blustering, anxious that nothing should delay him from getting at the girl. I assured him that all would be well and told him to mind what he got up to. His smile as he turned to go made his intentions quite obvious.

I went off to the wood to find Bert. Now you can drive a cow and calf, or a ewe and lambs, and usually they'll go quietly in the general direction in which you are aiming. But a sow and her litter are quite another matter. Piglets always have a hundred and one things to explore. They are apt to dive back between your legs, oblivious of abuse or a raised stick as they go snorting off in the opposite direction. And where they go, Mother goes too, bowling past you with a squeal, partly because she knows you're going to hit her and partly to let you know she's going anyway. When she's out of range she gives a couple of victorious grunts, which often sound like 'ha! ha!', and she veers to one side in case you've thrown your stick after her.

Fatso had found the hole in the fence and had gone to join the fun. By the time I reached the wood it was almost dark in there, but from the scurrying, squeaking and grunting it was evident that a great game was in progress.

'Where are you, Bert?'

'Yere I be.' His voice was angry, frustrated.

When I found him he was leaning against a tree and near to tears. 'Them buggers won't go. Every time I gets near the fence with 'em, one or t'other darts back and then 'em all goes. T'aint fair.' He hit the ground with his stick.

I laughed at him. 'You were in too big a hurry to leave the cowshed. If you'd thought to bring a bucket with you, you could've rattled it and they'd follow you out.' I gave him the bucket I was carrying. 'There you are. Lead the way and call them. I'll come behind.'

Just then Skinny decided to give her family a half-time drink. As she rolled over there was an unusual amount of squabbling and she refused to let her milk flow. Which made matters even worse. There was a real fight going on, not just the usual tussle for a teat. I went closer and in the half light I could see the trouble. Fatso's four were trying to get a look in. They'd been around when Skinny went down and evidently thought it a better idea to try and steal a quick slurp from her, rather than go to all the trouble of flooring Fatso. Anyway she was nowhere to be seen. She must have heard the commotion but she couldn't care less that her offspring were being torn to pieces by Skinny's mob. And now all thoughts of a feed had vanished for a time as tempers flared, ears got nipped and squeals echoed through the wood as the usurpers were driven off.

The victors returned to pummel Skinny and soon the milk came. The others trotted off, tails straight, grumbling and swearing as they searched for Fatso.

It took but a single rattle of the bucket to flush her out. She came crashing through the trees, agog, demanding, and hovered round Bert and the bucket, half squealing, half grunting, blaming him that tea was late today. Skinny cut short her feeding and soon they were all crashing and squealing after Bert, taken in by the hollow rattle of an empty bucket.

During the next few weeks 'Skinny's out!' became an oft repeated cry from us until the litters were ready to be weaned and sent to market. When any of us came in sight of the pig meadow during the course of the day's work, we would cast an anxious eye to see that all was well. It seldom was and the shout of 'Skinny's out!' would go echoing across the yard.

In the end we gave up and let her roam at will. The more we mended the fence, the more she took it as a challenge to her ingenuity to find a way out. She broke out for the sheer hell of it, often leaving her litter fast asleep in a heap in the meadow.

Sometimes she just fancied a walk and I'd meet her swinging

down the lane, with her family like ripples washing into the hedge-rows behind her.

Or, if the smells from the kitchen excited her palate, she would come face to face with Mother in the backyard and for a moment each of them would freeze.

'Go on, old thing, off you go,' Mother would say, hopefully, unconsciously banging a hand to her tummy in a habit which always betrayed anxiety.

At which Skinny would grunt kindly and take a step forward because the soft voice and the movement seemed more like an offer of food than a rebuke.

'Go on, I mean it now. Shoo! Shoo! Take your babies with you.' But by then the piglets would be advancing on a wide front, enticed by the tempting smells from the kitchen and Skinny's encouragement. So Mother was forced to clap her hands to produce some sort of order. Which only made them scurry in all directions and start Skinny swearing and advancing threateningly while Mother retreated.

Once I happened to come by to her rescue. '*Do* you think you could do something more to keep the pigs in, darling?' she asked, with her bright smile. 'They *are* dear little things but they're getting so adventurous. Soon I'm sure they'll be right in the kitchen. I don't *mind* shooing them away, but I'm really rather frightened when Skinny shouts and threatens to charge me.'

'Oh, that old sod won't hurt you.' I was impatient. 'Shout back at her. Throw something at her. Kick her up the arse.'

'Oh dear!' She sighed and looked forlorn. 'I do wish you wouldn't swear so.'

'She's enough to make a bishop swear. She's always getting out. I'm fed up with trying to keep her in the meadow.'

The bright smile returned. 'If at first you don't succeed, try, try, try again.'

I scoffed. 'The daft Victorian who first mouthed those immortal words had obviously never had sows and piglets to contend with.' And I stormed off after Skinny as she beat a smart retreat at the sound of my raised voice.

But I was often apt to forget how the regular sounds and smells of the farm made up the day for the various animals. To us, with our complicated minds, our worries and our hurry, these sounds and smells produced no pattern and passed unnoticed as a background. But not for Skinny. She savoured every moment of the day. To her each sound had a meaning and her flopping ears picked up each one in turn. Sometimes I saw her stand quite still and lift her head to listen, as though an alien note had struck a discord in the lilt of the day. To her each smell heralded happy thoughts. Each held the possibility of grub and demanded investigation. So she heard when a pan clattered in the kitchen and her long snout, with its blunt tip glistening pink and quivering around black nostrils, fastened on the broad smell of dinner cooking. So it was time to investigate. A couple of grunts and she was off with her swinging gait while her litter straggled, snorted and trotted to keep up with her. And always Little Willie came last, wheezing as he walked.

Sometimes Skinny's wanderings became too much of a good thing and we had to shut her up in her sty. It was all very well when she just browsed round the farmyard, rooting round the midden and getting plastered with dung, or sniffing the corn in the food store and wishing she could think how to get in there, or strolling across to the pond for a noisy drink before flopping down on the bank to feed her clamouring brood. Nor did I really mind when she established a bridgehead which gave her access into the orchard.

A stout spile fence ran from the backyard of the farmhouse across to the pond and ended up buried in the reeds which grew at the water's edge. It was proof against any animal which harboured thoughts of wandering down from the farmyard and into the orchard. On several occasions I'd noticed Skinny wedge her snout between the spiles and give an exploratory shove, but she never really tried because she couldn't get her snout under any-thing to lift upwards. So she lay on the side of the pond gazing at the fence while she fed her family. She could see the lush grass across the water and she could smell the heady tang of ripe apples. The fence loomed large and forbidding. It was a challenge. She became obsessed with the desire to go scrumping on the windfalls lying red and tempting under the trees.

In the end she made it. She wallowed in the reeds and worried at the spiles until she'd loosened one enough to squeeze through. Yet she could never get back the same way. When we called her, rattling a bucket and going towards her sty, she'd come charging across the orchard and go berserk, squealing up and down the fence. She made out it was our fault she couldn't get back. We had to let her out through the gate.

But when she started ranging out of sight of the farmyard we had to be firm with her. Time and again we'd go searching for her. We'd come dragging back with her from some far off hedgerow, chivvying, scolding, swearing, threatening to imprison her in her sty for good and all, but always relenting when she flopped down near home to feed her fagged-out piglets.

Finally I was shamed into shutting her up for a few days. It happened after old Jack, Pete and Bert's father, came shambling down the lane, driving her in front of him. He was looking none too pleased. His hands were deep in the pockets of his open raincoat and he was flapping his arms like an animated scarecrow, which struck terror into the piglets and proved to be a most effective way of driving them. His cap was resting firmly on his large ears, his jowls bristled with grey stubble and a revolting gurgling came from his pipe.

'T'aint right fer a sow ter be roamin',' he greeted me.

'What's up then, Jack?' As if I didn't know.

He took his pipe from his mouth and shook it, wiping the stem on his corduroy trousers. They were too big for him, trailing over his boots. Usually he hitched them up with a piece of string tied below each knee, but today only the marks showed where the string had bitten into the cord. He must have come out in a hurry. This was the first time I'd seen him surface before noon. He returned his pipe to his slack mouth and his bottom lip pouted and glistened. His face was grey and crinkled and two deep crevices ran like black railway lines from either side of his nose and down to his chin.

He pinched the dewdrop from the end of his nose, put his hands behind his back beneath his raincoat and drew himself up to his full five and a half feet. 'This yere sow, that's what's up. I see'd her through me window, in me garden she were, rootin' up me 'taters'.

I had to turn away and look at Skinny to hide my smile. I could imagine her glee at discovering Jack's potatoes, burying her snout in the soft earth and tossing it to one side for a joyful, guzzling share out of the white surprise.

'Good job Bob spotted 'er and barked,' he went on, 'else 'er would've cleared the lot the rate 'er was going.'

Bob, his lurcher dog, was skulking some yards back up the lane. He was behaving very warily, even for him. Usually he was never more than a few feet from Jack's heels, his ears back, his pink tongue lolling from his mouth and syphoning saliva in steady drips on to the ground. His long curling tail was perpetually between his legs and only the tip moved hesitantly to and fro as he agreed with

26

whatever Jack happened to be saying. And Jack relied on Bob's agreement, using him as a dumb back-up to prove the truth of a tale. 'Old Bob see it happen, too,' he'd say and Bob would agree, rolling his eyes, withdrawing his tongue for a moment to polish his yellow fangs and gently moving the tip of his tail. Pete often said he didn't know who was the bigger liar, his father or the dog.

Now Bob was sitting on his haunches back up the lane. He was pretending not to notice and denying all knowledge of a sow and her litter. He was facing the hedge so that he was half turned away from us, but the whites of his eyes kept shining and his ears twitched as he followed each and every movement Skinny made.

Jack noticed that he was not at heel, ready to confirm that Skinny had been stealing potatoes. 'Bob! Come 'ere, will yer!' he commanded in a low, growling voice that ended in a gurgle from his pipe.

There was no immediate response from Bob. While we had been talking Skinny had found something interesting along the verge and had worked her way back so that she was between Jack and his dog. Bob sat tight. His head was turned away as though he didn't want to know, but one eye was rolling, following Skinny's progress.

'Bob!' Jack repeated, surprised and annoyed at this unaccustomed disobedience.

Bob growled and shifted uncomfortably. Skinny lifted her head and stared at him as he got to his feet. She grunted, daring him to move and it was obvious they'd already had one confrontation. Bob was not anxious for another. The sheepdog in him urged him to round on the sow and drive her along and he felt compelled to obey Jack's call to heel. But to face a sow at bay twice in one morning was asking too much. His ears went even flatter, his tail hugged his bum and he slunk off up the lane pretending not to hear the names Jack called him. When he considered he was well out of range he turned and sat in the middle of the lane, bolt upright and inquisitive as he watched us negotiate Skinny and her mob into the yard.

We shut them in the sty and for a while we lolled over the wall and watched as the litter browbeat Skinny into a feed.

'Her've done they pigs well,' Jack conceded at last.

'Yes, not bad for a first litter.'

'Her's a good milker. Milked right orf 'er back, 'er has.' He removed his pipe and squirted saliva into the sty. Skinny rolled over and sat firmly on her teats. The piglets were getting big and boisterous now. Enough was enough. She had to be firm.

'Ain't you cut 'em yet?' Jack wanted to know.

'We'll do 'em this week, I was only telling the boys yesterday we'll soon have to castrate the pigs.' I laughed. 'They didn't seem too keen on helping. Afraid of what the sows might do.'

'They'll help,' Jack said, sternly. 'Pete's helped I cut pigs afore now. He knows how ter hold 'em. Sows'll be orlright once they be shut up.'

Just then Bob slunk into the yard, his belly close to the ground, his ears back, his eyes furtive. He sidled up to Jack and sat gingerly on his haunches behind him. Jack appeared not to notice. He went on gazing at the pigs, his arms resting on the wall. But presently he dropped one hand behind him and his fingers closed round Bob's eager nose.

I turned to go. There was work to be done and I felt Jack would be quite happy to hang over the wall chatting for the rest of the morning. I was obliged to him for bringing the pigs back. I was sorry they'd had first dig at his spuds. When he made no move to go I wondered whether he was expecting some recompense and if I ought to make an offer. So I wondered aloud if it was too early for a glass of cider.

He straightened up and put his hands behind his back under his raincoat. 'Aye, p'raps 'tis.' He turned to move away. 'But I could allus take some home in a bottle to have with me dinner.'

2

NONE OF MY immediate ancestors was a farmer. But my Father was a country parson in Kent, so I was within smelling range of cow dung almost from birth. He'd been a bachelor most of his life. He had waited until he was fifty-two before getting married and then wasted no more time; he sired five children before he was sixty. We were three boys and two girls and I was the next to youngest. As Father's increasingly boisterous family surged home for the holidays and swamped the quiet vicarage, he seemed forever shut out of harm's way in his study, or escaping with swinging walking stick on visits to his parishioners. Only at meal times did he appear at the head of the table, sternly trying to quell our squabbling and set us along the path to righteousness. And on Sundays, twice every Sunday, he was the tall white figure washing the sins from his congregation with words that went over our heads while, doubtless, he offered up silent prayers that the pew containing his wife and five children would not erupt before he was safely back in the vestry.

So our upbringing was largely left to our exuberant Mother who, after God and the Mothers' Union, lived only for our homecoming. She was twenty years younger than Father and she laughed with us, and sighed at us, through the mad days of the holidays. She tried to grasp and come to terms with the gusts of new words and new thinking that we brought home from our schools, and which must have blown sacrilegious blasts at a great deal of what she held dear.

But Father died when I was eleven and we lost our rent-free tied home. Mother came down the stairs from his death bed to where we all waited, sad and silent for once in a darkened room. 'Whatever *am* I going to do?' she asked as she sank into a chair and covered her face with her hands.

But dear old God was expected to provide and He certainly did His best. Mother found a rambling old farmhouse near Canterbury, Kent, in south-east England. It was called Twitham and I think it cost a ridiculous thirty pounds a year. But that was during the hungry Thirties and was probably as much as she could afford. At eleven you don't worry where the money comes from – except the sixpence a week pocket money, for which we were expected to make our beds and to take quarrelling turns with the washing up. It's still a mystery to me how she did manage *and* pay the school fees – although, admittedly, our schools had been carefully chosen by Father because of the special terms they offered to sons and daughters of clergy. Like *The Times* – he used to be able to buy that for a penny instead of tuppence.

Twitham farmhouse was a joy to come home to. Before Father died Mother had learnt to drive an old Morris Oxford, a luxury she considered it essential to hang on to because Twitham was such miles from anywhere. She drove it with determination and a crashing of gears, urging it up the steeper hills by jerking herself forwards and backwards over the steering wheel, crying, 'Come on, old lady, come on, old lady', while we all thronged round instructing her to 'Change down! Change down!', something she was terrified of doing because of the grinding battle to get into second.

We had triumphant journeys home from school in the old Morris, hanging from the windows, singing, arguing, assuring brother Donald he couldn't really feel sick and urging Mother not to slow down for the swinging, uphill turn through the narrow gate, and the bumpy ride across the field that separated the house from the road. We swept under a tall ewe arch to the front door and there lay the huge garden, with fruit trees and brambles and overgrown roses. And there was a fish pond with a fountain that worked – if you waded into the middle and turned on the big brass tap below the stone centrepiece. You always got drenched before you could get out of range. But it was fun for early morning dips in summer, and for catching visitors lounging in their deckchairs because it spread well beyond the bounds of the pond when turned full on.

There was even a tennis court, with posts firmly in place and a net mouldering in a shed. This delighted sister Ruth, then sixteen and in love with lacrosse and tennis, depending on the season.

Weaving her strange netted lacrosse stick above her head, she shied a hard white ball with unerring accuracy at innocent apple trees. It was Mother who toiled as much as any of us to keep the court in trim, especially before the summer holidays, attacking it with the mower and then spending long hours with the roller, trundling quietly to and fro while she practised aloud the talks she gave as a visiting speaker to Mothers' Unions far and wide.

For me the best thing about Twitham was the sprawling farmyard beyond the back door. It was not ours, but it was a new world that I loved at once. In winter I'd spend hours round the strawed yards full of blowing bullocks, or in the barns where heaving carthorses dumped tumbling loads of mangel wurzels. I'd help throw them into the root cutter and shovel away the shining slithers and mix them with great heaps of chaff. And on wet days the sheds and barns were full of farm men who smiled and spat and seemed happy – only sometimes I thought they were laughing at me when I couldn't understand their dialect.

During the spring holidays there were sheep pens and lambs and an old shepherd called Mr Terry. He told me he was a relative of Leslie Ames, the cricketer. So I hung on his every word as he worked among the sheep, telling me of the early days in the life of the great Kent and England wicket-keeper, who was my idol. Terry told me about when the young Ames was first picked for Kent: '"Now then, young Les," I says ti 'im, "don't ye get swelled 'eaded." And 'ee never has.' So old Terry became my friend and I always sought him out whenever I went across the farm. He was a loner, and I liked that because I could never feel at ease among the gang of farm men. He told me about farm work and let me help him and made me pick up and bury a dead lamb because he sensed I was afraid of it. Besides knowing the sheep and Les Ames, he was a fount of knowledge about everything on the farm, from cows and pigs to turnips and golden corn; from the intricacies of a reaper binder to the complicated lives of stallions and mares and what made horses fart.

So I reckoned I'd got nearer to farming than any of my ancestors. At any rate none of them were farmers. They seemed to be sensible men and sensible men don't farm. It's the romantics who do, and those who can't help it because they're born into it. Sensible men work from nine until five and live in a warm house close to all amenities. They don't get wet through, or feel the frost grip their fingers, or work in the sun with sweat in their eyes, or lie awake listening to the storm. Farmers are made fools of by Governments and Nature. They moan at the weather, groan at the prices, and grumble at the middle man's profits while thinking up new ways to quieten the bank manager. Yet they never believe there is any other worthwhile life. Sensible men can't understand this, save those who thrill to the sight of new grass in spring, an unlicked lamb, or a cow warm in a bed of straw in winter.

If it had not been for a long and tiresome illness in my teens perhaps I'd never have gone farming. But doctors had nodded wisely and declared I should have to lead an outdoor life from then on. We'd moved from Twitham by then, much to my grief. But John, the eldest, had launched himself on a career in the City and had persuaded Mother that London was where it was all happening. So we moved and rented a large Victorian semi in Dulwich. And the following year I had a sudden operation for a twisted gut, and had to spend the best part of the next year convalescing because they'd discovered some TB glands in my belly. I didn't feel ill, but bed and feeding you up was the cure in those days, together with a weekly prodding from the doctor and the laconic: 'Keep drinking the iodine three times a day, there's a good chap.'

I returned to school for my final year, a year behind my peers and all rather pointless. And from there I went straight into farming, finding a job for myself as a shepherd's mate in Worcestershire, and spending the next five years in hard labour on three different farms, learning skills and secrets from men to whom they came as a birthright.

After that it was really Mother's idea that I started to farm on my own when I did. I'm sure, secretly, she was rather horrified at the strange change that five years of close association with sons of the soil, and some daughters, had wrought in me. I was her little Dave. Frail from birth. Even at the age of five I'd knocked feebly on death's door suffering from double pneumonia and she'd devoted long days and nights to me, kneeling at my bedside in a little room in Maidstone hospital, tears on her cheeks as she prayed aloud for my recovery, while she peeled and pipped grapes because that was all I'd eat. The tough and tiring years on the farms changed the 'delicate' boy. I picked up the dialects of Worcestershire, Wiltshire and Staffordshire and took great delight in drawling them out in earthy asides on my fleeting and infrequent visits home. I'm convinced Mother had visions of my sinking permanently beyond salvation into the life of a stupid yokel.

So one day, she said: 'You seem suited to farming. Don't you think it's time you started thinking about having a farm of your own?' She was slim, wiry, with unruly white hair which she spiked into some sort of order with three curved combs. She was always terribly healthy, with bright red cheeks and a cold nose, which she had a habit of screwing up and blowing down when thinking hard. I looked at her in surprise. 'I don't know. Never really thought about it.' I had been completely and happily involved in my work – even more so because it was also war work. I had to fling my whole self into it because I was meant to be unfit for the army and felt guilty about it. And the harder I worked, the more I enjoyed it. I worked all day and every day, overtime and Sundays. And when it was too dark to work I drank and talked farming in the pub. Or cavorted at the weekly village dance and dallied with girls on the way home. Hard work, drink, love and deep sleep – there was never time nor inclination to ponder on where it was all leading and what I'd do after the war.

'You *should* think about it,' Mother insisted.

'She's right, you know.' Donald had joined us. Now he was the star of the family, the brainy one, the all-rounder. He'd got a First at Cambridge, he was a double Blue, and now he was a lieutenant in armoured cars and on leave after the first assaults following D-Day. He was going into the Church after the war and he and Mother were very close in that particular way. They involved themselves in deep religious discussions whenever he was at home, or exchanged long letters spattered with texts. He had come home on leave the day before and I had popped home for the weekend to see him. 'Farm life seems to suit you, old bean,' he went on. 'You're getting quite knowledgeable behind your caustic country comments. You should consider making a career of farming.'

'Perhaps,' I said. 'I suppose I could try for a job as a farm manager next. But I really need a degree for that. At least a diploma.'

'Then work for one,' Donald replied. 'You've got the brain.'

'Oh, sod the swotting,' I laughed, and he looked peeved at my language.

'It'd be fun to have a little farm,' Mother said, quickly. 'Lovely to live in the country again after stuffy old London. How I hate these hard pavements after dear old Twitham.' She smiled with a far-away look, and no more was said then.

But a few weeks later the telegram arrived. Donald had been

killed in action. Why did it always seem to be the brightest stars that were snuffed out?

It appeared as though Mother's faith had been crushed. The blow had fallen. She walked the house in a mist of tears. I heard her trying to work in other rooms and suddenly she'd cry out to God for her son. For two terrible days and nights I overheard her fierce prayers. 'Why, God? Why? Why have you taken away my son?' She seemed to be straying on the verge of accusing Him of forsaking her. For the first and only time in my life I was unable to reach her. I was insignificant. I was shut out, a stranger.

But slowly a tired smile returned and she threw back her head. She shouldered her Cross again, but it was heavier now.

I wanted so much to lighten it. 'Would you like to make a break from Dulwich? If I can find a farm, shall we go and live there?'

'Yes, let's.' She smiled. 'Donald said it'd be a good idea, didn't he? I'm sure it's the right thing to do.'

A few months afterwards I found Maywood. It was a sixty-five acre farm in a valley, on the edge of the Weald of Kent, and I managed to persuade the Agricultural Mortgage Corporation and the bank to lend me enough money to buy it.

Mother was then sixty and she left her warm and lively home. We moved together to Maywood, into an old farmhouse, two miles from anywhere and with a single cold tap in the kitchen, paraffin lamps and an outside earth privy.

And for company we had the two black and white sows, Skinny and Fatso.

3

When I learnt to castrate a pig my tutor was an old and experienced pigman on Paddy Taylor's farm. It had all been very straightforward in the security of the purpose-built pig house. It was just a case of opening a door, separating a litter from its dam by the judicious use of a large board and driving them down a narrow passage into another pen on their own. Once there we used to work our way through the litter, catching the males and castrating them, and their squeals were a remote echo, which evoked little more than an occasional grunt of concern from the dam. And when her litter returned to her she seemed unconcerned as she lay back to offer them a drink and we moved on to the next one. We could work steadily through half a dozen litters in the course of a morning without really trying.

I wish it had been as easy at Maywood. But we only had two pig sties and they had to double as castrating parlours as well. I could tell the boys weren't all that keen on the idea right from the start. It wouldn't have been so bad with only Fatso to contend with. I don't suppose she would have raised much objection were we to have cut her piglets' throats right beside her. But we all had a very healthy respect for Skinny's maternal instinct and would have liked a more secure place to operate on her offspring.

'But once we're in the pig sty with the litter we'll be okay,' I assured them. 'Skinny can stop outside in the meadow. She'll kick up a fuss I dare say, but that's all.'

Pete laughed. 'That's what you think. Her'll break in, see if 'er don't. You've only got ter tweek one of they little bums, an' if 'e squeals 'er's round on yer like a bloody tiger.'

'I ain't going in there when you cut 'em,' Bert declared, 'not nohow, I ain't.'

'Course you are!' I told him. 'You're both making a fuss about nothing.'

They thought about this for a while. Then Bert said, 'Tell yer what. Put 'er in the orchard. 'Er can't get out of there. Put 'er in the orchard, I say, and 'er won't bother with 'er litter. Not with some grub out there and all.'

It seemed a good idea and we set about the task of parting Skinny from her family. A rattling bucket soon brought them all careering across the meadow and into the sty. The piglets were already used to going into a creep feed at one end of the small yard attached to the sty, and they dived between the bars to their own food leaving Skinny at the long trough. We slipped a sheet of corrugated iron across the bars so that they were trapped as they guzzled away at their food.

Skinny soon finished and looked around for more.

'Off you go,' I called to Bert, 'rattle your bucket and lead her over to the orchard.'

The sow cocked her head and listened to the rattle in the meadow. For a moment she was torn between leaving her family and the possibility of more corn. She wavered, swinging her head towards the corrugated iron and then taking a step or two in the direction of the door. She couldn't resist the rattle and soon she was following Bert at a brisk trot, repeatedly calling on him to stand and deliver. By the time he had her through the gate into the orchard she was dribbling with excitement. And when he scattered the corn meal on the grass she'd forgotten all about her litter as she searched for every last crumb among the roots of the grass. Bert had reckoned it would take her longer to eat if he made her forage for the corn.

Now we were ready and the bottle of disinfectant and the sharp knife were at hand on the top of the wall.

Pete dived his hand behind the corrugated iron and caught the first male pig by the hind leg. He squealed with alarm as he lifted him up and grabbed to hold him by all four legs. He held him up against his chest so that his backside was thrust out towards me and his testicles were two little lumps just visible under the black skin. The pig had gone quiet now and was fixing me with a blinkless stare from between Pete's arms.

I dribbled some disinfectant over him, squeezed behind the first testicle so that it bulged up under the skin and I could make a quick incision. The testicle popped out, white and shining as I worked my fingers behind it and pulled so that it came away on a long cord like lengthening elastic. Finally it ruptured and I tossed the testicle over the wall into the yard, flicking my fingers to free it when the cord persisted in clinging to them. The pig appeared to feel nothing. With his head pressed firmly towards his chest as Pete held him, he continued to stare at me, watching carefully as I relieved him of his second ball.

I poured some disinfectant over the holes I'd made and Pete put him down. He gave a couple of grunts and scurried off into the sty, huffing about as he searched for his mother and his mates.

'That's one,' Pete said. He turned to grab for the next.

'Her's still eating,' Bert informed us. He was acting as look-out, straining on tip-toe to see across the pond and into the orchard. 'Her never heard that 'un squeal at all. Told you so! Told you the orchard were the best place fer 'er, didn't I?'

The next pig squealed as Pete lifted it up.

'Her 'eard that!' Bert called, excitedly. 'Her's lookin'. Her's comin'! Her's comin'!'

'Hold the bugger tight and he'll stop squealing,' I told Pete. 'Once you've got him against your chest he'll leave off hollaring.'

Pete tightened his grip and the noise stopped. As I set to work again Bert kept us informed of Skinny's movements.

'Gorne back now, 'er has. Good job I scattered that corn in the grass. Take 'er a long time to find it all, that it will. Greedy ol' bugger.'

There were seven pigs to do in Skinny's litter and we were getting on famously. Six were already snuffling about in the sty, comparing notes about their ordeal and asking each other what had become of Mum. Pete had got the knack of grabbing a pig quickly, gathering its legs and ramming it back against his chest so that he virtually throttled its squeal. And each time Bert reported on Skinny's behaviour with graphic descriptions of her reactions to the squealing. Twice his voice had risen to a scream as he had her on the point of bursting through the fence, and when the squealing stopped his voice lowered, almost with disappointment, as he told us that she had returned to search for corn.

The last pig that Peter grabbed was Little Willie. Being smaller than the rest he swung him up with nonchalance and gathered him to his bosom. But because he was the runt of the litter, Little Willie was used to having to fight every inch of the way. He squealed with gusto, only pausing for a second to nip Pete on the finger.

'You little sod!' Pete cried, 'you cheeky little bugger! Get back there.' He grappled to gather the legs together, but Willie's quick nip had given him a psychological advantage. Now Pete was treating him gingerly. The squeals were unending and ear-piercing as Pete tossed him around like a hot potato and Little Willie lashed out and wriggled to get free.

'Skinny's coming!' Bert squeaked, 'her's in the pond, buggered if 'er ain't found a way through. Her's coming! Coming!'

'Grab his bloody foot, for Chrissake,' I yelled to Pete. 'Hold the little sod, can't you? Stop his row.'

'I'm tryin', ain't I? 'Tis like trying ter hold a bloody cat.'

'Her's in the pond! Her's hollarin' like hell!' Bert was scrambling on to the wall.

'Come here!' I rounded on Pete again. 'Let me help you. Here, grab hold of those legs. That's it. Now told him tight. You great baby, fancy being afraid to hold a little pig.' I turned to the wall for the disinfectant. Willie was still screaming.

'I ain't afraid of 'im. Little sod bit me.'

'Shut him up, can't you? Can't hear myself think.'

'He won't shut up. Can't yer see I've got 'im tight?'

'Skinny's outside now,' Bert shouted down to us. 'Her's runnin' up and down outside the door. Her'll be through in a tick, that 'er will.'

At last Little Willie stopped squealing. He was breathing rapidly, wheezing in the way that he did as I fumbled to find his little balls. They were so small they kept slipping back into the folds of skin below his rectum. The castrated pigs had heard Skinny outside and were beginning to shout their troubles to her through the gap at the bottom of the door. She was grunting and blowing and pushing her snout to get at them, bashing her huge teeth against the wood, two hundred and fifty pounds of furious mother hurling herself to the rescue of her young.

'Her'll be in in a minute! That door ain't going ter hold 'er!' Bert was all prepared to jump for safety.

'Come *on*,' Pete urged me. 'What's up with yer? That bloody sow'll be here in a sec. And I ain't stoppin' here then, buggered if I am.'

'Hold him! Hold him! He's got such tiny little balls they keep slipping back every time he moves.'

I had the first one in my fingers again and cut quickly at the skin above. When it popped out I grabbed it and flicked it away and felt for the second one. The piglets were kicking up a great commotion now and the door was shaking as they attacked it from one side and Skinny from the other. I knew it couldn't be long before she broke through.

'Her's biting at the door now,' Bert yelled. 'Now 'er's got 'er snout under. 'Er's lifting it! 'Er'll be through in a minute.'

I was working feverishly at Little Willie and at last the second testicle was in my hand and coming away with its long cord. Pete was already sizing up his escape route over the wall behind him and as I reached for the disinfectant so he slackened his grip. Immediately Little Willie let out a piercing squeal which galvanised Skinny into a final attack on the door. There was a sickening, splintering crack and she burst through and charged in with a snort. She paused for only a second to greet the piglets in the doorway before crashing on into the yard to sort us out.

As soon as the door broke Pete dropped Little Willie and heaved himself over the wall as he'd been rehearsing so carefully in his mind. I started after him, leaping upwards as Skinny barged past Little Willie's greeting and came for me. I was almost clear, trailing my right leg as she lunged for me, open mouthed and determined to sink her teeth into me. She caught me. Fortunately it was only a glancing bite, which tore down my trouser leg and skidded down my shin as my leg disappeared.

I hobbled to the house and dived into the kitchen, nursing my bloody leg and abusing Skinny.

'That nasty old sow,' Mother sighed. She moved away from the long, low sink under the window, hands still wet as she pulled at my trouser leg. 'Dearie me, you *are* in the wars. I'd better find a bandage.'

I hopped across the brick floor and sank into the old, velvet covered armchair which filled the corner beyond the kitchen range. As I lay back feeling sorry for myself she scurried from the room. I heard her taking the stairs at her usual trot. She never walked upstairs, always ran.

Soon she came down, ripping a long strip from an old sheet. 'This'll do,' she smiled, 'we'll soon have you mended.' She flung the sheet on the table, moved to the sink and turned on the solitary

39

brass tap full blast. She filled a basin with ice-cold water and came over to swab my leg.

'I knew that old sow would get you one day, the way you swear at her so.' She was dabbing at the blood on my shin.

'Swearing's got nothing to do with it. She was just defending her young. Can't blame her for that.'

'No, but there *was* a lot of shouting and bad language going on.'

'That old sheet brings back some memories,' I said. It seemed a good idea to change the subject. 'Remember the hot fomentations? The boils we always seemed to be getting?'

She smiled. 'Like poor Job. But what cowards you all were!'

'Only because you used to get them too scalding hot.' I could see her now, plunging the centre of a screw of sheet into boiling water, and I could remember waiting with terror while the lump of lint cooked within it. And when she pulled it out and started to wring out the boiling water and unwrap the steaming lint, she would wince to show me that she was also suffering. Then, 'There's a brave soldier,' she would say as she slapped the scalding lint on the fiery boil and I tried to stifle a howl as she bandaged the heat in.

But now the antidote to Skinny's bite was a good stinging swab with iodine and a tight bandage of torn sheet, spiked home with a safety pin. She got up from her knees and leant over to kiss me. 'There you are. All better now.' And she laughed as she ran her hand through my hair.

As I stood up to leave, she said, 'One good turn deserves another.'

'Such as?'

'The quinces. I'm longing to make some jelly. It's a pity to waste them and you did say you'd pick them for me. Or I could if you're busy, but I'd need a ladder.'

'You can't go clambering up a ladder at your age.'

'Why ever not?'

'Well because . . .' But I knew there was no answer. She was still as agile as ever and would delight in the challenge of a ladder up a quince tree. It would be as nothing beside other acrobatic feats I'd seen her perform. Like the times in the tall-ceilinged house in Dulwich, when the ball-cock stuck in the cold water tank in the loft, sending water cascading from the overflow. The first time the plumber had been called. But that had proved expensive for the few minutes he'd spent aloft stemming the flow. So the next time it happened, Mother was alone in the house and saw no good reason why she shouldn't tackle the job herself. So she lugged the step ladder up to the top landing, set it up beneath the trap door in the ceiling, climbed to the top step and reached up to remove the hatch. And from there she swung herself up like a monkey and disappeared into the darkness to rescue the drowning ball-cock. It was a trick she performed several times, so I knew a ladder up a quince tree would be a cinch after that.

But the tree grew at an awkward angle in the backyard right next to the privy, its feet in the fertile depths while it leant forward to clasp the outside bog in a loving embrace, smothering its romantic benefactor with a thousand leafy kisses and offering branches loaded with golden fruit.

Which harvest Mother and I finally reaped between us. While I was poised, one foot on the slanting ladder, the other deep in the foliage clinging to the slippery roof of the privy, she stood below, emptying her shopping basket as I filled it and passed it down, and calling out and pointing to fruit I'd missed, lurking in the dark foliage.

Soon there was a rolling heap of quinces on the kitchen table and Mother declared she had enough.

Now Mother had several natural gifts—things she could do without really trying. Playing the piano was one. And the violin. Another was flinging on clothes without heed and looking just right. And another was cooking. By no stretch of the imagination could she be called a great cook, but she had the happy knack of being able to toss ingredients together, seemingly at random and usually while she was busy with another job as well, give them a quick stir and pop the mixture in the oven. And provided she didn't forget about it, out would come a sponge as light as a fairy, pastry that crumbled at a touch, or some concoction she herself could admit 'just melts in your mouth, although I say it myself' — her ultimate seal of approval. And if anybody asked her the secret to her success, she'd laugh and reply: 'Heavens, just luck!' But often her smile would soften and she'd add: 'And, of course, "doing what you have to do, in the Saviour's name".' We'd laugh at her for that quote. But we knew it was true and she put love into all she did for others and that was the secret.

And jam making was the same hit and miss romp as the rest of her cooking. She had a big, copper preserving pan which she kept highly polished. It had pride of place in the kitchen, poised on edge in the centre of the mantlepiece above the black kitchener, dwarfing the copper kettles and pots and pans ranged either side, relics of seventh wedding anniversaries. She stood on a chair to lift it down and shuffled it on to the table among the quinces.

'If you're going to stay you may as well make yourself useful,' she said, with a smile. 'Be a dear and put some more logs and coal on the fire. See if you can get the old thing to agree to blaze. Must have it nice and hot.'

I did as I was told. And she attacked the brick floor with a long kitchen knife, in the fond belief that she was putting an edge on the thing. But it was sharp enough to slice through the tough skins of the quinces and soon she was chopping merrily, piling pieces into the preserving pan.

The fire was beginning to lick at the logs with growing enthusiasm, so I stood for a moment to watch the carve-up.

'Skins and pips and cores and all?' I asked.

'That's the beauty of making jelly,' she laughed. 'You don't have to bother with all the fiddly bits. It all goes in together and all boils together. Which reminds me. Put some water in will you, darling? About up to there,' and she indicated the side of the pan with the point of the knife. 'Now, *where's* the sugar? Let's hope I've got enough.'

And before long the pan was glinting on the black kitchener. The fire was crackling joyously beneath while Mother was poised above, prodding and stirring with her wooden spoon, declaring that all that was needed now was 'a good thumping boil'.

I left her to it and came back an hour or so later. Now the kitchen was filled with a heady, sweet smell, drops of water were chasing each other down the window panes and steam was rising and disappearing among the black beams in the ceiling. There was no sign of Mother, but evidently the boiling was finished because the preserving pan had been heaved to one side of the range and was steaming gently, there was a plate of frothy skimmings on the table with the wooden spoon cast idly beside it, and a saucer in which a spoonful of the liquid had been left to see that it would gel.

I was in the process of dipping my finger into the saucer for a sample when Mother reappeared. Her face was flushed, and she swept stray hairs up her forehead with the heel of her hand. In the other she carried a piece of muslin.

'How does it taste?' she asked.

I smacked my lips. 'Lovely. Surprisingly tasty when you consider where it came from in the first place.'

'Hush! You don't have to think about that. Now, let me see, where's the big saucepan? This is the tricky bit.'

I carried the steaming preserving pan across to the table for her. And I watched as she wrestled with sieves and saucepans and muslin. Then I gasped as she plunged a jug into the molten mixture to ladle it across to be strained. 'Steady on! You'll scald yourself.'

'No! Pour boldly, that's my motto, then you're all right.' And most of the jam steamed and snuggled into its muslin bed, while the remainder dribbled in red tears down the sides of the saucepan and the pan and glistened in a sticky trail across the table.

While she waited for it to drain through, I left her chivvying it between hurried hunts for jam jars in the pantry.

And when I returned the job was done. The steam had disappeared, the kitchener glowed with pride and the sink staggered under a double armful of sticky washing up.

But Mother was happy. She looked up and smiled as she put the finishing touches to the golden-red jars, glowing across the table like a row of captured sunsets.

4

I BORROWED A boar from Ernie Carter. He came driving down the lane, with a trailer swinging behind his car, and rattled to a stop outside the gate.

Ernie was a big man, round, jovial, always dressed in a check jacket and a check cap, below which an abundant crop of black hair sprouted and curled. But when he lifted his cap his head was bald as a ball, a white anaemic dome above his ruddy face and around which the last luxuriant growth of hair clung like a fur fringe. The contrast was so startling that he took a great delight in raising his cap in front of strangers, just to watch their reaction. 'Aye,' he'd grin, 'fraid 'tis slippin' a bit lower each day.'

Ernie was of gipsy origin and he had come to rest on a small farm a mile or so away from Maywood. He lived there with his brother, Fred, their wives, a horde of children and an assortment of animals and machinery. They lived by their wits rather than their land, buying and selling, hiring out animals and machinery, always ready for a deal. Their farm was a Whipsnade of haphazard transactions, an agricultural second-hand shop where you could buy, or borrow, anything from a horse and cart or a hay turner to a ferret or an Angora buck.

Both Ernie and brother Fred never missed a farm sale of live and dead stock for miles around. Every auctioneer knew them and if ever a lot stuck without a bidder the cry was always: 'What about it, then, Ernie?' and he would raise his cap, laugh, buy it and cart it home to wait until he could make a few shillings on the deal.

In the spring they went to the orchard fruit sales, bidding for budding cherries on the trees, gambling on the final size of the crop and the amount it would fetch when picked by their lusty families and relations, swarming up the tall ladders. And when Ernie had bought a crop, and had paid over several hundred pounds from the wad he always carried in his back pocket, it was an anxious time of waiting to see how the cherries would fill out and ripen. The birds had to be scared away with bangers, or by turning out his sleep-filled children in the four o'clock morning to run about beating tins. The rain had to stay off, or the cold drops would split the tight skins of the cherries and spoil the sale. And when the crop was picked, and the round baskets glowed and glistened beneath the trees, the price had to be right to pay the pickers and still show a profit when the notes went back to his wad. Ernie never had a bank account. He couldn't read or write, so what was the use? He could reckon quicker than the next man and could remember every detail of every transaction among the multitude that thronged his fields and buildings.

I had been thinking about Ernie as I busied myself in the yard, waiting for him to arrive with the boar. I couldn't afford to buy a boar, not just for two sows, and I had arranged to hire this animal over a drink in the pub a few days earlier.

Several of us from the farming community were in The Six Bells that night, sitting on the wooden benches, behind the oak tables. Ernie and Fred were both there and the conversation had idled on to cherries and the profit taken by the wicked middle man. That year there had been a glut of cherries and the market price was low, so low that Ernie looked like being unable to show a profit, although the price in the shops was much higher.

'They buggers up Covent Garden were collarin' the lot,' he declared, thumping the table.

'Aye, collarin' the lot,' Fred agreed. He was smaller than his brother, younger and very much the junior partner.

'But us beat 'em, didn't us, Fred?' Ernie was beaming, his cheeks like polished apples, his teeth crowding to be noticed, his cap pushed back slightly and clasping the last of his hair. He was a born raconteur and already we were all listening and leaning forward on the table.

'Aye, us beat 'em,' Fred agreed, 'us sold 'em ourselves.'

Ernie scowled at his brother for jumping the gun. He would tell the tale and Fred could agree when requested to do so. And it was a long story, told with much detail and many a pause for effect while Ernie swigged his beer and sucked his teeth.

Because of the low price of cherries at Covent Garden they decided to set up as retailers to dispose of their crop. Among the tackle littering the farm there was an old lorry, bought as a speculation some time before and left with its nose stuck under a lean-to 'so's the ingin could keep dry'. It was coaxed into life, shuddering and smoking when on the move and fizzing ominously whenever it stopped. They loaded it with as many bushel baskets of cherries as they thought it would carry and added a few more for luck. They routed out an assortment of paper bags, yellow at the edges but each carrying a fine picture of a bull's head in red and the legend 'Prime Meat Our Speciality'; part of a job lot at a bygone sale of a bankrupt butcher: 'old Fullerton over Ham Street, him wot used ter graze all them ewes down Romney Marsh. 'E got mixed up wi' that young girl from Ashford wot worked fer him. Used to poke 'er in the shed behind the shop when his missus had gorne out. Kept customers waitin' and all sometimes, 'e did. You knowed 'im, didn't yer, Charlie?' Charlie was a shepherd who hailed from those parts and he nodded nervously, willing to enjoy the story but loath to be drawn into it. And from another shed on his farm Ernie unearthed a set of brass scales and weights, brushed off the dust, loaded them on to the lorry and slammed up the tailboard. They were in business.

They headed for London and parked in a side street leading up from a busy shopping area. And as they waited for their first customers, they decided that Ernie would stand on the back of the lorry to weigh up the cherries, while Fred would remain below to hand over the bags and take the money. They were expecting a busy trade and thought it only right to be properly organised.

It was a hot July day, hot enough in the country but hotter still among the shimmering walls of Lewisham. Ernie was a fat man. His clothes stuck to him and as he bent down to move a basket of cherries his trousers failed to give as they should and parted at the seam. 'It weren't much of a split,' he confided, bending forward over the table. 'But I slipped on me white overall ter hide it, like. You know what they town women be.' He smiled and winked. Then he frowned. 'T'wud have bin bad fer trade ter serve 'em wi' a split arse to me trousers.'

Everybody knew Ernie's white overall. He always wore it whenever he went to a sale. But it was neither white nor over all. The

46

buttons had long since gone, it was too short for him and there was a ragged tear in the tail where a barbed wire fence had taken a bite at it.

At first trade was slow as only the desultory shopper stopped on her way to and from the main road. Then some children happened by and gathered round in loud discussion as they pooled pennies to buy a bag. They crowded Fred at the back of the lorry and when Ernie bent to his task at the scales above, they sniggered and giggled, sharp elbows digging into neighbouring ribs. Ernie turned round and beamed at them, raising his cap to show his clown-like head and give them a little extra value for their money. They raced off down the road, laughing and shouting.

Soon a steady stream of women began to flood up from the main street. 'I said they'd heard we was cheaper than the shops, didn't I, Fred?' Ernie was scowling seriously.

Fred was smiling. 'Aye, we was cheaper right enough. But that weren't why. . . .'

'A lot cheaper we was,' Ernie cut in, severely. And very soon they were high busy weighing off and selling the cherries to the gathering crowd. Women thronged the back of the lorry. Fred kept protesting they weren't giving him enough room to move and Ernie perspired happily above them, shouting the praises of his cherries as he worked his way through the baskets, plonking handful after handful on the scales, shooting them into the bags and handing them behind him for Fred to take the money. There was great gaiety in the crowd below and Ernie glowed with pleasure. Both he and his cherries were a hit with these hard-bitten townsfolk and he kept up his flow of country comments they seemed to enjoy so hugely.

Fred had suddenly become silent as he took the money. He was becoming more and more agitated. Anxiously he began to call: 'Ernie! Ernie!' as he tried to attract his brother's attention.

Ernie kept on working, bent over his scales, loudly assuring his happy customers that the cherries were freshly picked, straight from the farm, cheap because no middle man had had his thieving hands on them.

'Ernie! Ernie! Your weights!' Fred was becoming more and more concerned.

'Me weights be orlright.' Ernie checked the scales impatiently. 'As good cherries as ever you'll buy! Sweet an' full o' sunshine.' He continued his patter.

Now the laughter was loud and long. Some women were throwing back their heads with open joy, others cackled behind a hand clasped to the mouth, some stood cross-legged, bent forward and helpless with mirth.

Fred didn't know where to look. He stopped taking the money for the cherries and leant forward to pluck nervously at Ernie's trouser leg. 'Your weights! Your weights! Turn round and see to 'em, Ernie!'

'I'll worry about me weights,' Ernie said, crossly. 'You worry about the money.'

A gale of laughter swept through the women, creasing their eyes and tugging at their cheeks and chins.

Fred sprang into action. He grabbed at the torn and swaying tails of Ernie's overall and pulled them together, trying to get them to meet across his large backside: 'Fer Chrissake, Ernie, yer balls are hanging out!'

Ernie drank his beer and his eyes were shining as we fell about with laughter. He put down his glass, sighed and belched. 'Same as I allus say,' he concluded, 'if yer wants ter make a sale you've got ter 'ave a gimmick.'

When Ernie arrived on the farm with his boar, I was there to meet him by the time he had manoeuvred himself out of the car. 'You didn't forget, then,' I greeted him.

'Forget? God bless you, no. I don't forget business. You said you wanted ol' Bill today and 'ere 'e be.'

We walked to the back of the small trailer. The boar was squealing with expectation, ramming his snout up into the pig net which covered him. He was well aware of the significance of a ride in the trailer and was anxious to get acquainted with his blind date.

Ernie started to undo the pig net and leant down towards the boar's upturned snout, staring him in the eye. 'You knows what's up, don't yer, Bill me beauty? A nice trip up the rind? Eh? Eh? How'd that suit yer?' He teased as the boar became more and more agitated.

'Good job he doesn't know we've got two lined up for him,' I laughed. 'If he behaves like that at the thought of one, the net wouldn't hold him.'

He was a powerful creature and the hairs bristled like faggots along his broad back as he strained upwards.

Just then Pete and Bert came sauntering across the yard and

hung around the trailer, ready to help drive the boar across to the meadow. Ernie finished untying the net, flung it back and lowered the tailboard. Bill huffed and blew at the open space, deciding the best way to lumber down, prancing a little with his front feet, anxious to get on with the job but wary of the short jump down to the ground. Eventually he flopped down, took a few paces into the yard and stopped. He stood rigid with his head raised, his tail tightly coiled, sniffing the air to see what dainty smells he could detect.

Pete stood behind him, gazing at him. 'Christ! He ain't arf got a pair of knackers on 'im!'

'Jealous?' Ernie enquired. His laugh rumbled up from his belly and his chins shook as it exploded from his mouth.

''Course 'e ain't jealous,' Bert piped up. He smirked when he found he had everyone's attention, turned to his brother and added, softly: 'If you had a pair o' knackers like that, them 'ud only split yer trousers, wouldn't 'em, Pete?'

And they both collapsed with laughter because Ernie's story in The Six Bells had already leapt around the village.

'You walked right into that one, Ernie,' I smiled.

'Ah, buggered if I didn't.' He laughed again as he turned away to fasten up the trailer. 'You 'ave ter mind what yer says ter boys these days. Sharp as needles 'em be.'

He clambered into his car and it sank with a lop-sided sigh. He grinned at me through the window. 'I'll be orf, then. Give us a tinkle when you'm done wi' ol' Bill and I'll fetch 'im back.' He moved away slowly in a cloud of exhaust.

The boys had driven Bill into the meadow to make the introductions. For once Skinny and Fatso were grazing within bounds on the far side and were oblivious of the arrival of their exciting new suitor.

Surprisingly they were both content to be on their own. They behaved as though they were glad to be rid of their clamouring families, delighting in the opportunity of a quiet graze without having to share each discovery with a squabbling brood; being free to do as they pleased, to walk without picking a path between exuberant offspring, to lie down and stretch out without becoming the target for battering snouts, needle teeth and scrabbling feet. True, there had been a vociferous parting when the young pigs had been shut up in one sty, ready to be loaded into the trailer for market, and Skinny and Fatso had been securely confined in the

49

other. Inevitably there had been a great deal of argument among the youngsters when Pete had gone into them to drive them into the trailer, backed with its ramp rising invitingly from the doorway. Ears had lain flat and tails swished as they tore round in a squealing circle, funking the open doorway, loudly demanding maternal protection.

'Come on, come on,' Pete had coaxed them, and making a dive he'd grabbed one by the hind leg and dragged it towards the door. 'Come on, this little piggy went to bloody market.' He bundled it up into the straw in the trailer. It darted back past him. It swivelled round, snorted and glared back at him, front feet firmly apart, ready for a dash either way: '*And this little piggy stayed home!*'

Thoughtfully we had provided Skinny and Fatso with food in the trough, hoping to distract their attention from the noisy plight of their progeny. But this had only made matters worse. At the loud attempts to load the pigs next door the mothers had shouted their disapproval with their mouths full. They had circled distractedly, each torn between her concern at the rumpus, her inability to stop it and her desire to gobble the food in case the other one pinched it all first.

But once the pigs had been loaded, and had departed, not even Skinny pined in the slightest for their return. Only Little Willie remained behind. Being smaller than the others he spoilt the look of the litter and I decided to keep him on and fatten him to kill for home-cured bacon later.

The sows raised their heads when they heard Pete calling. Skinny only glanced across for a moment, decided that it was not worth bothering about and continued rummaging through some leaves. Fatso thought otherwise. She had woken up that morning feeling distinctly romantic. It usually took about five days for this condition to arrive after the departure of a litter and Bill couldn't have swaggered into the meadow at a more opportune moment. Fatso was delighted to waddle across to introduce herself to him and she did so with as little modesty as a harlot in a high street.

She started talking to him when she was still several breathless yards away. Bill stood his ground, wary of this exuberant greeting. He grunted gruffly, a guarded 'good morning', prodded at the grass with his ugly, upturned snout and his top lip appeared to curl derisively. A fellow had to have a chance to get his bearings. He wasn't going to be rushed and he made it quite obvious he didn't reciprocate Fatso's fulsome display of love at first sight. He even turned his back on her. But Pete declared that this was just to show her what he could boast.

Whatever the interpretation of this manoeuvre, Fatso never faltered in her buxom approach. She cuddled alongside and her comfortable grunts became high pitched and staccato as she tentatively lowered her snout beside Bill's on the grass. Bill never moved. His tail curled tightly, his bristles stood above his shoulders like an upturned yard broom and only his eyes revolved as he debated his first move.

Fatso felt she was getting nowhere. She had declared her love for him. She had pressed her curves against him and the staccato grunts had surely been to assure him that she was ready whenever he was. But Bill was just not impressed. He was motionless, speechless, giving the impression that he couldn't care less if he never saw another sow again. I noticed the scars on his ears and I guessed he was an old hand at love making. He had long since learnt his lesson about making a too eager proposal to a strange sow. Those scars were the remnants of some pretty vicious love bites.

Fatso abandoned her vocal persuasion. She moved away, grunting deeply, and turned right round until her snout was lowered beside his back leg. Bill's eyes rolled as he wondered what she was up to and his snout twitched at the proximity of her voluptuous bottom. Yet even this provocation, this blatant supplication, left him cold and failed to elicit any worthwhile reaction.

So she decided that an even more positive approach was called for. Somehow she had to get the message across because he really was proving insufferably stubborn. Surely he realised how she'd been feeling since early morning? And how his very presence in the meadow was driving her to distraction? But if he wanted to play hard to get, well then, she had a trick or two of her own.

Suddenly she rammed her snout under his belly, rooted up sharply, lifted his hind legs clear of the ground and tossed him away from her.

Bill let out a horrified squeal at such precipitate foreplay. That this was a grave insult to his dignity was obvious from the way in which he regained his balance, held his head high and sucked his chops. The coil had sprung out of his tail on the impact and now it hung straight, fussily dusting over his testicles.

From far across the meadow the sound of Bill's squeal galvanised Skinny into action. She raised her head, realised she was missing

51

something of moment and came bounding across with a frolicsome gallop, her shrivelling udder now bunching into her belly and giving her increased ease of movement. She slowed to a trot, and then a wary walk as she prepared to introduce herself to Bill. But as she had yet to reach the same happy state in which Fatso found herself, her approach was quite different. She simply walked up to him with a powerful grunt or two, raised her head to get a better look at him from under her floppy ears and then drove her teeth smartly into his ear.

Poor Bill! He squealed again, took a few hurried steps away from this gaunt and evil-tempered stranger and shook his head and flicked his tail as, doubtless, he reflected on the hazards of his calling. Now that Skinny had made her point, had advised Bill of his place in the hierarchy on the farm, she strutted off to continue foraging and took not the slightest interest in the dalliance that followed.

Fatso was determined on satisfaction. There was an added urgency in the way she hurried back to him, cavorting a little almost as though she was inviting him to a session of slap and tickle. Her head lolled from side to side as she made her approach, goading him into action, threatening him with another bunt up the backside unless he responded. Bill raised his head, shuffled round to face her and assured her with a few sharp grunts that he was now becoming interested.

They stood facing each other, heads down and cheek to cheek, grunting endearments into each other's ear. It was quite a long conversation and now Bill was doing most of the talking as he worked his way through his usual line of patter. Every now and then he marked time with his front feet to emphasise a point and once he nudged her cheek and she responded with a little squeal of pleasure. Encouraged by this he edged forward and started to chuck her under the chin with his snout and she lifted her head and smacked her chops, delighted at his attentions.

Presently he lumbered round until he was at right angles to her and began to barge into her with his snout. She stood her ground, tense and silent and Bill lifted his head and plonked his chin firmly on her shoulders. Saliva frothed from his mouth and caught in the bristles on her back.

'Go on, Bill,' Pete urged him, 'can't yer see 'er's ready for yer?'

We were three interested spectators hanging over the gate, work forgotten while we were engrossed in the wooing.

Bill swung a little further round until his head was level with Fatso's belly. He grunted and put his snout under her, butting her and then lifting her up and down. She strained to keep her hind legs firmly on the ground. Now he seemed satisfied that she was in full agreement. He shuffled round in an elaborate preparation to mount her, prancing a little as he positioned himself for the take-off.

'Cor! Lumme!' Bert leant forward, pointing excitedly. 'He's got a cock like a corkscrew!'

It had appeared, red as fire, shining and revolving, a lengthening gimlet waving and apparently out of control as Bill mounted. It slapped about, screwing and searching for the place.

''Course 'e has,' Pete was superior, talking down to his young brother. 'Ain't yer never heard of screwin' somebody? That's where it comes from, see? That's what a boar does to a sow, he screws 'er.'

Bert was watching, fascinated. 'How the hell do 'e keep it twistin' like that?'

'Buggered if I know.' Pete shrugged.

'Nor me,' I said, when Bert looked at me questioningly.

Now Bill was comfortably in position, lazing along Fatso's back, now and then smacking his chops and grinning, his eyes half closed as he settled down to a long session. Flecks of white saliva fluffed down from his mouth and gathered on Fatso's shoulders like froth trapped in the fringes of a stream. She stood firmly beneath him, and apart from an occasional shuffle of her hind legs and a comfortable wriggle to press herself more firmly backwards, she never moved. And neither did Bill, except for infrequent thrusts.

Pete scratched his head through his beret and pulled it forward down his forehead. 'They say you can tell how many piglets 'ees puttin' into 'er.'

'Go on,' Bert said, in disbelief.

'Oh, aye,' Pete nodded seriously, 'you just have ter count the number of times. Each time 'e shoves, that's one piglet. 'Ees made six so far. I bin countin'.'

Bert and I laughed. 'That's just an old wives' tale,' I said.

'No. Honest,' Pete protested. 'Ol' Jack told I. When 'e used ter help ol' Dunnell with his pigs down Frog's Hole Farm. *He* said they allus counted and it allus came out right.'

'He was pulling your leg,' I laughed.

'Seven!' Bert shouted, 'I see'd 'im shove again. That makes seven, one more than ol' Fatso had last time. That last boar wot done 'er couldn't have stopped on long enough.'

'It's really got nothing to do with it, you know,' I protested.

'Eight!' Bert wasn't going to be put off now. This was a spell-binding spectacle. Any moment I expected him to cheer Bill on like a fan at a football match.

Bill was beginning to flag. There was no doubt about it. His head was drooping a little, his eyes were closed and his chops were still and no longer grinned. I thought he'd gone to sleep on the job. And evidently Fatso's flush had been satisfied because she was beginning to show signs of becoming bored with the proceedings. She nuzzled at the grass and began to reach forward to graze with impatient nibbles, like a bored whore reaching from beneath a long-finishing lover into a bedside box of chocolates.

Presently she took a couple of steps forward and Bill grumbled at her as he stirred and shuffled to stay mounted. His backside wriggled and his tail flicked and Bert was uncertain as to whether this was merely an effort to stay coupled or whether he was making another piglet. Anyway he called out 'Nine!' but without much conviction.

'No, you can't count that,' Pete decided, 'He'd have fallen orf if 'e hadn't shoved then.'

Fatso had had enough. She was more interested in foraging than in copulating and was being quite obvious about it. She was moving forward, one determined step at a time, carting Bill with her so that he had to strut hurriedly with his hind legs to stay mounted. His front legs dangled uselessly, now and then paddling the air as he strived to maintain his position.

'Nine! Ten! Eleven!' Bert shouted, triumphantly.

'Them wasn't proper shoves,' Pete said, coolly.

'Yes they was! Look at the ol' bugger. He's hard at it again. *And* 'er's stopped fer 'im now. That's eleven, right enough.'

In fact, Bill was panting. His mouth was open and he was blow-ing out jets of steam as he lolled forward. He looked askance and there was a desperate determination in his glance.

'I think it's time he knocked off,' I said. I moved past the boys to open the gate.

There was a shocked silence as they stared at me.

'Ain't yer going ter let 'im go on, then?' Pete was horrified.

'Yea,' Bert echoed. 'He can make a few more yet, I'll lay.'

'Good God, no,' I said. 'He'd stop on all day if you let him. Like as not old Skinny'll be on heat tomorrow. Just think how she'd knock hell out of him if he couldn't manage her.'

They laughed at that and followed me through the gate. Bill watched our approach with the desperation of a long distance runner being overtaken in sight of the tape.

'Go on,' I said, raising my stick, 'you've had enough for one session. Off you get!' I tapped him on the ear. He gave a tired squeal, shoved again and shut his eyes tight.

'Twelve!' yelled Bert, clapping his hands and laughing.

'Get off, you old sod,' I shouted and clipped him on the ear again.

He squealed and slowly rolled sideways while Fatso walked away from under him, grazing and without so much as a backward glance. Bill's front feet hit the ground, he staggered for a yard or two and then subsided with a long sigh as he stretched himself out on the cool grass.

As it turned out, Bert's calculation of conception at the round dozen was optimistic. But at least she improved on her first litter by producing eight piglets next time round.

Skinny had her turn two days later. But compared to Fatso's performance it was a matter-of-fact, almost clinical affair. Both the boys were thoroughly disappointed. They'd been looking forward to nothing less than a display of reckless abandon when Skinny's time came. There had been a great deal of comment and speculation ever since we had walked away, leaving the shagged-out Bill to sleep it off.

But when the urge came to her Skinny had simply set about the job of procreation with the same direct, purposeful manner that characterised all her activities. Not for her the frolicsome love play and wallowing enjoyment of Fatso. Just a determined walk across to Bill as soon as she had been let out into the meadow, a couple of stern grunts and a butt under the bollocks to tell him to get on with it. And he'd obliged immediately, perhaps remembering the salutory bite in the ear with which she had originally greeted him.

Bert declared it was obvious Bill preferred fat females. ''Else he'd 'uv stayed on longer. T'was her skinny backbone wot done fer 'im. I only counted eight proper shoves afore 'e fell orf.'

'He never fell orf,' Pete corrected him. 'T'was her fault. Her went marching orf when 'er'd had enough and 'e couldn't keep up. The way 'er was going it was a wonder 'er didn't pull his cock orf.'

Bert cackled. 'No, couldn't do that. Reckon he just unscrewed it going along.'

They laughed as they mounted their bikes and rode off up the lane together towards their home and tea. I heard no more of their conversation. Only Bert's high cackle was still crisp after they were out of sight, marking their progress through the autumn mist rising from the darkening meadows.

5

BETWEEN BATTLES with the pigs we worked at the cowshed to bring it up to the standard necessary to get a contract to supply the Milk Marketing Board. We cleaned out mountains of chaff from long forgotten corners of the old barn, slapped about merrily with buckets of lime wash and startled spiders that had always had it their own way. We built a dairy in one corner, a corn store in another and fixed up a line of drinking bowls along the mangers, one for each cow.

Meanwhile Mother had been coping with the installation of a bathroom and flush toilet, not only for our own comfort but because of visitors who might want to come and stay. As Mother pointed out, we couldn't really invite them to brave just a jug of cold water and a basin in the bedroom, not even for what she called a lick-and-a-promise. She'd been brought up to washing in cold water in the bedroom, so she found it no hardship. Even when we did get the bath she filled it with cold water and jumped right in every morning – good for the health, good for the soul. But we couldn't expect visitors to rough it. Nor, I agreed, would it be delicate to warn them to take a deep breath as they headed across the backyard, deep enough to last them at least part of the way through a speedy session in the privy. That was certainly no place for dreamers.

So Mother had waylaid Mr Boorland the builder after church one Sunday morning. She went to church every Sunday, twice and sometimes three times, on her tall bike with the basket on the front, two miles there and two miles back, down into a valley and up again and down the other side. Already she'd been welcomed into the fold and the Vicar had lined her up for good works. Perhaps she'd like to take on the Sunday School? Certainly the Mothers' Union. How blessed they were to have somebody of such valuable experience in their midst. Mother could never say no and refused to listen when I told her she was being talked into too much. It was her duty as she saw it and that was an end to it.

Mr Boorland was also a regular at church. He was a Sidesman, handing out the books and taking the collection, so Mother felt sure he was a builder one could rely on. He was also the local undertaker, a tall and anxious man who unwound himself sadly from his Austin Seven when he came to look over the job. And so sadly did he doff his trilby at the back door, for a moment Mother felt sure he'd misunderstood her and come prepared to measure for a coffin instead of a bathroom. But we soon discovered he carried his sadness with him whatever the job, and as the work progressed we became used to his lugubrious expression on his daily visits of inspection. Even when it was all over and we thanked him with obvious delight for the speedy and efficient job that enabled us to bath and bog in comfort, the gloom never lightened from his face.

Instead he asked me to accompany him to the orchard so that he could explain the workings of the new septic tank to me. And he lectured me on bacterial crusts and rates of flow, and almost had me swearing on oath that I wouldn't allow additional drainage water to enter and upset the delicate digestion of the bacteria. We surveyed the clear effluent, trickling away into the ditch, and he produced a small glass from his overcoat pocket. He filled it and held it high and only then did I see a flicker of a smile as he said: 'The effluent from a properly constructed, properly used septic tank is fit to drink. But I fear it's a little early in the day for me.'

However, the cows started to arrive before any visitors, much to Mother's delight. She was longing to get cracking making butter and suchlike and kept saying how it wasn't a real farm without foaming buckets of milk being carried into the kitchen. Pigs were all very well, but they didn't have the same appeal as cows. She didn't say so, but she thought it. I told her, as patiently as I could, that when we did start to send milk away every drop would be infinitely precious. I was going to rely on the monthly milk cheque to pay the wages, and the feed bills, and all the other bills that were beginning to form a paper mountain on my desk. It was only the thought of the milk cheques that stopped me worrying about the bills. I used to shuffle through them every now and then and con myself into believing that all accounting problems would be solved once the milk was flowing. So, I told Mother, she could forget all that old nonsense about Dick the shepherd blowing his nail while milk came home in pail—frozen or frothing. We'd just have a jug full for the house and the rest would go to the Milk Marketing Board and that way I'd keep solvent.

But it didn't dampen her enthusiasm and she came hurrying out of the house with me on the evening Lotty arrived.

Lotty was a big, brown and white cow with upright, curving horns. They gave her a surprised expression, as though she viewed everything with perpetually raised eyebrows. She was the first cow I bought and revealed her character the moment she arrived on the farm. The tailboard of the cattle lorry swung down and she peered out. Her long brown ears, blue veins streaking the greasy yellow skin inside, pricked as she watched the drover mount the ramp. Her large and surprised eyes rolled as he grabbed a handful of straw and scattered it down the ribbed boards leading to the road below. She sniffed the new air and her white nostrils glistened as she blew through them, sending two steamy jets melting into the autumn evening.

The drover walked past her into the lorry. She was his last delivery and he grabbed her tail and pulled it upwards to urge her down the ramp. Momentarily her ears twitched backwards to catch his 'Come on, yer bugger!' but she shifted her weight to her front feet, thrusting them deep into the straw. He might be in a hurry to get home to his tea, but she would go when she was good and ready.

The ride from the market had been the final indignity. She had lurched from side to side as the lorry creaked round the narrow lanes. All this on top of the hours hanging around the market, hours of bellowing and bullying, parading and prodding and she with a new calf continually adding its own protest to the unusual activity. And now it had been shut away from her, somewhere in the depths of the lorry and was bawling its head off.

The drover's language ripened. Mother looked away with a sigh and tried not to hear. Lotty looked round at him with surprise. Then she tossed her head to shake off his abuse and looked down to where we were standing, just beyond the foot of the ramp, ready to turn her towards the cowshed when she did come down. Now she paused again on the threshold of her new life, catching the earthy tang in the autumn flush of grass over the hedge beside the lorry, smelling the sweetness of the heated hay wafting up from the rick beyond the cowshed.

Suddenly she moved. Her back legs went up, she flicked her tail out of the drover's grasp as he hurriedly side-stepped, and she came helter-skelter down the ramp, bundling by us, her full udder swinging from side to side as she cavorted up the lane. Her high waving tail was as expressive as two raised fingers as she departed.

I lifted the calf from the trap in the front of the lorry. The drover heaved up the ramp and crashed it shut. He spat on the tip I gave him before pocketing it. Soon the lorry was roaring up the hill, leaving its exhaust to layer a blue stratum into the evening mist.

The lush growth of roadside grass and clover proved an irresistible temptation to Lotty. In her hunger she forgot her calf and I spirited it away to the calf pens. She never noticed. Her head was down and her tongue was curling, capturing and tearing off succulent mouthfuls of the bonanza which had leapt up from the hot, brown verge after the first autumn rain. She was so busy making up for the starving hours in the market that she never moved as Pete walked by her. And now that she had tasted what her new home had to offer she was quite happy to amble back down the lane when Pete urged her, stopping for a blow and a bite every few paces until we coaxed her into the cowshed.

We made a fuss of her with some corn in the manger and quietly fastened the chain round her neck. It was Pete who named her as he peeled at the round paper lot number still glued firmly to her rump. 'So, you be lot forty-nine, be yer?' He patted the number back when it failed to budge and ran his hand under her tail and down the silky folds of her udder. 'You ain't a bad old sod, be yer?' He laughed. 'Old Lotty!'

She turned her head and gave us her surprised look, the flour of the corn sticking to her wet nose and dusting her whiskers. She belched and blew a hot gust of clover-scented wind in our faces. She seemed pleased.

Mother came closer and slapped her on the rump. 'She seems a nice old thing.'

'Let's see how much milk she's got.' I hurried off for a bucket.

'What about her calf? Aren't you going to bring her back?' The calf was protesting loudly from across the yard. Lotty was too busy with the corn to bother.

'She stays where she is,' I called from the dairy. 'We'll feed her from a bucket.'

'Won't she be able to see her calf again?' Mother was looking hurt. She thumped her tummy in anxiety.

'They'll be orlright, Missus,' Pete assured her. 'We got ter separate 'em. The cow'll hold her milk else.'

'That's right,' I agreed, as I sat down beside Lotty. 'Now, let's see if she'll produce that foaming bucket of milk for you. Come on, old girl, some for your calf and the rest for us.'

And while Lotty was busy with the corn her milk flowed easily from her swollen udder. It was filling the bucket nicely when she abruptly looked up and turned off the supply. Milk was still there in the udder. I could feel it. But the teats had gone dry as she listened to her calf.

'Oh well, that's our lot for now.' I stood up and held the bucket out to Mother. 'There you are, then. We don't start sending it away 'til Monday, so you'll have gallons for the next four days.'

Her face lit up. 'Ooh! Doesn't it look lovely? Warm milk straight from the cow. What fun!'

But it wasn't so funny when Lotty spent the whole of that night bellowing at the top of her voice while her calf answered pitifully from across the yard. I kept waking up and listening. I felt dreadful. Like a baby snatcher. I could hear Mother moving about and I knew she couldn't sleep either. I knew she thought me heartless, which made it worse. Several times I resolved to get up, go outside and carry the calf back to its mother. And each time I told myself to let them shout it out, not to give in. You had to be cruel to be kind. No dairy farmer worth his salt would lose sleep over a cow bellowing for her calf.

Mother was already in the kitchen when I went down next morning. 'Poor Lotty, she's been crying for her calf all night long. I couldn't sleep. Are you quite sure it's right to part them so soon?'

'I knew you'd say that. Course I'm sure. Bloody cow. Never known one to keep it up all night like that before. It's a wonder she's got any moo left.'

'P'raps it would be kinder to let the calf go back to her just for this morning. What d'you think? Just to let her know it's all right and she needn't worry?'

'No! They've got to be parted so leave them be. The real trouble is she's had it with her for a few days, waiting to go to market. If it'd been taken away at birth she wouldn't have bothered so.'

'Poor Lotty,' Mother sighed. 'Such an upheaval for her *and* losing her calf into the bargain. She must think she's come to a dreadful home.'

'Oh, you worry about her too much. She'll be okay once I turn her out into some nice grass. She'll forget about her calf soon enough then. They always do.'

Sure enough we hardly had another moo out of her and she settled down, made herself quite at home and proceeded to flood us with milk. The stuff was everywhere. We had no separator and so the milk had to be left for the cream to set. Every basin Mother could lay her hands on was pressed into use, from buxom bedroom basins with flowery patterns to thin enamel jobs lurking in dusty cupboards. All were vigorously scoured, filled with milk and left to set, on the shelves in the pantry, on the wash-stand in the spare bedroom, even on the brick floor in the kitchen. And as soon as one lot of cream was ready for skimming Lotty had produced another couple of pails of milk to fill the basins again.

For Skinny and Fatso there had never been such times. They couldn't believe their luck, grunting in amazement when their troughs suddenly flowed with skimmed milk and it wasn't even feed time. They buried their snouts in it, blowing, gurgling, biting and sucking to make the most of the miracle.

Turning the cream into butter proved to be another problem. We hadn't got a butter churn either. But we did have Kilner jars so we poured the cream into them and shook them. And shook them, and shook them, and shook them and only occasionally a jar of cream condescended to turn into butter. I'd leave Mother after breakfast, crouched over the basins skimming off the night's cream and with fresh pails of milk waiting to be set. I'd return for the mid-day meal and she'd still be at it, shaking various jars in turn, urging them aloud to turn into butter.

In the end she gave up and tipped all the jars of cream into a basin, drew up the sleeve of her jumper and plunged her hand in with a 'Here goes!'

'Whatever are you doing?' I thought she had gone mad.

'I've had a brainwave. I remember I saw a farmer's wife make butter like this once.' She scooped the cream to and fro.

'Not very hygienic.'

'Rubbish! Anyway, you've got to eat a peck of dirt before you die.' And a minute or two later, a laugh. 'It's working. . . . I do believe. . . . Yes! Success! Just look at this lovely big lump of butter!' She was holding it up with both hands, squeezing out drops of buttermilk.

And she had a great time salting it, tasting it and patting it into criss-cross patterns with two old wooden butter pats she'd unearthed. Then she sat down and made a list of all the people she thought she'd post some to.

But I don't think she was sorry when Monday came and the frothing buckets of milk stopped coming into the kitchen. And I proudly took the first churn up to the top road on a handcart and left it there on a stand to be collected by the milk lorry.

After Lotty the herd increased by ones and twos as I bid at the auctions for the cows I liked the look of. More often than not the bidding ranged on beyond the optimistically low limit I'd set for each animal, in my efforts to buy ten reasonable cows for the money I had available. Ten cows which would give me a regular monthly milk cheque and, at the same time, breed calves which would eventually fill my cowshed with a line of young cows, in place of the ageing beauties with which I had to start.

Lotty retained her position as number one boss cow as each new stranger stepped down from the lorry and made her anxious entry into the cowshed. If she was tied up in her stall she would just look round, lowering her head slightly so that the newcomer had a good look at the terrifying hat rack she carried on her head. At the formal introductions in the meadow next morning, Lotty's usual greeting was a well placed hoick from the hat rack, just to make sure there was to be no argument.

To the timid blue cow, obviously called Bluebell, one surprised stare from Lotty was enough to keep her out of range. Bluebell was a gentle cow. She took the business of making and delivering milk very seriously. She ate delicately, always grazing a little apart from the others, and when she lay down to chew her cud her eyes never closed completely and her ears beat a continuous semaphore. And in the thunder days of summer, when the gad-fly drove the other cows berserk, tails erect as they careered across the meadow, Bluebell always came last, apologetically, running because she had to and as though she knew the havoc it was playing with her milk yeild. Gentle Bluebell, who bowed the other cows before her through the gate and was always the last to slip quietly into her stall.

Another cow, a big, cumbersome Friesian, never really had a chance against Lotty. She had a huge, swinging udder, so low that it was impossible to stand a bucket upright under it. Bert got landed with milking her and immediately christened her Big Tits as he grappled with her bulging teats, heaving them up to squirt nearly horizontal streams of milk into the tilting bucket clasped between his knees. How he used to curse her when she came in for the afternoon milking from the wet fields! Her udder dragged through the mud in the gateways like a spiked harrow and Bert had to fetch bucket after bucket of warm water to clean off the caked mud before milking. And sometimes, just as at last he sat down to milk her, there would come a stream of squeaky-voiced abuse when Big Tits raised a filthy hind leg and smeared a new weal of sticky mud across her clean udder. It seemed as though she did it on purpose because it was comfortable having her udder washed.

When she first arrived she made the mistake of lumbering past Lotty, evidently confident that her weight gave her preference. Lotty was furious. She gave a quick flick of her head, opening up a nasty gash just below Big Tits' fanny for her presumption. As I bathed the wound preparatory to smearing it with healing ointment, Pete stood beside me holding the cow's tail to one side. He shook his head with some concern. 'Another couple of inches higher, ol' gal, and you'd have been in real trouble.'

Then there was Daisy. She was a lovely, dark brown cow with a beautiful white udder. It fell wide and pliant from high under her tail and curved beneath her, long and level until it merged with the veins which clustered like knotty vines under her belly. When she sauntered into the auction ring I joined the bidding for her, but with little hope of success. And I couldn't believe my luck when she was knocked down to me while I was still below my limit. This, without a doubt, was the buy of the year. I hurried home with the good news and prepared for the arrival of the cattle lorry.

'Her be a real good 'un, then,' Pete remarked as he listened to my description. He was always as interested as I was at each new arrival on the farm.

'Aye,' I enthused, 'can't make out why she went so cheap. She's young, only second calver, full of milk *and* she's got a heifer calf. Auctioneer sold her as a five galloner, too.'

64

Pete eased his beret back and whistled. 'That'll be more'n Bluebell gives. Us'll be filling three churns a day afore long.'

'Who's going ter milk 'er?' Bert wanted to know. He'd never forgiven us for landing him with Big Tits.

'I'll do her for a start,' I laughed. 'See how we get on. If she's easy p'raps you'll be able to manage her later.'

Bert clasped his hands behind his back and under his jacket. Just like old Jack. His bottom lip pouted and glistened under his large cap. 'Reckon I've enough ter do wi' Big Tits.'

Pete scoffed: 'You'll have ter milk more'n one. When us gets a shed full o' cows you'll have ter milk three or four—even more when it's your weekend on.'

Bert smirked at me. 'Us'll have ter have one o' they milkin' machines. Ol' Dunnell's got one. Alice milks all 'is twenty cows by 'erself.'

'I know, I know. But it all costs money. Let's get the cows first and we'll worry about machines later.' I knew I would have to come to it before long. All the smaller farms were starting to use milking machines now. They were easier to buy now that the factories were producing more after the slim years of the war. And wages were rising so machines made economic sense.

But I hated buying machinery and often remembered some advice I'd been given by little Bill Checksfield. I'd bought Maywood from him when he sold up and retired to a small cottage in the village with, as he said when stressing the profits to be made on the farm, 'enough money to see I home'. He must have been nearing seventy, but his hair was still thick, very white, and his face was shining red and wrinkled like a walnut. Under bushy brows his eyes were blue as cornflower and he had a large white moustache with a yellow hole where a hand-rolled cigarette usually smouldered. Even with hob-nail boots on he was barely five foot four. I'm sure he regretted having sold the farm because he was always hovering around, cycling up from the village and finding odd jobs to do because time crept like a snail at home all day, getting under his tall wife's feet. While half of him wished he'd not retired, the other half wanted to make sure I didn't spoil the farm.

I'd bought an old tractor and on his next visit Checky had seen it skulking in the cart shed, right next to the stall where his young black carthorse used to stand. We'd often had the usual old man, young man argument about horse versus tractor, so when he saw it he came hurrying to find me. He was shaking his head sadly as though my downfall was now certain. 'You should always buy what's growing into money, my lad, growing into money. Not summat dead and growing into rust.'

The lorry arrived bearing Daisy and her calf from the market. She walked down the ramp and into the cowshed with the confidence and grace of a prizewinner. She only gave one low moan of protest when Pete lifted her calf into his arms and carried her off to the calf pens. But then how could she know she wouldn't see her again for months?

Anyway, she forgot her calf as soon as we chained her in her stall. She blew at the corn in the manger, sampled it with a tentative lick and tucked into it with evident relish.

'Her's hungry,' Bert observed.

'Her's a beauty,' Pete said. 'Look at 'er bag, will yer? There's a five galloner, right enough.'

'Least 'er's got some good tits,' Bert conceded, 'not like they bloody great bananas of ol' Big Tits. Wouldn't mind milking this 'un, that I wouldn't.'

I brought a bucket of water and a cloth. I began to wash her udder. It was hot and tight and as I dried it off the milk began to weep from her teats.

'Christ, 'er's got some milk,' Pete exclaimed.

'The sod who sold her never milked her out this morning, I know,' I complained. 'Why *will* some bloody heathens still stick to that old trick?'

'What trick?' Bert asked.

'Not milking 'em out before they sell 'em, of course. Let their udders swell right up so's it looks as though they give more milk than they do. Must put them through hell. Like as not cause mastitis.' I patted her on the rump. 'Never mind, old girl, I'll soon relieve you of that lot, make you more comfortable.'

Pete had brought the milking stool and bucket. Daisy was still snuffling at the corn. I took the bucket, placed the stool behind me and sat down quietly beside her.

I pressed my head gently into her flank. 'All right, gal,' I crooned quietly, 'let's have it.' I stroked my hands over her udder to reassure her before clasping her two front teats. You could never tell. The hurly-burly of the market was enough to fray the nerves of the quietest cow.

Daisy went on eating as the first squirts of milk hit the side of the empty bucket with ringing pings. The milk flowed freely and soon

66

there was a warm gurgle as strong streams buried themselves in the rising froth in the bucket. This was a delight. It took but the slightest pressure from my curling fingers to draw the wealth of milk from the wide udder. Even the rapid alternation from hand to hand seemed too slow to keep up with the speed with which Daisy wished to release her milk. Even as I worked on the front quarters, so thin trickles dropped to the floor from the other teats and I began to think that a machine really would be necessary to cope with this cow, a machine with a cluster to embrace all four teats at once. She really was a bargain. Half a bucket of milk already and I had hardly started to relieve the pressure in the front quarters. I was dreaming away. A few more cows like Daisy and there would soon be plenty of money to buy a milking machine from the fat cheques I would be getting for each month's milk.

Then it happened. With the accuracy of a first division striker her leg shot forward, crashed fair and square into the side of the bucket and sent it flying out of my grasp in a clattering cascade of milk.

'You sod!' I jumped up. I leant forward to retrieve the bucket which was rolling around near the manger. The white lake of milk was veined with brown as it slipped round my boots and dribbled idly into the dung channel.

Daisy turned her head and her eyes rolled. 'You!' I fumed. 'You bloody sod! No wonder you went cheap!' As I said it I wondered how the other farmers at the market had known. She had seemed quiet. Perhaps they had guessed. Perhaps their years of experience told them this cow was too good to be true. Nobody would sell such a promising young cow unless there was a hidden fault.

Pete was shaking his head and clicking his tongue with concern. Bert just said: 'Her's a kicker, then.'

Amongst cows there are kickers and kickers. There are those who kick at the slightest touch, a sort of nervous reaction, a 'leave me alone, do,' which is usually easy to deal with because you both know where you stand. A hobble on her hind legs, or even a head thrust firmly into her flank when milking her, will calm her. And then there are those who kick for the sheer hell of it. Hobble them and they jump and cavort, bellow and groan as though they are suffering the most terrible torture. Even if you do manage to quieten them enough to sit beside them with a bucket between your knees, they hold on to their milk as though each teat contained a tightly turned off tap. The next auction sale, or a couple

67

of thirsty calves who will bunt back when they get a biff or two as they booze, are the only ways to deal with these kickers.

And there are the kickers like Daisy. The calculating kickers who wait until you least expect it, who fool you into believing they are co-operating and then let fly with a winner. They never kick at every milking. Just once in a while when they suspect you're off your guard. And always when the pail is almost full. Such a kicker was Daisy and from that first demonstration of her failing we tried every known remedy to cure her.

We tried hobbling her. She stood quietly while I tied the rope and there was a dreamy look on her face as she chewed her cud and released her torrent of milk. But when she judged the opportune moment to kick, the hobble only provoked her into more violent action. The first time I managed to rescue the bucket of milk in the second or two of respite which the hobble provided; at least it prevented the sudden, deadly accuracy of the unfettered kick. But soon she got the hang of it and in a flash she'd be bucking, both hind legs clear of the ground, see-sawing when they landed in an effort to be rid of the rope. Once, in a frantic manoeuvre, she managed to splash both feet into the full bucket. For a moment she stood stock still while the remaining milk sloshed out the muck from her cloven hoofs. Her ears were back and I knew, like me, she was wondering just how she was going to extricate herself. She was only half listening to my colourful abuse. She was waiting for me to make the first move and when I did, by standing up, she shot both legs backwards like a rampant stallion and sent the pail flying across the cowshed, a silver sputnik with a milky trail.

Bert suggested we fix a plank between her legs. He maintained old Jack had once done this with success in controlling a fractious cow. And it puzzled Daisy for two or three days when we tried it. She never even tried to kick. She was hoping to lull me into a false sense of security as she worked out how to overcome this new obstacle. Certainly I began to feel we had found the answer to preserving all the frothing buckets of milk which gushed from her, so that they ended up in the churn instead of spreading in sickly sadness through the straw and dung to the drain. The heavy plank was a solid barrier between the bucket and her wickedly accurate hoof. As each milking passed I became more confident we had found the answer. She stood quietly, her eyes half closed, her ears flopped, her jaws slowly chewing as each new lump of cud quivered up inside her dewlap from her first stomach. Her belly rumbled reassuringly against my ear and there was a dull ache in my forearms as I kept up the long, steady rhythm of milking.

Then she was mixing it with both hoofs. Like some bovine Houdini she had freed herself from restriction, the plank flew behind her with a soggy splash along the dung channel and yet another bucket of milk swirled across the floor, hooked out of my grasp as I tried to cradle it.

In the end we reached a sort of compromise. I let her stand unencumbered. But I made sure the bucket was never so much as half full before I emptied it and came back for another go at her. Now and then she flashed a kick at it. Sometimes she scored. More often than not I saved the milk. I never did discover what made her kick. A sore teat could do it. Or a sudden sound. Sometimes there could be a protest kick when the corn in the manger was finished. And in summer, when the flies defied all sprays in their angry raids on succulent, sweating hides, captive in a cowshed, then you could expect a kick or two. But these were desultory kicks, ones you could parry with your arm before they hit the bucket, kicks about which you'd had due notice, usually in the form of a warning whip round the ear from a shitty tail.

Only Daisy knew when she was going to kick and what made her do it. Yet she was a lovely cow and I never really regretted buying her. Her milk flowed unstintingly. Throughout the long winter of her lactation she never dropped below four gallons a day. Not even during the lean and draughty month of March, when the winter tack had become monotonous, fusty with no green kale or ox cabbage to enliven it; only the dull hay and the dusty corn in the manger while the wind whispered tantalising promises from outside, of new grass flushing in the far meadows beside the stream.

By the time that first autumn at Maywood began to shiver into winter I had my ten cows. After Daisy had come a dainty Ayrshire heifer, doe-eyed and long-eared who was called Bambi the moment she stepped from the lorry. She had a neat little udder with teats so small that it was only possible to milk her with the tips of thumbs and forefingers.

''Tis like workin' on a bloody virgin,' Pete complained. But the milk flowed rapidly and in surprising quantities while Pete's tongue darted to and fro along his lips as he worked at the delicate task. It must have been an unconscious reaction.

Then, in two buying sprees of great daring had come Popsi,

69

Laura, Blackie, Myrtle and Florrie. They were a line of comfortable matrons who completed the Heinz image of my dairy herd and enabled me to fill another churn and a half of milk a day. With the exception of Popsi they were all freshly calved and she was to distinguish herself with a rather special performance early in the New Year.

So milking time was either a joy or an abominable chore. Just which largely depended on the weather or the pressure of other work crying out to be done. If we were busy, with crops demanding long hours of attention, with yet more work piling up while time ran out, then it was often a curse to have to down tools and become the slaves of dairy cows. But if it was wet, or snowing, or when the east wind came snapping up the valley, then it was a joy to come from the cold fields into the warm cowshed, snug with the rich smells of chewed cud, hot hides, sweet hay and crisp straw mixed with dung. And on a cold, dark morning, straight from a warm bed and with a swinging hurricane lamp chasing the blowing shadows across the yard, it was a delight to slip into the cosy company of the cows. They knew the time. They were waiting and when the latch clicked on the door and the shaft of lamplight glowed on the straw and was lost in the high, dark beams, heads slowly turned, chains clinked, eyes rolled and the lazy ones still lying down reared up, dipping their backs and curling their tails as they stretched out of the long night.

The small dairy led off the cowshed at one end. With each clank of bucket and churn echoing from inside it, long ears twitched backwards, gauging each sound in the regular routine of preparing for milking. They listened for the footsteps across to the corn store, waited for the squeak of the door and the dull thud as the lid of the corn bin banged back against the wall. Now heads turned, ears came forward and sometimes a long tongue rasped up a nostril, perhaps to improve the sense of smell. The veins began to pulsate in the tightening udders as the familiar sounds and smells worked as a crescendo towards the release of the gathering milk.

But Lotty had her own special habit just before milking. She stood in the stall at the end of the line, next to the dairy and the corn store. Because she was the nearest, and also close to the hanging hurricane lamp lighting the comings and goings, she could watch the preparations while the others had to rely on only sounds and smells. And when the sights and sounds and smells built up towards the moment when the scoops of corn would come tumbling into her manger, when the bucket would clank behind her, the head press into her flank, the hands clasp her bulging teats, it was all too much. Then she hunched her back, shuffled forward, raised her tail and peed. Steam rose and quickly disappeared while the overpowering, acrid smell drifted slowly up into the rafters and we could make a start.

Winter

6

UNFORTUNATELY COWS HAVE to be milked twice a day, seven days a week and on high days and holidays. And that includes Christmas Day.

'We'll all have to muck in over Christmas,' I suggested to the boys, a few days before.

Pete shifted his beret to the back of his head and drew imaginary patterns on the dairy wall with his finger. He always showed embarrassment when decisions had to be made out of the general run of events. 'Reckon so,' he said, at last. 'Might jest as well be down 'ere milkin' as hangin' about at home. Won't be nothin' special there.'

'Not at Christmas?' I was surprised.

Bert sniffed and wiped his nose with the back of a milk-sticky hand. 'Dare say ol' Jack'll kill a rooster—if he don't have no luck wi' a pheasant. Last year us 'ad a rooster. Tough 'e was, too. Mum said 'twas Jack never killed 'un soon enough. Her didn't arf go on at 'im when 'e kept waitin' and waitin' ter get a pheasant in 'is traps.'

'Traps?' I tried to sound casual. But as soon as I said it I realised I'd sounded too eager.

Pete turned back to the wall and drew some more imaginary pictures. Bert smirked and shuffled a bucket loudly across the floor with the toe of his boot. 'I've often wished I could trap a pheasant,' I went on, casually. 'I can't shoot for toffee and I always hear them squawking in the May Wood.'

Bert giggled. 'Jack gets 'em on ol' Dunnell's stubbles.'

'He uses a special light gin trap,' Pete chipped in. 'Spreads the

75

jaws and sets 'em ever so light on the clip, 'e do. So light he has a job ter leave it without it springin' orf. Then 'e drops a few grains o' wheat between the jaws. . . .'

Bert squeaked: 'And along comes the ol' pheasant.' He started mincing across the dairy, pushing his head forward and rolling his eyes with each step, 'and 'e sees the corn and "ha! ha!" 'e says and 'e gives a good peck at it. And up comes the jaws and cops 'im by the neck and there 'e is, all ready fer pluckin'.' He grabbed his own neck in his hands, stuck out his tongue and uttered a long gurgle.

We all laughed and Lotty turned round, winding a tuft of hay into her mouth as she looked at us with surprise.

'So pr'raps you'll have a pheasant this year.' I finished scrubbing a bucket and upended it on the rack to drain. 'What about presents? Going to hang up your stockings?' I teased them.

'Not bloody likely,' Pete said. 'Us don't give no presents up our 'ouse. Not since afore we left school. Except p'raps Mum'll give us a pair o' gloves, or some socks—maybe sommat like that.'

'And Jack'll get hisself a bottle o' port down the pub,' Bert suggested.

'Aye,' Pete agreed. 'Mum'll have a glass and Jack'll get pissed on the rest. He'll mumble and dribble an' shake the 'cumulator on the wireless if the tunes fade.'

Bert prodded his brother. 'Least you won't be there. I'll lay you'll be out givin' darlin' Rose 'er Christmas box.' He gave a filthy cackle and leered at Pete.

Pete blushed, shuffled his beret and suddenly clapped his hand with a resounding smack over Bert's mouth. Soon the two of them were giggling and wrestling, their shadows dancing on the wall as they tussled along behind the cows. Long ears flicked backwards but the munching of hay continued. Only little Bambi looked round and peed with concern.

We made as many preparations as possible to minimise the work over Christmas. In the corn store we shot sacks of ground oats on to the wooden floor, added bean meal, fish meal and a shovelful of brick red, powdery mineral salts. We mixed them all together, Pete and I turning the white heap with shining shovels, spluttering in the dust laden gloom while Bert hovered round with a bass broom, sweeping up behind as we piled the corn bin to overflowing.

We stamped out into the yard like three dusty millers, smacking our clothes and wiping our faces. Skinny and Fatso ambled over, grunting enquiringly, lifting their heads to peer, just in case we had left the door open.

'I'll bet they buggers get out Christmas,' Pete said.

'Sod 'em if they do,' grumbled Bert.

I hastened to say we'd shut them firmly in their sties, just to forestall any possibility of a lively pig hunt through the woods over the holiday.

There was kale to be cut and carried down to the cowshed. It was a wet and shivering job, hacking at the base of the tall stems, getting showered with water if it was wet or a tinkle of ice down your neck if it was freezing. Whatever the weather your fingers became numb as you piled the cut kale on to a spread out piece of sacking, gathered the two soggy ends to wrap the bundle and then hoped it all stayed together as you heaved a hundredweight over your shoulder. Then there was the long trudge through the sticky mud, the clever manoeuvre through the gate without hooking the load to pieces on the gatepost, and lifting the gate shut with one hand while the weight of kale threatened to topple you over backwards, or the slimy sacking to slip from your grasp. By the time you reached the cowshed you were in a muck sweat and it was only the obvious delight of the cows at your arrival which seemed to make it all worthwhile.

In the warm dry cowshed in winter, kale time was almost as exciting as corn time. As soon as the heavy wet marrowstem kale plonked into the mangers, cow chains rattled, heads and horns waved as tongues groped to tussle with the thick and fleshy food. The leaves went first and then there was the glorious chew down the juicy stem. Heads would come up, ears flop back, eyes half shut while tongues dripped as they steered great green lollipops into slowly masticating jaws.

We needed a cartload of kale outside the cowshed to last over the holiday. And this meant catching Colonel and harnessing him up.

Colonel was an ancient carthorse, a bay gelding who seemed to have been kicking around the farm for as long as anybody cared to remember. Bill Checksfield couldn't say for certain how long he'd been there. He seemed to have come clopping through the mists of time and the old man had been adamant that I bought the horse with the farm. It was almost an ultimatum. No Colonel, no farm. Checky was quite prepared to let him go for only a tenner, rather than chance the knacker man getting his filthy maulers on him.

So the old horse stayed on the farm and there was always the odd carting job for him to do. There was dung to be shifted out into the fields on the frosty days in winter, when the ground was iron hard and the heavy cartwheels bumped over frozen ruts, hard mud clinging to the red spokes, metal rims gleaming and the bulbous, grease-filled hubs clonking as they lurched against the axles. Colonel could pull a loaded cart clean through the middle of the roughest gateway without being led. But once he reckoned he'd done enough for one day, or if he didn't feel like work anyway, then he'd make sure that one heavy hub clipped the gatepost and knocked it askew. His ears would flick back to catch the oath he knew would come ringing after him and he'd veer off, deaf to the 'Whoa! Bugger you, whoa!' of whoever was following.

There were many jobs for which Colonel came in useful. When you could find him. He liked to wander and over his long life he'd made a great study of escapology. He would chivvy at a gate until he'd loosened the latch and could barge through. Tie it with string and he'd rip it off with his worn, yellow teeth. Bind it with wire and he'd turn his arse to it and kick his way through. If the gate was strong enough to resist these cracking blows, he'd shake his mane, swish his tail and plod off as though it didn't really matter. Somewhere around the field the hedge would be weak. Maybe there was a place where a few spiles had been driven in to block an old gap through the blackthorn. It only needed a few deft blows with a hind hoof and there was room for an old horse to squeeze through.

He knew his way everywhere. Long before winter set in he knew which farmer had made the sweetest hay—and the best way to get at the hay rick. Perhaps late at night, or early in the morning my 'phone would ring. 'That you, Dave? Old Colonel's at my hay rick. Fer Chrissake come and fetch 'im back, will yer?' And the call could have come from two or three winding miles away. Colonel knew every farm in the parish and every farmer knew Colonel. I'd grab a halter, mount my bike and pedal off to mumble my apologies and swear at Colonel.

'Sorry about this. Dunno how he got out. Must've kicked his way through again.'

'He's made a hole in the side of my rick, right enough. Big enough to crawl in, it is. Pulled out and trodden more hay than he's eaten.'

'Yes, yes, so sorry.' Of course Colonel had pulled out a lot of hay. You wouldn't catch him eating the weathered outside of a stack. He liked the fragrant middle. 'Come on, you sod! Break out again and it's the knacker yard for you, my lad!' I'd grab him by the forelock and he'd meekly follow.

'So sorry, again. Have to keep him tied up. Let me know if you find you're short of hay later on.' Fortunately nobody ever did. Otherwise I'd have never had enough.

On the way home, with the halter rope trailing behind my bike, Colonel would start to dawdle. His steps would get slower and slower until I was forced off the bike when he stopped completely. He'd hang his head as though he was dead beat. A sad look in his eye would accuse me of pacing him with a bicycle as though he was an unbroken two-year-old.

'Come on, you devil! I'll bet you clipped along this lane fast enough when you were after that hay.' I'd tug on the halter. No movement. I'd shorten my grasp and whiz the end of the rope by his ear. A nod of his head would be followed by a few desultory steps forward, which stopped the moment I bent down to pick up my bike.

'I'll make you move, you crafty quadruped.' A walk to the hedge-row. The choosing and the loud snapping off of a stick. A watchful, blinking eye, a sudden flick of ears, a clumsy clatter of hooves as he swivelled and made off away from me along the way we had come.

'I'll teach you, you cunning bugger!' A rapid chase. A grab at the dangling halter. A submissive nod of his head. 'I'll come quietly.'

'You'll bloody move, mate!' A resounding thwack on his ribs and for the next few hundred yards we would make good progress as he kept up with my slow pedalling. Almost imperceptibly he'd lag behind. He knew I couldn't hold the halter, keep my balance and lean back to use the stick all at the same time. I had to dismount and he could stop.

'Don't make out you want a breather, you crafty sod. I've got work to do. Buggered if I don't find some for you too, when we get home. Help you shift that gut full of hay.' Another flick of the stick and so we would finally reach home in a series of stops and starts and swearing.

In the end I won the battle of containing Colonel. I bought an electric fence. This simple device was but a single strand of wire, fixed to stakes over insulators and strung along the inside of a hedge. Coupled to a six volt battery through a ticking circuit breaker, an electric current pulsated along the wire to give a tidy jolt to any animal that touched it. Or any human for that matter, and even wearing wellies you could feel the shock bite through your body.

The dew was heavy on the grass on the morning I gave Colonel his first lesson in electricity. I grabbed him by the forelock and together we walked across to the side of the field. 'I've got a surprise for you, old lad. Just come along and have a look at one of these new fangled inventions.'

He nodded along behind me, now and then blowing through his nostrils. I was using the tone of voice that usually heralded a bowl of oats at the end of the walk. He had a tight little moustache that curled at the ends, like that of an old fashioned sergeant major, and it twitched and it glistened with dew.

We neared the fence and his ears shot forward as he caught sight of the shining new wire. 'Yes, that's it, my old friend. You've seen wire before. Remember that bit of barbed wire you trampled into the mud last week. *What* fun you had, didn't you? Well, this is a very special bit of wire. I want to introduce you to it so's you'll be quite sure you recognise it again whenever you see it.'

Now we were right beside the wire. I still held his forelock and I pulled his head down towards the wire. 'Now you just dab your old moustacho on this lovely new wire, like this!'

I could feel the jolt tingle through his forelock. With his four wet, iron clad hooves embedded in the wet grass he must have received a real belt. His head reared up in alarm, he gave a disgusted snort and trundled off across the field faster than he'd moved for years.

So long as he was surrounded by an electric fence he never broke out again. Provided the current was switched on. But if it was off, or maybe a stray branch or a crooked insulator had short-circuited it, Colonel knew in an instant. He would blandly walk through the fence, hooking the wire round his fetlocks, tearing it from the stakes and dragging it along until it lay in a tangled mess impossible to unravel.

But for all his faults he was useful. However exasperating, he was lovable. Whoever happened to be working with him would chat away to him as though he was another mate, fairly certain there wasn't much in farming parlance he didn't understand.

And we cut and stacked a fine load of kale which Colonel pulled down into the yard behind the cowshed. We unhooked it and left it there, enough to last well over Christmas with only a few minutes work to feed the cows from there each day.

There was the laborious job of cutting and carrying the hay from the rick in the stack-plat at the end of the buildings. The heavy, wide-blade knife had to be sharpened, keen as a razor, or it would bounce off the tightly packed hay causing sweat and bad temper. There was no surer way of generating both heat and bad feeling on a frosty morning than a stint with a blunt hay knife. You never found it was blunt until you came to use it, high up on the rick. Of course I was always in a hurry. There never seemed to be time to stop, go down the ladder and sharpen the knife. A few minutes of brute force, perched up on the square shelf of hay and I could hack off a two foot deep layer. Or so I always thought. But the knife refused to penetrate more than a few inches. I'd discard my jacket. The whole rick quivered under my renewed efforts while I cursed the hay, the knife and the last person to leave it in such a condition. When I thought about it, it was usually me. The wind whispered in the rick, plucked at my wet shirt, fanned it with a breath straight from the Arctic and slapped it back against my clammy body.

But take the trouble to pull the whetstone from its hiding place, plunged deep in the shaven face of the rick, lay the broad knife across your knee and liven the edge with steady, rasping strokes. Then up the ladder and on the shelf of hay it was a different story. When you grasped the heavy handles and plunged the knife, it sank with a satisfying scrunch and sheared off a thick layer as you sliced along the sides of your perch.

By Christmas the hay had long since finished heating in the rick. Now it was a golden brown with a rich smell of nuts and rubbed tobacco. As you drove the pitchfork into the middle of the cut flake and lifted it clear on to your shoulders, so you disturbed a dead summer. Down the ladder you carried tight layers of tangled grasses pressed to rest, captured in full flower but now each head a shatter of seeds. Amongst the tangle here lay a still yellow buttercup, there the faint trace of blue in a flattened swirl of vetch, and a tall, crisp thistle, its cluster of purple blooms now a silver pillow for a huddled bunch of wild white clover. Here was a sense of summer in the midst of winter.

There were many such flakes to be cut and carried for Christmas. One by one we humped them into the cowshed and stacked them upon each other in the dark, back corner. The cows studied our activities and pondered upon them as they lay on their straw and chewed their cud. The rich aroma pervaded every dusty cranny and hay seeds crept past our up-turned collars to nestle in the sweat on our spines.

81

'Ol' Dunnell bales all *his* hay,' Bert observed. He pulled a grubby rag from his pocket, leant forward and rummaged beneath his collar.

''Twudn't be no trouble if us had bales,' Pete agreed. 'Us could soon carry 'em down from the stack-plat.'

I pointed out that only the bigger farms could afford to buy or hire balers. Small farmers had to be content with their lot. A horse and waggon, eager arms with pitchforks, and loose hay carried home and stacked neat and solid under a golden roof of thatch.

'Bet you won't find old Jack using a baler on his field of hay,' I concluded.

They laughed. Pete said: 'He says balers make musty hay.'

'Yea!' Bert agreed. 'Jack, well Jack borrowed one o' Dunnell's bales, like. Brought it home on 'is bike 'e did. When he undid the wire and broke it open, t'were all mouldy in the middle.'

I thought: serves him right. I said: 'Ah, hay sweats out and heats up better in a stack.'

'But it be a bugger ter cut 'n carry, all the same.' And Pete sloped off with his pitchfork, gathering up the tufts of hay we'd littered on our loaded journeys.

For Mother and me this was a quiet Christmas as far as the usual celebrations were concerned. The family was still scattered by the war and memories of Donald were still raw. So we were going to be on our own, with business almost as usual. In spite of all the preparations you make on a farm, some work has still to be done when animals are involved. You can never just leave them and relax. And as Mother had planned three cycle trips to church and back, including a special session with the Sunday School, that was going to take up most of her day as well.

The special treats of Christmas fare were still hard to come by. So we settled for a roast cockerel, and a pudding from a wartime recipe, with gravy browning as one of the ingredients to give it the authentic colour because the lack of the correct amount of fruit left it looking anaemic. And for booze we had a bottle of sherry, although Mother would only ever drink 'just a teeny-weeny glass, darling. Any more makes me feel quite swimmy.'

But one of my pleasures at Christmas was listening on the wireless to the Nine Lessons and Carols. It had become one of the vital, nostalgic parts of Christmas, as much a part as the food and drink, the holly and the tinsel, and that special feeling that came when the candle first lit the bedroom in the morning and I peered round the curtain at the cold, dark sky. The feeling that lurked through the years from the first memories of an outstretched hand in the dark, groping for the bulging stocking hanging from the bedpost and knowing that Christmas Day had dawned.

In the days at Maywood radio reception was spasmodic in the valley. The bulky, portable wireless set had to be swivelled with great accuracy in order to pick up the strongest sound waves. The battery had to be good, so I made sure of renewing it as I looked forward to the Christmas listening.

Then I discovered that the time of the broadcast of carols had been changed. Now it clashed with the afternoon milking.

'So the cows will have to enjoy the carols with me,' I said to Mother. 'I don't suppose you want to listen in, do you?'

'Gracious no. I'll sing carols in Church.' And I knew she'd be glad if I didn't listen indoors. Religion over the radio was anathema to her. She switched a service off whenever it started. It was a lazy man's way of worship. There was no hardship, no sacrifice involved in sitting back in a comfortable chair and listening. It cheapened the Church, as well as helping to empty them.

So on Christmas afternoon I left her by the fire going through her cards and presents, and I marched off up to the cowshed with the wireless under my arm.

Above the hill to the north, and beyond the wood, the sky was full. A heavy mass of black spread overhead and mingled with the early-coming night. The stark branches of the tallest oak trees seemed pewter plated against it and a bitter wind scurried through the steading, flicking at the thatch so that the hay rick looked as though it had taken fright. It was a wind which snapped at every hindrance, the sort from which countrymen turn weather beaten faces, muttering: ''Twill be warmer when it snows.'

Inside the cowshed there was a rich, warm gloom, centrally heated by the hot breath and the glow from hides and full udders. I lit the hurricane lamps, hung them up and a feeling of cosy contentment came over me as the yellow light stroked life into the colours of the cows. The wind moaned outside as it was forced to leap over the high roof and I was glad for the cows that they had warmth and shelter, sweet food piled round about and water waiting to bubble into the drinking bowls at the first press of a wet nose. How much nicer it all was for them than for others, whose owners believed it was healthier, or cheaper in labour costs, for them to stand hoof deep in cold mud, rumps to the wind and backs hunched as they waited for the winter to pass.

And now I was going to treat them to some music into the bargain. Carols for Christmas in a cowshed. Suddenly it seemed right. Here was where carols ought to be sung. Were not cows watching and blowing hot breath over the manger where Jesus was born?

I set the wireless on a spare milking stool against the wall behind the line of cows. I switched on as the announcement of the programme was being made and swung the wireless to catch the maximum sound. Reception was perfect. The volume was only turned low and yet the announcer's voice resounded up the bare wall.

The door opened. Pete and Bert clattered in, red cheeked and finger blowing.

'Christ, ain't it cold?'

'Reckon 'tis goin' ter snow.'

They bustled off into the dairy, pulling off their jackets as they went. Evidently they'd decided that milking was to be done in record breaking time. Water splashed, buckets rattled and hilarity suggested that perhaps Jack had shared his bottle of Christmas port after all.

Then there was silence. Pete walked out into the cowshed. 'Who's that talkin'?' He peered into the shadows behind the cows. 'What yer got there, then? A wireless?'

Bert joined him and giggled: 'What's this? Workers' Playtime?'

They laughed and nudged each other, bubbling with high spirits.

'Shut up and listen!' I was bending over the wireless. The announcer had finished setting the scene. I increased the volume as the first clear and passionless notes of the boy soprano climbed up and stroked the high rafters.

'Once in royal David's city, stood a lowly cattle shed.'

The boys listened in silence. They had a sense of occasion which straightened their faces and I half expected to see them stand to attention. Instead they swayed slightly and looked puzzled at this unexpected turn of events.

And the lonely notes called and echoed and found an answer in the tingle of nostalgia which crept through me.

While the silver soprano sang alone through the first verse the cows paid little attention. Here and there a chain rattled and

Lotty turned to stare at us, puzzled at the unusual break in the routine build-up to milking.

But when the second verse began and the whole choir and the organ swelled into sound, there was immediate participation. Heads shot up and ears pricked forward as they tried to trace the tumbling sounds. Lotty shook her head in disbelief; there was a soft moo from Bluebell, as though she was tuning-in to the right note, and Daisy kicked at the trembling air because she couldn't think what else to do. Big Tits lumbered backwards, plonking her large feet down the step into the dung channel, her rump swaying as she positioned herself so that, for a moment, I thought she was limbering up for a slow rumba.

I stood behind the line of cows and began to conduct, singing and encouraging them in their participation. The boys hooted with delight and joined in with words well remembered from Sunday School days. It was a rousing overture.

When the carol ended I turned the volume down. We had to get the milking done and evidently too much sound wasn't going to help. Pete and Bert had gone back into the dairy and had started the carol from the beginning again while the lesson was being read by the choirboy on the radio. Their singing was disjointed, interspersed with clattering buckets. First one would sing, and then the other, and then would come a line or two in unison.

I walked across to the dairy. Bert was lolling in the corner, beating time with a bottle of port. Pete's beret was well back on his head, his black eyes were shining and with both hands outstretched, a bucket on the crook of one arm, he aimed at the highest note at the start of the penultimate line.

At the sight of me the singing trailed away, but revived again as I conducted and joined in to the end of the verse.

Bert held out the bottle. 'Wanna swig?'

The port was already more than half gone. 'Thanks.' I took a mouthful.

'Bought it down the Six Bells dinner time, us did.' Pete's smile was wide and proud.

'Oh? It's not Jack's bottle, then?'

'Nope!' Bert was emphatic. 'This is our'n.'

He wiped the top of the bottle with the palm of his hand, spat dryly as farm men will when preparing to drink and took a swig like a veteran. He swallowed with only a slight wince and handed the bottle to Pete. 'Your turn.'

'You two got through that lot between you?' I asked.

''Tain't much.' Pete was happily repeating Bert's performance before drinking. He held the bottle high. 'Merry Christmas!'

On the wireless the first lesson had finished and now the singing had started again. It was softer and with no vibrations the cows had calmed down and seemed to be enjoying the tune. The usual keen awareness of our activities in relation to the corn bin had been replaced by a rapt appreciation of the singing. I had read of some farmers' favourable experiments in milking to music and had been inclined to scoff at the idea. Now it seemed they were right. Even Lotty's head was lolling slightly and there was almost a far away look in her eyes.

She snapped back to reality when Pete barged past her with a scoop of corn. She ate it with her usual gusto. Pete treated her to his own rendering of the next carol as he sat beside her with a clatter and started to milk her. He knew the tune right enough, but was short on the words so that most of the time he crooned: 'Lotty, Lotty, Lotty, I love Lotty.'

Meanwhile Bert wrestled with Big Tits. He heaved at the great udder as usual only now, instead of the usual stream of squeaky obscenities, his version of the carol became almost a mellow madrigal intoned into the cow's belly. Twice he broke off from his work, placed his bucket and stool with exaggerated care against the back wall, and drifted along to the dairy for another spot of refreshment.

We milked to the music. When a carol finished and the sombre sounds of reading took over, then we treated the cows to a ragged encore until a new tune demanded our attention. The milk came from the cows with ease and there was more than usual for an afternoon. Maybe it was the music that soothed the hormones. Maybe it was just because of a feeling of goodwill all round and an extra touch of tenderness generated by the port. Maybe it was because of the over generous dollops of food dropped into the mangers that morning because it was Christmas.

There was no doubt that carols in the cowshed were a huge success. Even Daisy behaved herself after her first startled foray at the reverberating sound waves, and as I milked her and sang to her, I had the certain feeling she'd be good. Somehow a kick at the bucket seemed out of the question in the general air of bonhomie and I showed my trust in her by milking her right out without emptying the bucket half way through.

With each visit to the dairy I noticed that the port in the bottle had diminished. Soon only a swirl over the bottom remained, evidently left there for good manners. By then the rate of milking had slowed down appreciably and I wondered whether either of the boys was going to need my help in finishing off their last cows. The choir had drifted through yet another faultless performance and now there was a glorious rumble from the organ as the choir drew breath to exhort us to 'Hark! The herald angels sing.'

I looked at Pete. He was sitting sideways on to little Bambi, lolling his head against her flank, plucking at a tiny teat with his right hand while he conducted the music with his left. Squirts of milk spurted with each beat, sometimes going into the bucket, more often fizzing into the straw on the floor. His beret had slipped off and was trapped between his shoulder and the cow and his black hair sprouted and fell like a luxuriant tuft of grass. He finished the verse a bar behind the choir, gave me a wide, glazed smile and blinked slowly.

'Better let me finish her off, old lad,' I suggested. 'You best start to feed round.' He'd be safer carrying hay.

He saluted slowly with his left hand and stood up unsteadily. He flung his arm over Bambi's back for support as he stooped to pick up the bucket and stool. She stood still with her eyes half closed, enjoying the music and chewing her cud as though he didn't exist. Then he saw his beret lying under the cow so he carefully replaced the bucket and stool and went down on all fours to retrieve it. As I looked down at him I wondered if he could ever manage to keep his date with Rose that night. Certainly he'd never be able to raise her Christmas present.

Finally he joined me behind the cows and sauntered off towards the dairy, bucket over one arm and beating time with the stool. 'Glory to the new born King!'

I stripped the rest of the milk from Bambi as the choir crashed into the last verse. Pete was carolling louder than ever from the dairy, singing glory to each cow in turn and even the sows and old Colonel got a mention.

There was no sight nor sound of Bert. Only a half full pail of milk and a stool tucked against the wall marked his passing. But we found him eventually when we went into the dark corner where the hay was stacked. He was sound asleep, snoring gently into his large cap, which was dragged down for comfort over his face.

7

A FEW DAYS after Christmas it snowed. At first it was only a light dusting, just enough to cover the scant grass and powder the hedges. But it perplexed Skinny and Fatso when they waddled out of their warm sties to greet the morning. They'd been imprisoned since Christmas Eve so that we didn't have to go searching for them over the holiday. Doubtless they'd thought longingly of the meadow during their incarceration. Indeed, whenever I'd passed anywhere near their sties, other than at feeding times, they'd come belting out into their little yards, reared up so that their front trotters rested on the wall and sworn at me with enthusiasm.

Now that they were at liberty at last, Fatso's immediate reaction to the white carpet stretching before her was to take a bite at it. As it was tasteless she shovelled along with her snout until a snow-ball gathered and she tossed it aloft with a disgruntled snort. The snow was a hindrance to foraging. So she stopped, stood still with her tail hanging limp like a frayed sash cord, and cogitated on this new situation. She was grubby, sty-worn and the broad white stripe over her shoulder looked grey against the bright snow. Finally she turned back with a peevish grunt and sidled up to the outside wall of the sty. She thrust her rump against it and started to rub. Her tail sprang into a coil, she uttered tiny, high pitched squeaks of pleasure while dust rose from her like incense and drifted down to sully the snow.

Skinny's reactions were altogether different and caused us some exciting work. To her the snow was a sprinkled condiment, obviously adding relish to the grass which it covered, even enhancing the subtle fragrance of the grubs and bugs hibernating in the white forests of roots beneath the surface. And before she had taken a dozen paces into the snow, her head went down with determination and her strong snout broke through the turf like a plough share. With a flick of her head she rolled a lump over and by a delicate mincing of her front teeth against her tongue, she extracted the harvest hidden there.

By nature pigs are rooters. But ever since their introduction to the great outdoors, Skinny and Fatso had found an abundance of acorns and other morsels littering the surface of the meadow and the wood. There had simply been no incentive to root. Because of this I'd been lulled into the belief that they would continue to forage and graze on the surface and that there was no need to take steps to prevent them tearing the pastures to pieces.

Bill Checksfield had warned me about rooting pigs on one of his cycling tours of inspection. It was the first time he'd seen the sows in the meadow, soon after they had farrowed. I had seen him come free-wheeling down the hill, perched on his old black bike, a tall, narrow handled machine which must have been the son of Penny Farthing. He dismounted in a hurry, running the last few yards and heaving at the high handle-bars to bring the thing to a halt. He had to back pedal to work the hub brake and usually he drifted on, with all his little weight on the pedals, to where the lane started to climb again just past the buildings, and the additional pull of gravity brought him to a halt beside the stack-plat. If he arrived from the other direction, and this meant he was coming from a session at The Six Bells, many years of practice in all weathers, and on the darkest of nights, told him the precise moment to start leaning on the brake. With a gentle hush-hush from the hub he would glide past the stack-plat, past the stable and the cowshed, slowly losing speed as he turned into the yard at the back of the house, circle it past the edge of the pond and round until he came to rest against the well head outside the back door. And he could do this to perfection even when he was too drunk to walk.

But the sudden sight of the pigs in the meadow brought him scurrying to a halt. He leant his bike against the fence, toddled across to the pig sties and stood gazing out across the meadow. Cycle clips still gripped the bottoms of his baggy trousers and he pulled a large red handkerchief from his pocket, raised his cap and mopped his brow.

Checky never came looking for me on his visits to the farm. He'd lived there so long that his feeling of responsibility for the place was unlikely to die. I accepted this in an old man. Although I had the enthusiasm and ideas of any young man starting on his own, I knew there were many local wrinkles to be learnt from old Checky. Best to keep in with him.

I greeted him from across the yard. He turned, wiping the inside rim of his cap with the handkerchief. He pulled on his cap leaving a tuft of white hair frothing over his forehead. His fingers were stubby, as thick as the cow teats they had squeezed for years and his nails were long and yellow, ridged like the age rings on a cow horn.

'Mornin',' he replied as I reached him. He smiled and held out his hand. It was always important to him to shake hands at each new meeting. 'They sows,' he nodded at the meadow, 'you'll have to ringle them, you know.'

'Oh, I don't think they'll root,' I said. 'They're too busy eating acorns for that.'

'Never knowed a sow what didn't root. That's a good little meadow, that. Nicely sheltered from the north, it be. Full of early grass, you'll find.'

He thrust his hand deep into his jacket pocket and brought out a spherical silver tobacco case, cupped in his horny hand. For a moment he stroked it lovingly with his thumb and then he flipped open the inlaid, hinged lid with his nail. He pulled at a twist of shag, coiled like a sleeping slow-worm in a nest, broke off a small piece and buried it in his palm behind the case. With surprising delicacy for such thick fingers he extracted a cigarette paper from the packet squashed in with the shag and stuck it to his bottom lip. He snapped the lid shut, returned the case to his pocket and began to rub the shag with a slow, deliberate motion.

'Aye, you'll have to ringle they sows, right enough. Acorns won't last for ever and they'll tear that turf to pieces, come the winter. You mark my words. Tear it to pieces, 'em will.'

The cigarette paper shivered as he spoke. He pulled it from his lip and teased the black tobacco into it, rolling it and prodding it with a calloused forefinger until the gummed edge overlapped and could be drawn along the pink tongue peeping from under his generous moustache. He pinched the strands of shag protruding from one end of the cigarette, popped it into the yellow hole in his moustache and lit it with a huge flame that flared with sudden magic from a large and battered lighter. The strong smoke drifted lovingly up over his face.

'There's a pair of ringling pliers among that box of tools in the stable,' he went on. 'Dare say there's a packet o' rings there too. Used to be all sorts o' tack on that old shelf, there did. Stockholm tar, creosote, horse oils, all manner o' tack. Used to be a spare set of shoes for ol' Colonel up there too. And some frost nails. He'll need some frost nails if we get some slippy weather, mind.'

I assured him, nodding, that no doubt all the articles he had mentioned were still on the shelf. As yet I hadn't got around to rummaging among the dust and cobwebs to find out all that I had inherited. 'But I'll see if the ringling pliers are there,' I concluded.

'Aye.' He blew another cloud of smoke. 'You find 'em and give us the wink and I'll come up and ringle they old sows for you.'

I thanked him and told him I'd see how the sows behaved. But he seemed to have lost interest now. He took the cigarette from his mouth and tickled the ash from the end with his little finger. The paper glowed where it hadn't burnt back along the line of spittle and he tore this off carefully before having another puff.

He started to chuckle. 'Funny about that old shelf,' he mused. 'You've met old Frank Weller, ain't you? Travels for Higgins and Jenkins, he do. Sure he's been round here trying to sell you fertilizer and this and that.'

I agreed. He was the fat man, with thick glasses, who had driven down one day and overflowed from a Morris Minor. A keen salesman he was, and had I agreed to buy the vast list of essentials he considered I needed—from his long experience of serving the farming community, mind you—I'd have gone broke trying to pay for it all.

'Aye, old Frank,' Checky went on. 'Been coming for years, he has. Nosey old bugger, too. One day he came and it were raining heavens hard and he wanted to pee. Nipped into the stable, he did, into the corner under that very shelf. Suppose he thought he'd see what I got up there while he was standing there having a pee. See whether I was short of anything so's he could sell me some more.' Checky chuckled again, removed his fag and spat. 'Anyway, he stretched up and copped hold of an old paint tin. He tipped it forward to see what was in it. Full of creosote, it were, and it slopped down all over his John Thomas.'

I laughed and said: 'How very unpleasant.'

Little sparks flew from Checky's fag as the wind from his chuckles blew past it. 'Come running out, he did. Right old state he were in. Reckoned it felt as though 'twere burning orf. Kept waddling up and down, up and down, holding it and blowing on it so's I didn't know what to do for the best. I couldn't very well take him indoors; not with the Missus in the kitchen.'

He paused. I agreed it would have been improper and begged him to continue. 'Didn't know what to do, I didn't. I suggested some udder ointment. There was some of that up on the shelf. He'd sold it to me. Never been opened. But no, Frank wouldn't hear of it. Said it'd be too heating. Said it were something to cool it down he wanted. So I thought, water. And I slipped down to the well by the back door, drew a nice bucket of cold water and carried it back to the stable fer old Frank.'

Checky pulled his cap further down his forehead, shook his head slowly and smiled at the memory. 'That were the only time Frank Weller never managed to sell I anything,' he said, as he walked back to his bike.

I'd never ringed a pig so it seemed a good idea to get Checky to do it. So when Skinny started to root in the snow covered meadow, I sent him a message. The same morning he came wheeling down the lane with a piece of cord draped over his handle bars.

A search along the shelf in the stable had produced the pliers. With a drop of oil the rusty jaws were made to open and shut freely. Each jaw was curved and channelled so that when they were fully extended a split ring could be bent open and lodged in them. The rings were made of stout copper wire and the two open ends were filed to points so that they would pierce through the gristle on the snout of the unfortunate sow when the pliers were squeezed tight. Three or four such rings embedded around the top rim of her snout definitely discouraged her from digging. Until she got them out.

But first catch and hold your sow. Pete and Bert had driven them into their respective sties, bolted the doors and smartly taken up the position of spectators, hanging over the wall from the outside. They had examined the pliers, tested the sharp rings with the tips of their fingers, whistled appreciatively and decided it was wisest to keep a stout wall between them and the sows when the rings were squeezed home.

Checky fumbled with his piece of cord. He ran it round his thick fingers and wound it round the palm of his hand as he looked down at Skinny from outside the sty. She, wise creature, had guessed that something unusual was afoot. The unexpected bowl of corn to entice her in had been welcome, but it had only taken a minute to eat and now she raised her head and fixed Checky with a beady eye. He was a stranger. Something to do with her confinement in the sty again. Just when she'd discovered all that succulent food that lay under the turf. She grunted sternly, demanding release.

Checky slowly tied one end of the cord into a slip knot. He looped it round his hand and pulled until it bit into his rough knuckles. 'That'll hold her,' he decided. He eased the knot and handed me the rope. 'You catch her. Just drop the loop over her snout and pull it back so's it slips between her jaws and tightens over her snout.'

'Anything you say, guv'nor,' I replied, trying to sound as though it was simple, something any fool could do.

Skinny slewed round at the sound of the bolt. She was all for making a dash for it as I slipped into the sty. I urged her to calm down, lied to her that there was really nothing to get so het up about and told her I'd come for a chat.

She backed away giving a series of staccato grunts, half inquisitive, half apprehensive. With her head in the normal position she could only see my legs under her long ears and obviously she felt this put her at a disadvantage, so she threw up her snout with a belligerent grunt, stared me in the eye and challenged me to make the first move. She'd never seen me carry a length of rope before, but evidently she placed it in the same category as a stick. So all the cards were on the table. Rather foolishly I was dangling the rope in front of me as I tried to decide on the best method of attack. I knew I had to score first time or we were in for a rodeo.

'Get behind her, get behind her,' Checky urged. 'You'll have to slip it over from behind, else 'er'll back out of it afore you gets it tight.'

I made a move to rub her back and my fingers started to scratch into the bristles. I was making the appropriate endearing noises, the ones that usually put her at her ease and produced the high pitched squeaks of pleasure. But she remained wary. She knew I'd not come in for a back scratching session. Not now she had seen the rope. She'd no intention of relaxing.

'Scratch 'er tits,' Bert suggested, from the gallery, 'her always likes that. Her'll go quiet if you scratch 'er tits.'

'No 'er won't,' Pete sneered. 'Her knows summat's up. Give 'er some grub, I say. Nab 'er whilst 'er's eating.'

I agreed and suggested he brought another bowl of meal. 'And you stay in here,' I told him when he produced it, 'grab her ears as soon as I've got the cord through her jaws.'

'Her'll bite.'

'No she won't, not if you hang on. Go on, give her the grub.'

At the smell of more corn Skinny forgot her alarm. She barged up to the trough in front of Pete, shouting at him to tip the food in.

I moved behind her and waited until she was hogging it back. Then I dangled the loop of rope in front of her snout and snatched it back so that it flicked into her mouth and tightened over her snout.

She was furious. She squealed, loud and long and made a desperate effort to rid herself of the pinching cord by charging forward.

'Grab her ears!' I yelled to Pete, as the cord bit in where I had twisted it round my hand.

Between us we heaved her to a standstill. With her ears pulled back and her mouth open she rolled her eyes and uttered a low moan of menace.

Checky bustled in. He held the pliers with the jaws open and a ring slotted in them with the points ready to bite.

Skinny watched helplessly. She looked down her long nose and saw the ring being positioned over the quivering, wet rim of her snout. She felt the points scratching slightly as they were pushed well back to the base of the rim. She wanted to move but the tight cord seemed to paralyse her. Then Checky's heavy hand clenched the pliers shut and the sharp stab released her squeal of anguish.

Checky had three more rings pinned on the lapel of his jacket. And one by one he slotted them into the pliers, puffing sparks from his fag as he did so, and pinched them into Skinny's snout. But with these she just watched and never objected. She knew when she was beaten, but perhaps the pressure of the cord had made her snout numb so that she lost all feeling.

Fatso couldn't help hearing all the commotion from her sty next door. But when I went in to her, with the cord behind my back this time, she was snuggled down in a heap of straw, grunting gently and pretending not to notice anything out of the ordinary.

'Come on,' I greeted her, 'your turn now. How about some nice pretty rings in your old snout?'

She grunted again, smacked her chops and continued to lie there. This was too easy. I leant over her, told her what a beautiful

94

creature she was and yanked the loop of cord through her mouth.

She squealed with horror as it tightened over her snout. And she went on squealing as she got to her feet and, quite unexpectedly, sat back on her ample bottom like the picture of a porker in a kiddies' painting book.

Somehow the loop slackened and slipped out of her mouth as she came backwards instead of lunging forward as I'd been expecting. But she seemed not to notice. It must have still felt as though her snout was being gripped by a ring of steel because she continued to squat there, howling for the whole parish to hear.

Pete grabbed her ears. 'You great baby. Nobody ain't touched yer yet.'

But she continued to squeal, hardly pausing for breath, deafening us all, and she was putting so much effort and concentration into it that I believe she scarcely felt the rings piercing her snout.

8

WE WERE NEARING the end of an afternoon milking when Jean first arrived. There had been some more flurries of snow and now the lane outside the cowshed had merged in with the verges of the hedgerows. The only traffic to mark the light covering had been the postman's bike and the thin wheels of the handcart, on which we pulled the churns the half mile up the lane to the collection point on the road at the top. Usually one of us could manage this job on his own. But today it had needed Bert to push and Pete to pull and even then their feet had slipped on the fresh snow on the uphill, loaded journey. But coming down had been another story; full tilt, empty churns clanking and threatening to topple and the boys shouting as they slid behind the swaying handcart.

Of course Colonel's footprints had marked the snow, scuffling along during the day between the heavy tracks of the cart. But no cars or lorries had left their marks along the lane. Very few came at the best of times because the lane was just a lazy loop down into the valley past Maywood, up again to curve by Jack's white, clapboard cottage and offer an exit to a track which led to a couple of isolated farms farther up the valley. Then the lane dropped again into another steep valley, past old Dunnell's farm at Frog's Hole, then up again to join another parish road leading down to the village in the next valley.

So the sound of a car rolling to a stop in the dark outside the cowshed caused immediate comment.

'Who the bloody 'ell's that?' Pete enquired of nobody in particular.

I was walking across to find out when the door opened slowly and a girl peered into the lamplight. She had blonde hair curling just above her shoulders, a green beret perched on the back of her head and a wistful smile.

'Is this Maywood Farm?' she asked. Her voice was soft. It fitted her face and was an added attraction to this unexpected vision. 'Er,' she went on, 'this was the only light I could see, so I barged in. This *is* Maywood, isn't it?

I was still staring at her, nodding vacantly. (She told me later she thought she'd stumbled on the village idiot.) Then my voice returned and I agreed that this was indeed Maywood and how could I help her?

She took a couple of steps forward, thrust her hands deep into her overcoat pockets, and hunched her shoulders: 'Well, actually, would you believe me when I tell you I've come to catch your rats?'

I stared at her for a moment. Then: 'Quite frankly, no. But do come in and make yourself at home.' I gestured into the cowshed with a bow.

Pete and Bert had frozen in mid stride. Pete's mouth was open, his bucket over his arm and he was staring vacantly. The brim of Bert's cap was over his ear, where it usually ended up after a tussle with Big Tits, and he too stood with his mouth open while his nose dribbled unattended. Lotty turned her head, stared and flourished her horns with a rattle of her chain, while Bluebell quietly raised her tail and shat, slowly and seriously with a sound like slow applause from a single pair of hands.

'As a matter of fact I work for the Ministry,' the girl went on, 'your farm's next on my list. I'm due to start on your rats to-morrow, actually, but I thought I'd drop by on my way home tonight, just to see the size of the job. Only I'm later than I meant to be. I couldn't find this lane and it started to get dark, and what with the snow. . . .'

Her voice trailed. Obviously she wasn't used to such an attentive audience. Pete and Bert were still staring and three more cows had turned to look, either at the unaccustomed sound of a female voice or because the expected hay had not arrived.

I turned to Pete, pushed my hand under his chin to shut his mouth and told him to get a move on. He smiled sheepishly and started towards the dairy while Bert came to life and shuffled after him, with a leer at me and a snigger.

I grabbed one of the hurricane lamps and suggested we made a quick tour of the buildings. Once the boys got together in the dairy I could imagine their comments and, however discreet they thought they were being, their excitement would mean that remarks were not made sotto voce.

'Funny job for a girl,' I remarked as we plodded through the straw-littered yard to the calf pens, 'you're hardly my idea of a rat catcher.'

'And what's that?'

'Oh, I dunno, some grisly old man with dead rats tied round his belt by their tails.' Her laughter and only the flickering light to break the darkness gave me the courage to add: 'Certainly not a ravishing blonde.'

She never answered. I wondered if she always ignored farmers if they got fresh with her. We reached the calf pens and went inside in silence. It was a low, thatched building, running along the top side of the yard and at right angles to the end of the cowshed. It used to be a bullock lodge, where steers chewed through the winter days, growing fat and sleek on chaff mixed with chopped mangel wurzel, on oats and barley and beans and prime meadow hay. But now half of it had been railed off and turned into calf pens. There were six small loose boxes, each with its own door, a little hay rack in one corner and a wooden frame in another to hold a bucket of milk from spilling when an excited calf drank and bunted at it. The other half of the building remained as it was, open to the yard. From the darkness in there three yearlings turned to blink at us as we entered. Then they turned and went on pulling at the hay in the rack along the inside wall.

I stood the lamp on the waist high wall of the first calf pen and Daisy's calf peered up at me. She knew milking was over and she thought I'd come with her bucket of milk. Her brown coat shone in the lamplight, her ears were pricked forward and her wet nose thrust up expectantly.

'Let me introduce you to Daffodil,' I said, as I hung my hand over the wall. The calf immediately sucked at my fingers. 'Daffodil, this is?' I looked up.

'Jean,' she said, 'and I know your name because it's on my list.'

She turned away and held out her fingers to the calf in the next pen. 'And what's your name?' she asked it. It tottered to her and gave a feeble cry.

'That's Buttercup,' I said. 'Only born yesterday. We're still having to teach her to drink.'

98

'You've *not* taken her right away from her mother?' The calf was nuzzling eagerly to hold on to her fingers.

'Oh, she'll be okay. So'll Mum. They'll soon forget each other and Mum'll give us her undivided attention and all her milk.'

She sighed: 'I suppose you're right. But it always seems a bit hard.'

'Women always think that. Anyway, the next calf's called Primrose and the big one on the end, that's Lucy, daughter of Lotty, but she's weaned now and so she's not expecting milk like the others.'

'So they're all little girls, no little boys?'

'All little boys go to market. Nobody wants bull calves, I'm afraid; leastways not from dairy cows.'

'What happens to them?'

'They go for baby veal.' I was leaning over the wall while Daffodil was sucking and bunting at my fingers. She was stamping her back feet and swishing her tail, furious that no milk was forthcoming. I looked up at Jean and she glanced at me. 'D'you like veal?' I asked, smiling.

'Don't be horrid.'

'Well, I expect you like roast lamb, don't you? So why not veal?'

'You know what I mean.' She wrinkled her nose. 'You shouldn't think what happens to the unfortunate ones when you look at these dear little things.' She pursed her lips and leant down to shake her head slowly at the calf still hanging on to her fingers. 'But you're going to grow up into a nice big, beautiful cow, aren't you sweetheart?'

I thought she sounded softhearted for a rat catcher. But I didn't tell her so. Instead I enjoyed looking at her. Her hair had fallen forward over her cheek and her ear peeped through like a delicate shell.

There was a movement in the darkness of the shed. I looked round and the three yearlings had ambled over to see what was going on. They leant over the rails, stretching their heads towards us, blowing at the lamplight.

I stood up. 'While we're at it I'd better introduce you to Elsie, Doris and Brutus.'

Jean looked up. 'Brutus? So there's a boy here after all?'

'Well, yes. And again, no. I bought these three off the previous owner of the farm. Elsie and Doris will become cows in a couple of

99

years and we thought Brutus would make a good bull. But he's not turning out to be quite the right shape, I'm afraid.'

I walked over to the rails and held my hand out to Brutus' outstretched nose. His tongue came out slowly, touched my fingers and sloshed back into his mouth. He shook his head as though I tasted rotten. So I scratched him where a fringe of brown hair sprouted between his thickly budding horns, each of them already a couple of inches long. He liked that and when I gripped one, hot horn, he cocked his head and challenged me to hang on.

'No,' I said as I tussled with him, 'I'm afraid you're not growing up as beautiful as you should do. You'd only turn out to be a nasty old scrub bull and I don't want a nasty old scrub bull on my nice, pretty cows.'

He broke away from my grasp and snorted at me, shaking his head in victory.

Jean walked over and leant on the rails. 'He looks all right to me. Look at his cheeky face! He's lovely, aren't you, Brutus?'

'I'm afraid one of your Ministry colleagues wouldn't think so. He'd have to be licensed to keep him on for a bull and he wouldn't pass the inspection. Too weak in the forequarters, they'd say.'

'So what'll happen to him?'

'Well, he'll lose his manhood—or should I say his bullhood? I'll have to get the vet out to him before long, before he starts getting ideas about Elsie and Doris.'

'Poor old Brutus,' she said, holding out her hand to him, 'it isn't fair, is it?'

He stretched out his tongue again to see if her hand tasted better than mine. But instead of a tentative lick he suddenly rasped his tongue on her sleeve.

She jumped back, snatching her hand away. 'Oh! I thought he was going to bite me.'

I laughed: 'He just wanted to see if your coat was worth eating.'

She looked at me and smiled. I felt taller. Work didn't matter any longer and I just wanted to stay talking to her.

'Well,' she shrugged, 'we're not getting round your buildings very fast, are we?'

'Does it matter? You in a hurry?'

'No, not really. I've only got digs and a bitchy landlady to go back to. I'll be late for tea and she'll moan anyway, so who cares?'

'You could have some tea here. That's a good idea!'

'Oh no! No, I couldn't. Thanks all the same.'

'Why not? Mother won't mind. She's used to having people barging in unexpected.'

But Jean was adamant. We stood in silence looking down across the dark yard. Beyond the railings at the bottom was the pond. And beyond the pond was the circular yard at the back of the house. A single light yellowed the kitchen window and sparkled in a path across the black water.

'How many are there in your family?' Jean asked.

'Oh lots,' I laughed. 'But they're all scattered about. Only Mother and I live here on our own. It's a bit dull for her, I'm afraid, after the busy house full she's always been used to before she came here. Still, she finds plenty to do. Always pushing off on her old bike, rain or shine, in a round of good works. Wouldn't think she was sixty.'

'You've not been here long, then?'

'Less than a year. Still, it's better now than when we came. Very primitive, it was. As you see, we've still only got lamplight, but at least we've now got a flush bog and a bathroom upstairs. One better than the privy across the backyard and the tin bath in front of the fire.'

She laughed. 'Especially in this weather. My last landlady had an outside lav and it used to freeze up with the slightest frost.'

'Ah,' I said, 'there's the advantage of an earth closet for you. May pong a bit, but it never freezes up. Our's is a very palatial one, as a matter of fact. A double seated job, room for one adult and one child. And there's a marvellous quince tree growing just behind it, too. Loaded with fruit it was and Mum made jars and jars of quince jelly. Lovely stuff. I always make a point of telling visitors where it comes from when they remark how nice it tastes.'

'I think you're horrid.' But she was smiling beautifully.

'No, not horrid. Just—er—basic, shall we say? Your outlook tends to be basic when you're farming. You're so close to the root of everything.'

She was looking at me with her head on one side, as though she didn't quite know how to take me. She just said, slowly: 'I see.'

'Anyway,' I continued, desperate to hold her attention, 'to finish the saga of the privy. Now that we've no further use for it, it's been taken over by Mrs P.P.'

'Mrs who?'

'Mrs P.P., Mrs Puffy Pecker. She happens to be a rather dilapidated old hen. She got left behind somehow when all her mates were rounded up and sold at the farm sale. She didn't seem to miss them a bit and spent long and happy days on her own, scratching round the farm with the pick of all the perks she uncovered and with absolutely no competition. Mum fed her with scraps at the back door and named her after some hen character in a children's book. She's become very tame and steps slowly into the kitchen whenever she finds the door open, tilting a sharp eye for anything worth eating and crooning quietly. Then suddenly she disappeared. Couldn't find her anywhere. We knew she'd been laying somewhere because her comb was bright red and we'd see her come sauntering across the yard cackling with pride. I searched everywhere. All the likely places. Never thought about the privy. Hadn't given it a thought since the builders departed pronouncing the lovely new bog usable. But one day I happened to pop my head round the door in passing and there she was, sitting on the seat on the adult side, broody as could be and being fiercely defensive of a huge clutch of eggs, overflowing from under her and threatening to roll down the hole.'

Jean was enjoying the tale. 'Did she hatch them out?'

'Heavens, no. Not that lot. The eggs weren't fertile. Poor old Mrs P.P. is a widow. She hasn't had the pleasure of being chased by a cock for many months—not since they all departed with the highest bidder at the farm sale. But it wasn't a wasted effort on her part because I nipped off and bought a fertile clutch of eggs from a poultry farmer and swapped them for her massive clutch. I gave her a nice nest of hay. I even nailed some boards over the holes in the seat while she just sat there and swore at me for interfering. Still, she hatched out twelve nice chicks in the end and has lived in the bog ever since.'

I turned and picked up the hurricane lamp off the wall. 'But I've given her a perch now. She finds that more to her liking than the seat and she doesn't get into such a mess. Old hens tend to get a bit bedraggled and seem to give up trying to keep themselves clean. A good scratch in the dust once in a while and Mrs P.P. thinks that's all that's needed at her time of life.'

'You *are* a fool,' Jean said. Her eyes were shining as I held the lamp high. I could see they were hazel and I'd expected them to be blue. 'But seriously,' she went on, 'I'm glad you mentioned chickens because I must be careful about them. I have to make sure

I don't put any rat poison down where they can get at it. I'd hate to go round picking up dead chickens instead of dead rats. It hasn't happened yet, touch wood, but there's always a first time.' She stretched out her hand and clasped the wooden rail. 'D'you mean to say *all* your chickens live in the lav? D'you shut them up there at night?'

'God, no. Only Mrs P.P. She rules in solitary state. She kicked her brood out as soon as they were old enough to fend for themselves. No fixed abode, most of 'em. They perch wherever it takes their fancy. Since I bought an old tractor and parked it in the cart shed, they've taken to perching on the beam above it. Must be something to do with the heat it gives off after it's been at work. One even settles on the steering wheel with a terrible fluttering and commotion. She *will* leave it until it's too dark to see properly and she slips about trying to get a grip and swearing horribly. Can't think why she likes it. It must be very uncomfortable, especially as the others spend the whole night bombing her.'

'Why don't you keep your chickens shut up properly at night?' Jean sounded nonplussed.

'Well, there's not many of them and they do so enjoy themselves roaming at will. They pick up all manner of food that would otherwise go to waste, you know. And they lay well. And the eggs taste rich, when you can find them, and it's always a lovely surprise when you do. Anyway, they always perch well up out of harm's way at night. I defy any fox to get at them—except perhaps the one who fancies herself as a tractor driver, she's a bit vulnerable.'

Jean sighed. 'Oh well, I shall just have to be very careful where I put the poison.' She turned and looked round her to where the light danced into the corners of the shed. 'Ever seen any rats in here?'

'Now and then. Sometimes you see the odd one scooting along a beam under the thatch.'

'Um, I'll have to look for signs of runs tomorrow. I just wanted to find how many buildings there were altogether tonight, and how big. The trouble is I never know the size of a farm until I get there, not having worked in this area before.'

Bert appeared from the cowshed. He came clanking across the yard with three buckets of calf milk on his arms. 'You pinched the other lamp,' he complained.

I'd forgotten he'd need it to see to feed the calves. I held it aloft for him as he plonked buckets into two of the pens and gave a scoopful of calf nuts to Lucy. The calves sucked greedily, banging their noses into the buckets while their tails went wild. Lucy rattled at the nuts as though she had a mouthful of loose teeth.

Bert opened the door of Buttercup's pen and held out the bucket towards her. 'C'mon, mate, grub's up.'

Buttercup bunted at his leg, looking for a teat. He stood astride her and pressed the palm of his hand against her nose and curled his fingers into her mouth. She started to suck noisily. With his other hand he brought the bucket towards her and slowly lowered the fingers she was sucking into the milk. The milk was yellow and glutinous, the sticky colostrum of the newly calved cow, full of antibodies and the essential first food of the calf.

But a calf looks upwards to find its mother's kindly teat. That's where it expects the milk to come from. Not down in a bucket. And it is surprising the strength with which it can bunt upwards when it finds its head being lured in the wrong direction.

Which is exactly what Buttercup did just when Bert thought he'd got her to taste the milk. With all her natural urge her head shot up out of Bert's grasp, clipping the rim of the bucket and slopping the milk on his trousers.

'Whoa! Yer little sod. Where d'yer think you're orf to?' He held the calf between his legs, dipped his fingers in the milk and started again.

I leant towards Jean and quietly warned her that the language could well become colourful. She shrugged, 'I expect I've heard it all before,' and peered over to get a better view.

Now that the calf had tasted the milk she became even more convinced that she must push upwards to find some more. And the more determined Bert became that she should realise it was in the bucket and not under his armpit. The tussle became vigorous and Buttercup was now quite certain that the figure bending over her was that of her mother and the bucket had nothing to do with either of them. She jerked a wet nose under Bert's chin.

He was working himself into an impossible position. He had moved the bucket to the safety of the frame. The fingers of his left hand were in the calf's mouth, his right hand was on top of her head pushing it downwards towards the milk, he held her body between his knees and his mouth was tight shut to contain the abuse appropriate to the way the job was going.

'Isn't he being rather rough with her?' Jean wanted to know.

Fortunately she spoke quietly. Anyway Bert was too busy to hear.

'That's it, Bert,' I said, 'let 'er come to it gently. Don't force her too much.'

I turned back to Jean. 'They can be very obstinate, you know. Most of them get the hang of drinking from a bucket in just a few minutes. The odd one behaves like this and requires more patience than most of us possess when we're busy.'

Jean leant over the door towards the calf. 'Poor little thing. You don't understand, do you, Buttercup?'

Bert straightened up, took his hands from the calf and placed them on his hips. 'Bloody awk'ud, that's what 'er is!' He let the calf totter off from between his legs and looked at Jean. 'There 'er is. There's the bloody milk. Why don't you have a go?'

'All right! I will!'

She pushed open the door, picked up the bucket and stooped towards the calf. Bert smirked at me and leant back against the wall.

And we both watched as she talked quietly to the calf, let her suck her fingers and gently drew her towards her. She held up the bucket of milk, slowly directed the calf's nose into it and in a moment there was a loud sucking as the milk gurgled past her fingers.

She looked up, smiling. 'There you are! Nothing to it! It only needed a woman's touch.'

'Beginner's luck,' grumbled Bert.

She turned to Buttercup. 'You don't understand the silly men, do you?'

By way of reply the calf gave a violent bunt and the milk slopped. But Jean hung on to the bucket and Buttercup blew the milk from her nostrils and settled down to sucking again. Soon the milk was finished and Jean handed the empty bucket back to Bert with a smile. He took it from her, gathered up the other buckets and went back towards the light streaming from the cowshed door, muttering to himself.

Jean was still in the pen petting Buttercup. The calf was shaking her head and looking a trifle bewildered after her exertions. Presently she moved away from the girl, knelt down and flopped gently into the straw. Her long ears twitched for a moment or two and then she blinked slowly as the warm milk soothed her.

I bolted the door when Jean came out. 'Want a job as a dairy-maid?' I asked.

'I'll have to think about it,' she laughed, tossing her head to shake the hair from her face.

I caught hold of her hand as she walked away from me. She stopped and looked at me over her shoulder. 'Come on,' she said, 'better show me the rest of the place.' I thought I felt her squeeze my hand very gently as she pulled her own away.

A door led through the back of the building into the stack-plat. Wisps of hay clung to the rough lintel where fork loads had scraped on their way through to the feeding rack. The heavy door creaked as it swung outwards and the lamplight spilled over the snow and was lost in the bulk of the hay rick, brooding above us with its high head glinting white against the night sky. The smell of it flavoured the sharpness of the north air, which bit our faces after the comparative warmth of the bullock lodge.

'Where are you taking me?' she asked, and there was a slight shiver in her voice.

'Out into the cold, cold snow,' I leered. I grabbed her hand and this time I held it tightly as I pulled her after me. We ran through the snow, our feet sinking through it and into the scattered straw and hay which carpeted the stack-plat underneath. The lamp glass rattled and the flame flickered wildly and when we stopped by the gate leading into the lane I caught the hot, homely smell of burnt paraffin.

I raised the lamp on to the gate. It was between us and I sniffed loudly. 'Ah! I love the smell of a warm lamp on a cold night.'

'What a strange thing to say.' She was smiling and the close flame flooded her face and highlit the colours there.

'Oh no, not strange. It reminds me of being snug and cosy while the wind whistles outside. Lying in bed and looking at the patterns on the ceiling made by the hot chimney of the oil stove—a special treat on very cold nights.'

She laughed, merrily. 'I'm afraid I've always lived with electric light—and fires.'

'Then you don't know what you've missed. A flame moves and flickers. It's alive and personal. And you've no idea how marvellous your face looks in this lamplight.'

'Oh, thank you,' she nodded with a mocking smile. But she never looked at me and she ran a finger along the top of the gate, scraping off a tinkle of snow. I wondered what she was really thinking. How long had it been since she first walked into the cowshed? An hour? Perhaps not that and I seemed to have known her for ages and nothing else mattered. In the background the familiar noises of the farm were of no real importance any more. The rattle of a cow chain, the bang of a bucket on concrete, the voices of the boys. They were finishing off my share of the work and I couldn't have cared less. For the first time since I'd come to Maywood my thoughts had been wrenched away from it. I'd lived and breathed the place every waking hour. It had filled my life to the exclusion of all else and had been the dominating factor in my every decision, action and thought process over the past year. A year since any girl had held a smiling face close to mine.

'I'm beginning to freeze to this spot while you stare at me,' she said, laughing.

'So sorry, I was carried away by your beauty!' I picked up the lamp and opened the gate for her. 'There's an oast house over the road. You'd better have a look at that. We store corn in there to the delight of both rats and mice. Certainly a place requiring your attention.'

The tall, conical roof of the oast was like a stubby finger sensing the wind. At its tip the white, weather-boarded cowl hunched its back to the elements, swivelling to and fro and pointing accusingly after the wind with a slender vane protruding from its mouth. I led the way through the small door leading into the ground floor storage area, which was a rectangular building joined on to the roundel with its conical roof. The lamplight sunk into the low, regulars row of dark beams and only reflected on the grey cobwebs, now clinging in ragged tatters after yielding their rich harvest of autumn flies. Sacks of corn were piled in rows, two high and resting on boards across the earth floor, and here and there a tuft of hay sprouted from the side of a bulging sack, plugging a hole nipped by a hungry rat. There was a musty smell of cold corn and dead fires and in the back of my throat I could sense a trace of the acrid yellow smoke of burning brimstone still clinging in the beams.

Jean peered between the lines of sacks. She nodded and pointed to the door leading into the roundel. 'More corn in there?' she asked.

'Oh no. The fires are in there for drying the hops upstairs.'

'You still use it as an oast?'

'Yes, I've got five acres of hops out the back. It's a real old fashioned hop garden with a pole for every plant and God knows how many miles of string to put up every year. It keeps us out of mischief, I can tell you. But there's a two ton quota goes with this farm so we have to keep busy.'

'A quota?' She looked puzzled.

'Only certain farms are allowed to grow hops these days. Stops overproduction and the Hop Marketing Board will only guarantee to buy your quota. Over and above that you have to take a chance whether you sell or not, depending on whether your factor has any spare quota on his hands. But it's an expensive crop to grow, terribly time consuming and, of course, you have to have an oast house like this to dry the hops and press them. It's daft really. This place is used for just three weeks in the year and the rest of the time it stands idle. So we use it to store corn and odds and sods.'

I showed her the three fireplaces let into the big, round chimney in the roundel. Smokeless fires, started with charcoal to light the lumps of shining Welsh anthracite and set them glowing. And the heat gathered and was sucked up through the green hops piled on the round, latticed floor above, and was drawn out, steaming, through the mouth of the twisting cowl. And when each new load of green hops was set to dry, three or four sticks of brimstone were placed on a metal dish and set to roast on one fire so that the thick fumes killed all the insects in the hops. For half an hour or so these fumes seemed to invade every corner of the oast house and send those working there spluttering for fresh air.

We went outside again and I led her up the wooden steps clinging to the side of the building and up to the floor above. Here the smell of hops was strong. The shattered, oily seeds crammed the crevices between the boards on the floor, left behind from the piles of dried hops that had lain there over the years. They had been turfed hot from the drying floor, cascading down to cool before being swept and pressed into the tall pockets. The heavy press stood like a scaffold at the far end of the floor, the plunger down and resting on the loose boards blocking the hole to the floor below, through which the pockets hung when they were being filled.

Five short steps led up to a door into the circular drying floor above the fires. Jean wanted to look inside so I gave her the lamp and she climbed up and stood on the hessian stretched over the latticed floor. She turned to face me. She had unbuttoned her overcoat and underneath she wore a pair of khaki jeans, curving and nipped tight into her slim waist, and above them she filled a green sweater to perfection. I was just thinking how cuddly she looked when she pointed behind me.

'Oh, we're not alone, I see. Who's that watching us from that pile of sacks over there?'

I looked round. 'That's Henry. He's a tom cat who just appeared here one day, unheralded and unsung, and decided he'd take up residence.'

'I love cats!' she exclaimed, and in a moment she was down the steps and approaching Henry. He stretched out a paw of claws and yawned a greeting.

He was a tabby tom, with a dirty white shirt front because he always seemed too tired to clean it properly. When he came to settle down anywhere, first and foremost he would hold one hind leg high, while he paid particular attention to those parts which he considered the most vital to him. Once that was over, he never ever lavished more than a few desultory licks to the rest of his coat before curling up to sleep soundly in his own stink. He'd disappear for days on end and then reappear, lean and lacerated about the ears and front paws, his wide white whiskers bristling with importance and his yellow eyes scowling as he demanded milk at the dairy door.

Henry was obviously a very successful lover. He travelled miles on his rounds making sure that no female in season missed the opportunity of his skill. I often thought how much easier it must be for a town tom, with maybe fifty females within sound of a good catawall, whereas poor old Henry had to tramp miles of wet and lonely fields in search of love. But once he solved his problem by bringing a girl friend home with him. She was a dainty little black and white thing, obviously infatuated with Henry. He installed her in the bottom of the oast house as a love nest and evidently left strict instructions that she wasn't to move from there. He himself would come squeezing out through one of the ventilation holes at the bottom of the roundel and go striding about his business—a saucer of milk at the dairy, a good scratch half way across the yard, a swear-up at Mrs P.P. because she always wanted to start something whenever she saw him, fluffing up her feathers and thrusting her beak at him with a menacing caw. Then he'd lope off up the lane on the off chance of a bit of fun with one of Jack's several cats and come back an hour or two later and make for the oast house. And from there would come the most blood-curdling screams as he put his adoring mistress through her paces.

We never did see her outside the oast. On several occasions we tried to catch her, but it was impossible. She was as wild as a weasel. If she was curled up asleep on a sack when we came in, she would be awake and off before we were through the door. All we would catch would be a glimpse of black and white as she scurried off into her secret maze of runs between the sacks. Or perhaps, disturbed from another spot, she would leap up the wall to the beams and disappear through a small hole into the loft above. And it was useless to try and trap her there because she would take to the rafters in the dark roof and fly from one to the other with feline assurance. Once she dived into the darkness of the fireplaces and we did think we had her cornered. A flurry of dust told us she'd taken refuge in the chimney, and when I peered up through one of the fireplaces, I saw she'd scaled the inside wall like a lizard and was crouched high up on a dark ledge staring defiantly down at me.

Eventually Henry must have tired of her and given her her marching orders. She disappeared as suddenly as she had come, no doubt with Henry's offspring squirming in her womb. Which was just as well in a way, otherwise the farm would have been overrun with unapproachable cats and Henry would have had the time of his life with a series of incestuous relationships.

Sex was the main preoccupation in Henry's life. He was definitely not a keen mouser. I know his mistress made considerable inroads into the rodent population of the oast house during the long and solitary hours spent waiting for his return. For this reason I welcomed her presence. I left her the odd saucer of milk in gratitude, but I could never be sure that she ventured out to drink it before Henry had it on his return, and then ordered her to dance attendance on him.

The mice and rats were more evident again after she'd gone. They appeared to treat Henry with disdain. Probably they knew he was always too shagged out to catch them. I suppose he did manage to catch one or two because he never had any food from us other than his milk. But we only actually saw him with a mouse on one occasion. We were milking and he came marching into the cowshed, swishing his tail and growling importantly with a mouse lying doggo in his jaws. After he'd made quite sure we all knew he was there, he put the mouse down and played tip and run with it on the hard standing behind the cows. I was rooting for the mouse and thought it had beaten him to the drain when he pounced on it in the nick of time and carried it out to the lane, growling in triumph. Then he let it go again and dribbled it down the lane like a centre forward. But the mouse dived into touch, nipped through the long grass on the verge and found sanctuary in the hedgebottom. Poor old Henry was livid. For a long time he crouched in the grass, waggling his backside and pouncing at every whispering movement as blades of grass straightened their bent backs. In the end he turned his back on the spot where the mouse had disappeared, sent a stream of urine into the hedge and pushed off up the lane.

Jean sat on the sprawling heap of sacks and stroked Henry while I sat beside her and told her about him. He sat up on his haunches and tried to look important. He curled his long whiskers forward, purred loudly and was obviously convinced I was giving him an excellent reference. But his eyes began to close as he stared at the lamp on the floor, his battered old ears drooped and he sank down with a sigh as sleep got the better of him.

It was then that Jean moved away from him into my arms.

'You're rather late,' Mother greeted me, when I went indoors after Jean had gone home. 'Is something the matter with the cows?

I laughed: 'No, they're all fine. Everything's fine. Couldn't be better. I've just had a visitor, that's all.'

She shuffled the saucepans on the kitchener as she prepared to dish up the evening meal. She opened the black oven door and peered inside. 'I hope the pie's not over cooked. No. *Just* right. Pass me the oven cloth will you, darling?'

It was sitting in the middle of the table, half draped over a glass, just where she'd cast it after the last pie inspection. I pushed it into her outstretched hand. 'Don't you want to know about my visitor?' I asked.

She carried the pie over and plonked it on the table, slamming the oven door with her foot as she did so. 'Of course I do. Who was it?'

'A rat catcher.'

'A *rat* catcher?' She frowned, brushed the unruly wisps of hair from her face with one hand and tossed the oven cloth in the direction of the sink with the other. 'Whatever did he want at this time of night?'

'It wasn't a he. It was a *she*—a charming blonde with a figure like Venus.'

She attacked the pie. 'Now you're telling me one of your stories.'

'No, honestly. A beautiful, blonde rat catcher. I never even dreamt that such a creature existed. Drafted from the Women's Land Army to this work of National Importance—ridding Maywood Farm of rats.'

Mother laughed. 'I don't believe you. If she was so marvellous why didn't you bring her in? I'd like to have seen her.'

'I will tomorrow. She's coming again to kill the rats tomorrow. I'll ask her in for a cup of tea. Then you can see this vision with your own eyes.'

She put down her knife and fork with a clatter. 'Oh dear! I shall be out all day tomorrow. I've got to go and give my blessed Flower Talk all the way over at Ivychurch. They've asked for it specially. It'll take ages getting there and back on the buses.'

I shook my head slowly and looked serious. 'That's the penalty of fame. News of Mrs Creaton's Flower Talk is sweeping the Kent countryside, released to the Mothers' Unions in the Provinces after its record breaking London run.'

'Go on with you!' She reached across and jabbed my arm.

'Never mind,' I laughed, 'the lovely rat catcher will be coming every day this week so you won't miss her.'

And now she looked at me and smiled because she was happy at the excitement she saw in my eyes.

9

THE FOLLOWING DAY there was more snow and I was afraid that Jean wouldn't be able to make it. She'd told me her digs were in Ashford and although there was barely two inches of snow on the lane, I was convinced that great drifts would have swirled across the open stretches of road nearer town to prevent her coming.

Of course Pete and Bert had plenty to say and the snow was only of secondary importance to them that morning. The oast house stood on a rise of ground and apparently the light from the loft window was clearly visible across the snowy valley from Jack's cottage. My stay there with Jean had been timed.

'It were gorne seven when the light came down the steps,' Pete was delighted to inform me, anxious to get his own back for the times I'd ribbed him about Rose.

Bert agreed from somewhere under Big Tits, made a remark I never caught, but could well make a guess at judging by his loud snigger into his bucket.

Every aspect and implication of Jean's sudden appearance on the farm had been thoroughly discussed. This was a great new topic of conversation which had to be savoured and commented upon to the full. They worried at it like two terriers at threshing time, determined to shake every last ounce of life from a dead rat as they flung it to and fro between them. I even heard Bert discussing it with old Colonel as he humped the harness on his back in the stable. I happened to walk through the door just as he was pushing the collar over the old horse's head. He never saw me. He was busy hanging on to the collar and Colonel was lowering his head as though he was listening attentively. 'Did 'em come in here last night, Colonel?

Did 'em, eh? Lookin' fer rats they was. So *he* says. You seen any ol' rats in here? Have yer, Colonel? Or what else did yer see when 'em was in here? Eh! Eh?' He laughed softly and rubbed his hand over the horse's nose. Colonel blew through his nostrils and rattled his bit with his tongue. I wondered what that was supposed to mean.

Since the snow we had tied Colonel in the stable at night. Now we had to use him every day, carting hay and kale to the top field by the road to feed a flock of thirty in-lamb ewes, now that the covering of snow had denied them their main means of livelihood.

This flock of ewes belonged to Bill Checksfield and I was keeping them for him on what was known as a 'half crease' basis. I fed them and looked after them and in return, half the lambs due to be born in February and March would belong to me. It suited us both very well. He was able to retain an interest in the farm which had occupied the major part of his life, and which he was loath to leave altogether, and I could start my own flock of sheep by cashing in on unused capacity on the farm and without having to put my hand in my pocket. As there was certainly no spare money to be found there, I needed little persuasion when Checky suggested the idea. 'You ought to have some sheep,' he'd said, when I'd been talking to him about the cows I was going to buy. 'You need sheep to follow cows. Keeps the pastures sweet 'cos they clean up behind the cows. And there's good steady money in sheep, what with the wool and all. Always has been. Sheep allus paid when things was bad. You ought to have bought some of they old ewes of mine at the sale.'

At that I'd laughed. 'I would've needed money for that. By the time the mortgage company and I had paid you for the farm there wasn't much left to splash around. I have to have these cows to bring me in a regular cheque every month, for the wages and the feed and the fertilizers and all the rest of it. Or have you forgotten all the expenses there used to be now you're in flush retirement?'

He'd raised his cap, relieved an itch with a gnarled fingernail and blown a shower of sparks from the last soppy half inch of fag. He'd started to laugh but it developed into a series of little, tickling coughs. Then he'd come across with the 'half crease' suggestion he'd been hatching all along.

And we'd gone together to the autumn sheep fair in Tenterden where he'd bought a pen of thirty big Romney Marsh ewes. And a week later a bright-eyed young ram with a neatly clipped backside to display him to the best advantage, had been added to the flock.

Pete immediately called him Bollocky when he arrived and he watched him go swinging off into the field to introduce himself to the bevy of bleating blind dates. We had plastered his chest with raddle and over the next few weeks the tell-tale red marks appearing on the rumps of the ewes told the tally of his attentions.

The ewes came swaying through the snow to meet me when I arrived with the food. Bobbles of snow clustered on the loose wool on their legs and bellies and they moved in a cloud of hot breath, peppering the snow with anxious droppings. They crowded round the back of the cart and slowly formed themselves into a squirming line as they followed the hay and kale I flung out from the moving cart. They ate with quick, nibbling bites, chewing fast as they hurried from place to place, certain the food was better farther along the line and trampling the hay into the snow in their anxiety to find out. As I watched them, I told myself again that I really must make a hay rack. One that could be moved about the field. It could be kept full and the sheep could help themselves from it whenever they liked. But I remembered I'd given myself this instruction every day since the snow had come. There was always so much other work needing immediate attention. But a hay rack was essential. It must take preference. Already some of the ewes were getting heavy with lamb. Perhaps not more than a month to go. And there were hurdles and straw to bring up to make windbreaks. And the long, galvanised feed troughs. We needed them up here too for the corn and chopped swedes to bring on the milk. And the hay rack. Yes, the hay rack. God, I hoped the snow soon cleared.

This field formed the corner with the road at the top of the lane. I stood in the empty cart and urged Colonel on a detour over to the hedge bordering the road. I wanted to see whether cars had been passing all right. But Colonel could think of no good reason why he should have to tramp any farther afield in the snow. The gate into the lane was in the opposite direction and it was thither that he should go. So he stopped. No amount of shouting and swearing would make him budge. He hung his head, lay back his ears, blew jets of exhaustion from his nostrils and he knew I hadn't got a stick. So I left him and plodded off on my own while he swung round smartly and made off down to the gate.

As I reached the hedge the milk lorry drove by and stopped to pick up the churns from the stand at the corner. I shouted a greeting. How was the road to Ashford? He didn't know. He hadn't come that way. But why should it be bad? He heaved the full churns on to the lorry, flung tomorrow's empties into the ditch and I walked back across the field feeling despondent.

Jean arrived early in the afternoon.

'I thought you'd got lost,' I greeted her.

'Why? I told you I had to visit another farm first.'

'Did you? I didn't hear you. I've been expecting you all morning. I thought the snow had stopped you coming.'

'You don't listen.' She got out of her van and walked round and opened the rear doors. 'Well, let's make a start.'

She put on some gloves with gauntlets and I stood close behind her looking over her shoulder. She prized the lid off a gallon paint tin filled with bait and poison and picked up a torch and a stick with a spoon tied to the end. As she turned round I kissed her full on the lips. For a moment she responded and then turned away.

'There's a time and a place for everything,' she said, suddenly prim.

'I couldn't resist you.'

'What about all the work you had to do? Last night you were telling me how busy you were.'

'So I am. I've got loads to do. But it'd take more than work to stop me kissing you.' I closed the van doors. 'D'you want me to help you?'

She laughed: 'And have you molesting me all the way round? No, I can manage. One person's enough for this job anyway. Too many people thumping around frighten them and they get suspicious of the bait and won't eat it. I'll find you when I've finished.' She started to walk away. 'Promise,' she called back, looking round at me.

'Good. Then we'll have a cup of tea. Mum's gone off to give one of her holy Talks. But I can just about manage to boil a kettle so we'll be okay.'

I went whistling off to the cart shed. The hay rack for the sheep had to be made and I felt just in the mood to go tearing into that job.

An hour or so later I'd knocked up the long V-shaped frame and had begun the tedious job of sawing and shaping the slats to contain the hay. It looked rather rustic but it was strong. It would serve the purpose and was far cheaper than buying. That was a big consideration.

Jean came in without my hearing her. She laid cold fingers on my neck and darted back from my grasp. 'You're meant to be busy,' she laughed. She pointed to my handiwork. 'Whatever's that?'

'What's it look like? It's a hay rack for sheep, of course.'

'You could have fooled me.' She tried to evade me but this time I caught her and held her. There was no resistance. Her arms went round my neck and she folded herself against me in a slowly yielding movement. A minute or so later, she said: 'I mustn't be late. Not like last night. Mrs Wilkes will throw me out. She told me she was very displeased. Thought I should have more consideration about the time of the evening meal. A right old lecture she gave me and never let me get a word in edgeways.' She had been speaking into my ear. Now she moved back to look at me and her hands were resting on my shoulders. 'I'd a good story ready, too. But she swept out of the room before I had a chance to explain.'

'Oh? And what would you have explained?'

'Don't be silly. Not that. I'd a good story ready about losing my way in the snow. The trouble with my landlady is I think she feels she ought to mother me. She keeps referring to me as "one of my young ladies".'

'Are there more like you?'

'No. But I think she's had a female lodger . . . ah, excuse me . . . paying guest, ever since her husband died years ago. She always refers to past guests as "business ladies" and I don't think she quite knows how to deal with a rat catcher.'

'It's a wonder she took you on in the first place.'

'Ah, but I was wearing a smart dress and told her, very truthfully, that I worked for the Ministry. Business lady material. Poor old soul, her face fell a mile when I came down to breakfast the first morning wearing jeans and a sweater. Come to think about it she must've been worried stiff about how to explain me away to the neighbours. Hardly a business lady mincing off to work in jeans and wellies.'

'I'm surprised she never threw you out, conning her like that.'

'I never conned her! I'm as good as any snooty shop girl or secretary and I'll wear what I like.' She was really quite cross. Her eyes were wide open and her body stiffened.

My arms were still round her. My hands had been gently exploring the contours of her body while she spoke and now she broke away. 'But of course,' I said, quietly, 'I think you're marvellous.'

'Well, you shouldn't accuse me of conning people.'

'Just a joke. Sorry.' I moved to hold her again but she avoided me.

'About your rats,' she said, coldly. 'I've fed them in all the runs I can find today. I'll put some more poison down tomorrow wherever they've eaten it. *And* the next day, that's Thursday. On Friday we should find a few dead ones, only mostly they go away to die. Then I'll clear up any poison that's left.'

There was a long and uncomfortable silence. I was looking at her but she was avoiding my gaze. At last I said: 'I hope we don't find any dead chickens.' I hoped I sounded stern.

'If we do, that'll be your fault for not having them properly controlled.'

She was looking at the tractor, standing darkly at the other end of the shed. I couldn't be sure but I thought I saw her mouth twitch. 'Come now,' I said, 'you know how much the chickens enjoy roosting up there—especially the driver.'

The twitch turned into a smile. I put my arm round her again. Soon I said: 'Why take offence so easily? I didn't mean to hurt your feelings.'

She smiled. 'I know you didn't.'

'Well then, why? P'raps you didn't like me fondling you. Was that it?'

She looked up quickly. 'Oh no, *that* was rather nice.' She shrugged her shoulders. 'Anyway, why bother? I can't always explain to myself why I behave like I do sometimes.' She walked away as far as the tractor and pulled idly at the cumbersome steering wheel. 'You ought to cover this up. Or move your chickens. They're making a mess of it.'

I agreed and she wandered back towards me. 'I suppose it's old Ma Wilkes really. She's the one that annoys me. Makes me feel like a child, looking down her nose at me in her prim way. I feel trapped there and dislike having to conform to her rules.'

'Then move. Find some other digs. Or get a flat of your own.'

'Ha, ha. On my money? Even if I could find one. No, I suppose I shall have to stick the old bitch until I hear of somewhere better. So long as I can just make her realise that all she's responsible for is my board and lodging. Nothing more.'

I laughed. 'Then you'd better tell her. And if she throws you out there's always a spare room here.' The words were out before I'd consciously thought about them. A spur of the moment idea prompted by my desire for her.

She just said: 'Thanks, I'll bear it in mind.'

I reminded her that I'd promised to make her a cup of tea and we walked towards the house.

'Remember,' she said, 'I can't stay long. And it looks very much as though there's more snow on the way.'

I squeezed her hand. 'You worry too much, that's your trouble. There's plenty of time for a cosy chat by the fire.'

'Huh! You're not the one who'll get caught in a snowstorm.'

'Or have to face the wrath of Ma Wilkes, I know.'

Mother had swept the snow from the backyard. Mrs P.P. was parading up and down with slow, measured steps and crooning rather crossly. She gathered her claws together each time she picked up a foot as though she was trying to warm them between steps. She hadn't moved far since the snow. Apart from a few wary ventures across the yard, to scratch through lumps of dung left by passing pigs, she had been content to mooch up and down between the back door and the privy, on the look-out for scraps or a quick warm up in the kitchen if the door was left open.

As we reached the back door I saw that it *was* open, just resting on the latch but with not enough room for Mrs P.P. to squeeze through. Now Mother had never locked a door in her life. She placed implicit faith in her Guardian Angel and for sixty long years that benign spirit had worked overtime on her behalf, making sure that a succession of handbags, hats, umbrellas, cases and coats, left on buses and trains, never failed to be returned to her. He even steered the flying shrapnel away from her during the blitz, when she consistently ignored the shells bursting overhead because she had to patrol her beat as an Air Raid Warden. And once, before the war, hurrying home one wet London night, when her carrier bag split depositing greengrocery in all directions, her Guardian Angel had appeared dressed in top hat, white tie and tails, fielding rolling oranges and gathering up sticks of rhubarb, which he presented to her with a bow. But although she relied on the angel to keep burglars at bay as well, she usually did her best to help him by at least banging the door shut after her as she hurried through. Yet I knew she never would get used to the Suffolk latch on the back door at Maywood. She called it 'a bother', because so often she had to return to latch it when it failed to catch as she swung it shut after her.

So I shrugged as I pushed it open. 'She must have gone tearing

119

out in a greater hurry than usual, off to do battle with the snow on her bike to the bus stop,' I said to Jean. And she laughed as we went inside and I explained about the Guardian Angel.

It was warm in the kitchen. There was a red glow from the fire bars of the kitchener, squatting comfortably in its ingle-nook. The kettle was singing quietly at the back and I thought, good, it won't take long to make the tea.

I pulled a chair back from the central table, scraping it across the brick floor. 'Take a seat. Or d'you want to wash away the rat poison first?'

I pointed to the long, shallow sink under the window. The old brass tap dripped sullenly, jealous of the bright, new hot water tap. 'There's hot water, soap, towel and . . .'

'What's that noise?' she asked, suddenly.

I listened. The door to the large pantry leading off the kitchen was ajar. The sound was coming from there. There was no mistaking the noise I heard.

'Whatever is it?' Jean asked again. I held my finger to my lips as I crept across.

I reached the door and took a silent step inside. Skinny had her back to me, her tail tightly coiled. Her head was buried in the bread bin.

I didn't know whether to laugh or shout. Instead I beckoned to Jean to come in and look. Skinny was champing with gusto.

Jean clapped her hand to her mouth. 'Oh!'

At the sound of her voice Skinny's head shot up, caught in mid chew with the end of a loaf in her jaws. She stood quite still while she made up her mind what to do. She couldn't see us directly behind her. She just knew we were there. I think she was half hoping that if she stayed motionless and absolutely quiet she'd get away with it.

But Jean started to laugh. Skinny made a desperate bite to get a better grip on the loaf, spun round with a mouth-stuffed grunt, saw she was cornered and charged out between us. Jean tripped and sat with a thump on the brick floor. I was thrown against the pantry door and Skinny discovered that the back door was firmly shut against her. She squealed with fury, ramming at the bottom of the door and trying to polish off the loaf at the same time.

I came up behind her. I was sorely tempted to boot her up the backside. It was swaying in front of me as she worried at the door. But there was no escape for her and it seemed wise not to aggravate her further. Instead I started to make my way past her to open the door, trying to talk to her nicely.

As the door opened inwards it meant that Skinny had to give way. Try asking a cornered sow to step back a pace or two. At the first sight of my leg coming in front of her she made off under the table and came to an abrupt halt, face to face with the red faced kitchener. In a moment I had the door open and was bounding round the table to drive her out. She swung round in the confined space, found herself surrounded by a forest of chair legs and dived through them carrying a chair clinging drunkenly to her back. Convinced that she'd been captured at last she squealed with intense chagrin, swerved through the door sending the chair flying and galloped across the yard with great grunts of glee at her sudden freedom.

Jean was still sitting on the pantry floor, helpless with laughter. I picked her up, dusted her down and steered her to the commodious old armchair in the shadowy corner beyond the fire.

A little later, I said: 'Mother doesn't really believe you exist, you know.'

She sat up on my lap and looked at me with her eyes wide. 'I feel real enough to you, don't I?' There was a trace of the same defiant look I'd first seen earlier.

I pulled her back against me. 'I should say so. I haven't stopped thinking about you since you first crept into the cowshed.'

'And you greeted me with your village idiot look,' she laughed. 'What with your vacant stare and Pete and Bert looking like a couple of morons, I wondered what I'd let myself in for. Even the blessed cows all stared at me as though I'd no right to be there.'

'But I'm so glad you did come. After you'd left last evening I couldn't wait to tell Mum about you.'

'Then why doesn't she believe I exist?'

'It's the rat catcher bit she can't go along with. I'm sure she still half believes I'm pulling her leg.'

Jean pouted and picked a stray hair from her jumper. 'Why doesn't anybody believe me when I tell them what I do? After all, there's no reason why a girl shouldn't catch rats just like any man. There's nothing much to it and most times the rats go away to die. You don't even have to touch many.'

'There's just the dead chickens to pick up, that's all,' I suggested. Almost immediately I had to fend off a determined attack. Which turned into a fierce kiss and dissolved in softness.

When she drew away she said: 'I'll bet you anything you like none of your chickens die from eating my poison, careless though you are with them. I've hidden the stuff too well, I can tell you.'

'Only time will tell,' I said, with mock gravity. Which again provoked the desired attack.

Then I said: 'But seriously, now. Tomorrow you must meet Mum. I won't be forgiven if I haven't formally asked you to tea.'

'Really?' Jean laughed. 'You make her sound very formidable.'

'That's the last thing she is. Mind you, though, she's curious. She'll want to know all about you.'

Mother always wanted to know everything about everybody.

After Jean had left, and when Mother returned from her Talk that evening, flushed with the bike ride and happy at another successful reception, I told her I had asked Jean to tea the following day. Whereupon she pulled off her coat and hat, flung them in the old armchair and threw herself on the kitchener, tempting it with crackling kindling and the driest logs, coaxing it with kind words to produce an oven hot enough for a cake and a batch of buns.

'I wonder if I dare try an 'all-nighter' as well,' she mused, when the baking was under way. She had one hand against her red cheek and was staring into the fire. 'I haven't made one for simply ages because I never know how this old brute's going to behave.'

'But that's just how the all-nighter was born originally,' I reminded her. 'Ages ago, you remember, when the oven went out half way through.' It was a treacle cake which, because it had been cut off in mid-cook, subsided into a sorry hollow. And Mother had taken one peep and slammed the oven door on it in disgust, forgetting about it until the following morning. Then she had removed it and cast it with a sigh on to the sideboard until she could pluck up enough courage to throw it away. Waste of food was abhorrent to her. But mysteriously the cake had disappeared, slice by stealthy slice as the family and paying guests passed that way, returning again and again for more of the chewy delight.

So she decided to risk one now. And the following morning she removed the all-nighter from the oven, poked her finger into its golden hollow and pronounced it to be another success.

Jean came again in the afternoon and the first thing she wanted to know, as she got out of her van, was whether I'd counted the chickens.

'Of course,' I nodded.

'And they're all there?'

'All present and correct.'

'There you are, I told you so. I'm careful of the stock of even the most careless farmers.'

'But there's just one thing,' I said, frowning seriously.

She looked at me quickly and her smile vanished. 'What's that?'

'Henry's looking a bit queer.'

'Oh, no! *Don't* tell me he's picked up a dopey rat.' She gripped my arm and looked wretched. 'Where is he? Has he been sick? Let me have a look at him.'

She saw me looking beyond her and she swung round. Henry was sitting bolt upright on a wall near by, his whiskers proudly curled forward and his yellow eyes glinting with friendly recognition. Jean walked quickly towards him and gathered him into her arms. He looked at me smugly over her shoulder, purring like a well tuned engine.

'There, poor Henry,' she crooned as she stroked him. He half closed his eyes and his engine roared approval. She turned to face me, looking slightly relieved. 'There doesn't seem *much* the matter with him. I don't think he can have caught a rat.'

When I couldn't keep a straight face any longer, she opened her eyes wide, took a deep breath and stamped her foot. 'You rotter! And to think I believed you! You're *cruel*!' Henry turned his head in sympathy and gracefully rubbed his cheek against her face. Then she laughed happily when I put my arms round them both.

'Cats and dogs are okay anyway,' she said, as though she had known all along. 'Even if they do happen to pick up something they can be sick and it doesn't do them any more harm. But rats and chickens can't be sick. That's why it kills them.'

'I see,' I nodded, wisely.

She insisted that I left her to her work on her own. When she had finished, pleased to tell me that all her secret little piles of poison had been sampled, we went off to find Mother.

She was in the garden—or what passed as a garden. Once it had been nice, spreading away in an L-shaped quarter of an acre to the front and one side of the house. But as Checky and his missus had grown older, so the weeds and brambles had closed in, relentlessly creeping forward year by year until only the lawn remained, shaded by a towering cherry tree and fringed with an overcrowded herbaceous border. But Mother had decided to tackle it. She was determined to bring it back to its former glory. As she had always considered herbaceous borders to be her speciality, she had started with that. And that meant giving it a good digging. Which, in turn, meant removing all the plants. And the job had been on the go, on and off, since the autumn.

So when I pushed Jean in front of me through the little side gate, Mother was hard at it. The snowy lawn was dotted with huge up-rooted clumps of Michaelmas daisies clotted with clay, with piles of pale-rooted poppies and with the rest of the gamut of perennials to the stark stalks of phlox and the green, broad leaves of purple iris. And the roots of each clump were covered with sheets of newspaper, held in place with a dollop of clay in the belief that it would keep the frost off.

Mother looked round when I called out. Her hair was a halo of white wisps, her cheeks glowing and with a quick upward flick she brushed the palm of her gardening glove over the tip of her nose to remove a budding dewdrop. 'Hello!' She gave a gay wave with her smile, threw down her fork and came towards us, kicking lumps of snow and clay from her shoes. '*How* nice! I'm so glad you've come.'

She pulled off her gloves and shook Jean's outstretched hand as I introduced them. 'Oh, how cold your hand is. You must be frozen! Come along in and let's find the fire.'

She led the way to the front door, hurriedly scraped a little more mud from her shoes and marched into the tiny hall. The stairs led straight up, on the right was a room which the agents particulars had described as 'second rec.' and which I used as an office-cum-junk room, and on the left was the sitting room. The kitchen led to the back from that.

We followed Mother in. A log fire was blazing on the open hearth in the ingle-nook, the Aladdin lamp was already alight casting its shadow into the beamed ceiling and the afternoon tea table was opened out in the middle of the room. It was bright with a white cloth, the best tea service and plates laden with enough food to feed a large family.

'Oh, what a lovely room,' Jean exclaimed. She looked at me and smiled. 'Yesterday I was only allowed into the kitchen.'

'Nonsense,' I laughed. 'That was only because it was warm there and this fire wasn't alight.' But I was glad of her remark. It showed she was feeling at ease.

'Well, sit you down,' Mother said. She frowned at me: 'Come along, David, where are your manners? Take her coat.'

'Oh, excuse me, Madam,' I said, with a flourish.

'That's it,' Mother said. 'Now, I'll just go and *mash* the tea,' making great play of the local expression she'd learnt.

When she had gone through to the kitchen, Jean hugged my arm. 'Oh, she's *nice*,' it sounded like relief, 'she's so—so natural.'

I laughed, softly. 'You wait, my girl. You haven't had the inquisition yet.'

Tea came in the silver teapot and there was clotted cream to go on strawberry jam. And while we worked our way through it, and Jean was introduced to the special stick-jaw qualities of the all-nighter, between mouthfuls she managed to persuade Mother that she was, indeed, a rat catcher.

'Ugh! Horrid creatures,' Mother shuddered. 'I don't know how you dare pick them up.'

Jean laughed. 'You get used to it. I used to use the tongs provided by a thoughtful Ministry at first. But now I don't mind picking them up by the tails so long as I've got gloves on.'

'This is a nice teatime conversation, I must say,' I remarked.

Mother had finished tea and she put down her cup. She shuffled her chair closer to the fire. She spread her rough hands towards the flames and moved her fingers as though she was playing an imaginary piano. 'Now, let me see,' she said, 'where's your home?'

And I thought: hello, now we're off.

Jean caught my eye with the flicker of a smile as she said: 'Well, I've got digs in Ashford, but my home's the other side of Canterbury.'

'Oh, really? How interesting. We used to live near Canterbury. Dear old Twitham farmhouse. I wonder if you know it? Near Wingham.'

Jean frowned and shook her head slowly.

'What fun we all had there.' Mother was smiling into the fire, lost for a moment in far-off memories. Then she asked: 'D'you live in a village?'

'Sort of. But outside a bit, on a farm.'

I sat upright. 'Is your father a farmer?'

She laughed: 'Yes, anything wrong?'

'You never told me!'

'You never asked.'

'Well, you could have said, instead of letting me traipse you round as though it was all new to you.' I felt foolish.

'But it *was* new to me. It's not a bit like Dad's farm. He just grows corn and cabbages. The only animals are bullocks and sheep

125

that come for a few months in the winter and are sold again. Your animals are all part of the family and I got so interested in them it would've spoilt it to tell you about our farm then.'

'Yes,' Mother said, 'the animals are fun, aren't they? Except perhaps the sows. They're better from a distance.'

I laughed and turned to Jean. 'She's afraid of them, that's the trouble.'

Jean said: 'I don't know how she puts up with them—not when they come right in and eat out of her bread bin.'

'Oh dear, yes!' Mother exclaimed. 'Naughty old Skinny.'

'It was your fault for leaving the door open,' I said, 'It wasn't really fair on the Guardian Angel, you know. After all, he was busy getting you through the snow on your bike.'

'But I'm *sure* I shut it,' she persisted. We laughed again and fell silent.

Mother changed the subject. 'Didn't your father want you to work for him on the farm?' She smiled at Jean.

'I started to—when I left school and joined the Land Army as my war work.' Jean shrugged. 'But, you know how it is, farmers are difficult enough to work for at the best of times.' She laughed. 'When it's your own father, it's impossible. Especially when I seemed to spend all my time hoeing rotten old cabbages.'

'How tiresome for you, my dear,' Mother agreed. She really only liked digging. Hoeing was much too fiddly.

Jean smiled. 'Anyway, it was time I left home. And I'm always glad I did because now they all mean so much more to me each time I go back.'

'Is yours a big family?' Mother wanted to know next.

'Five—four girls and a boy.'

'Poor fellow,' I said, quietly.

Jean opened her mouth, but before she could think of a suitable rejoinder, Mother exclaimed: 'How jolly! Ours is a big family too. Such fun. And is your brother the eldest?'

'No. Actually I am, worst luck.'

Mother looked surprised. 'Oh! Why worst luck?'

'When you're the eldest you always get the blame for everything.' Jean laughed and her cheeks were flushed. 'It's always your fault if there's an argument and you're always expected to set a good example. So boring.'

'Yes, how trying that can be,' Mother agreed, with feeling.

'I don't think any good example ever stopped us from arguing,'

I observed. 'We seemed to be at each others' throats morning, noon and night.'

'Rubbish! You weren't as bad as all that.' Mother frowned.

And so we chatted on while Mother discovered that Jean had been to school in Canterbury and had also been a Girl Guide. Which was a point in her favour because Mother herself had been talked into the job of Guide Commissioner when we lived at Twitham. So there was plenty of talk about tracking and singing and roaring camp fires. I sat back and listened, glad that they seemed to be getting on so well.

But it was later that Jean, quite unconsciously, delivered the final clincher. Mother had been describing her journey to Ivychurch the previous day, to give her Talk to the Mothers' Union there.

'Oh,' said Jean, innocently, 'my mother belongs to the Mothers' Union.'

After that she was home and dry.

Soon the fire got the better of her and Mother dozed off. And Jean said it was time to go because she was afraid of more snow. So we roused Mother, who protested that she wasn't really asleep, just thinking, and she came to the back door with us.

When Jean had driven off and I came back in, Mother was at the sink with the washing up.

'Well?' I asked, 'what's the verdict?'

'Of course I like her, darling. You knew I would. She's a nice country girl and she's very pretty.' She paused and thought for a moment. Then she said: 'I'm sure she comes from a good home.'

'You make her sound like a stray cat.'

She plunged her hands into the water and sighed. 'Oh dear, you know I didn't mean it like that.'

I leant over and kissed her cheek. 'I know. She likes you too. She thinks you're super, so that's okay.'

And I found I was whistling as I walked across the yard to help the boys finish milking.

10

Whenever Margaret Featherstone-Kelsey came to call it was like opening the back door and letting in a gale. She was a spinster of the parish, and as a keen member of the Women's Institute, the Women's Voluntary Service and a Friend of Canterbury Cathedral she had latched on to Mother soon after our arrival. They really had very little in common apart from their membership of these bodies, but Margaret was the sort of woman who bubbled over with fatuous ideas, imagined she had a flair for organisation, threw herself with gusto into strange causes and inflicted herself on anyone who would listen.

Secretly, I am sure, Mother loathed her. But she was too staunch a Christian to show hatred. She felt it was her duty to help Margaret when possible. However, whenever Margaret's big, black, pre-war Humber came swelling into the yard, Mother would yield to temptation, clap her hand to the side of her face and exclaim: 'Oh dear! Here comes that awful shallow woman from Brenchwood Hall again. I wonder what she wants this time.'

Everybody always came to the back door, and thus the kitchen. Nobody ever discovered the twisted little gate set in the hedge along the lane and leading to the front door. So I was often trapped in the kitchen whenever one of Mother's friends called. Usually an excuse of work to do on the farm gave me an easy exit. But not so with Margaret. She was a hobby farmer and swept me into the conversation with a torrent of chat about her Jersey cows, her horses and how were my darling pigs?

Margaret was a big, tweedy woman in her early thirties. As I was ten years younger, of course she seemed ancient. Unconsciously I slotted her into the maiden aunt category and was naive enough to think that the reasons for her visits were solely to rake my long suffering mother into helping with a jumble sale, or contributing in one way or another to further the schemes she was perpetually hatching. Once she came suggesting that Mother should make something for what they were pleased to call 'a sale of work', in aid of some nebulous charity. And this gave us a good laugh after she'd gone. Mother had raised a large family and was therefore able to patch clothes, cobble a hole in a sock, sew on a button or run up a curtain as well as the next Mum. But that was as far as her talents went in that direction. Any attempt to knit or sew a garment from scratch ended up, after weeks of toil, sighing and remaking, in a creation as unlike the pattern as it was possible to imagine and often only suitable for a freak. Margaret had kept trying to persuade Mother to make something, even if it was only a knitted tea cosy, or perhaps an embroidered tray cloth. In the end Mother had persuaded her to accept three jars of quince jelly as the best contribution of her work, and a sharp scowl at me had sealed off the information about where the quince tree was situated.

It was Bill Checksfield who had first suggested to me that there was a side to Margaret's character which I had not suspected. He'd arrived at the farm one hot, July day, just as her car went off up the lane, in a haze of dust and swirling strands of hay.

'That's 'er from Brenchwood Hall, ain't it?' he asked.

I agreed and informed him that she'd talked long and loudly and wasted my time.

His moustache had lengthened while his eyes creased and sparkled in a smile. 'Her's hot under the breeches, that one.'

'You don't say!' It had never occurred to me to think of her in that way.

'I do say. You want to watch her, me lad. They do say as how 'er likes young men. Likes to smother 'em with love.' And he'd laughed and blown sparks from his fag.

As Margaret had just driven off after extracting a promise from me to visit Brenchwood Hall, I began to wonder. She was going to show me over her farm the following Sunday afternoon and I was invited to have a swim in her mill pond, which, she told me at length, she'd equipped with a diving board and a landing stage.

Even before Checky spoke of her I'd not been looking forward to this visit with any great enthusiasm. I was interested in the farm light enough. She'd told me plenty about it and I wanted to see the neat dairy buildings she'd converted from the old stables. And her pampered little herd of Jersey cows. But I wasn't too keen on the swim in her pond. Even at the best of times I was never enthusiastic about immersing my body in cold water for the sake of the doubtful pleasure of swimming. And as I was extremely self conscious of my long and very skinny body, I didn't relish displaying that either.

And I'd looked even skinnier when Margaret unveiled herself. I was in my swimming trunks, squatting hunched up on the side of the pond after our inspection of the farm, watching the deep, dark water and thinking how cold it looked. Margaret had come prancing across the lawn from the house, draped in a voluminous bathing wrap, the tight auburn curls bouncing on her head, which looked too small for her body. With a wide, red smile she'd swept the wrap from her shoulders and stood clasped in a tight pink swimsuit. It barely contained her. I was almost afraid to look at so much woman. Somehow her breasts managed to find lodgings, and she had a surprisingly slim waist, but with wide hips and a large, low-slung bum.

'Not been in yet? Dear me, that won't do. Come *on*! I'm simply dying for a dip.' And she walked to the end of the diving board with springing steps, dived in cleanly, surfaced and bobbed up and down like a pink and white buoy. Then she drifted on her back and kicked her feet, propelling herself across the pond in a shower of grey spray.

Just to show willing I dived in quickly, made a rapid circuit of the pond and paddled back to the bank. I sat there trying not to shiver under my towel. Margaret was still splashing happily in the pond. The water rippled and gurgled into the rushes around the bank and she waved cheerfully to me whenever she paused to bob. Several times she called to me to join her again but no, I called, swimming wasn't my forte and anyway I found it too cold.

I was just thinking of taking a quick run around the lawn to warm up before getting dressed when she emerged, dripped up the steps and subsided beside me. She was very close to me and I remembered Checky's warning about being smothered by her. I was mesmerised by the large, soft body heaving and dripping silently so near me. A violent and involuntary shiver shook me and immediately her arm was round my shoulder, drawing me closer to her. A huge breast slipped its mooring and was eyeing me eagerly with a cyclopean stare. I felt trapped. I was unable to move. I was to be engulfed by the soft white flesh straining to burst from its tight, pink sheath and break over me like a tidal wave.

She turned to complete the clinch with her other arm and as the staring cyclops bore down on me I was galvanised into action. With a resounding thwack on her wide, wet thigh, I sprang to my feet declaring how late it had got and I really must hurry back or the milking would never get done.

Strangely this abrupt brush-off made no difference whatsoever to Margaret's visits to Maywood. She was far too ebullient for the woman scorned act and she behaved as though it had never happened. And I made sure I avoided any situation where it was likely to occur again.

She came a couple of weeks after Jean's first visit and we became involved in a discussion about my cows. She was leaning against the open door of her car and had been on the point of getting in for the last five minutes. She had a long, striped scarf wound round her neck and every now and then she made great play of throwing one end over her shoulder, which would then slip back at her next attempt to bow into the car.

'You're *not* going to experiment with that *dreadful* Artificial Insemination, are you?' She stood up abruptly.

I had mentioned the problem of getting my cows in calf that month. Artificial Insemination centres had recently been set up by the Milk Marketing Board and now the service was available to farmers. I thought it was a wise and progressive move to take advantage of it.

'But it must be better than a trip down the lane to old Dunnell's bull,' I protested. 'A.I. gives you the advantage of semen from better bred and more expensive bulls. And with no chance of disease either, not like there is from a communal bull. It's got to be better.'

'And what about the poor cow?' she asked. 'Have you thought about her, my dear? I think it's positively too scientific for words. I'm absolutely convinced it can't be right to interfere with nature to that extent.' Her scarf went flying over her shoulder again and her bubble cut quivered as her head shook with revulsion.

'We've interfered with nature so much already that I can't see that as an argument against it.' I laughed at the piercing look she gave me. 'When you think about it, there's precious little natural about the way we farm dairy cows these days. And their milk yields keep getting greater so it can't be bad. A.I. is just the next step forward in improving the breeds as I see it.'

She was shaking her head quickly again. 'No, no, I don't agree. The poor cow must miss the *stimulus* of the bull. I'm quite sure of that. I mean to say . . . well . . . a glass rod!' She shook her head and shuddered. '*And* a man's arm up her back passage at the same time. Well! I ask you! Oh no, I'm sure that can't be right. Poor things!' She was deadly serious and had gone quite white at the horror of it all.

So I kept a straight face. 'Yet they get in calf. They say the conception rate's higher with A.I. than with a bull. And they have some fine calves, too.'

'So they may. But it can't be right, I'm sure it can't. Not in the long run. If the cows never see a bull, or even smell him, if the only contact they ever have with him is through a glass rod, well . . . I mean to say . . . no stimulus. Why, in a generation or two, say five or six years, they'll forget that such a creature as a bull exists. Then we shall run into all sorts of trouble. Silent heats. Maybe no heats at all. It's difficult enough to spot some of 'em even now. Takes a bull to smell them out.'

I wanted to tell her she was talking nonsense. But she seemed upset enough as it was. She was very fond of her little Jersey cows. Evidently she wished most fervently to spare them the frustrations which she experienced herself, poor woman.

In the end I shrugged. 'Oh well, A.I. or no, I've got six cows to get in calf this month and three next or my milk cheques won't be worth having next autumn.'

She stooped towards the driving seat again. Suddenly she straightened and banged the roof of the car with the lambswool glove she was wearing. 'I have an idea!' she declared. 'You shall be the first to try out Hercules!' Her brown eyes were wide open, her cheeks were rosy again and the heavy lipstick glistened into a smile.

'Hercules?'

'Yes, of course, you remember Hercules. I showed him to you that day you came for a swim. He's the little Jersey bull I've been rearing to take dear old Agamemnon's place. Why, he'll be just right for you.'

I remembered Hercules. He was the fiery little brute who had snorted and hoiked at me with his new horns when I had greeted him in his paddock. And he had glowered at me as though he meant it, too. I ventured to suggest that perhaps he was a trifle small to use just yet.

'Good gracious, no! He's a fine little bull now. I've had him licensed and the vet's been to put the ring in his nose. I'm going to use him on Agamemnon's daughters first. But they won't be ready until March. You could have him here until then. That would give him some practice. Now I think that's a splendid idea, don't you?'

I was hesitating, wondering what to say. I wasn't too keen on Jerseys. I always thought of them as gentlemen farmers' cows and they had a reputation for being delicate and needing fussing. But, on the other hand, their milk was rich in butterfat. For just this once it might not be a bad idea to inject some Jersey blood into some of next autumn's crop of calves. Already a lot of attention was being paid to increasing the national minimum level of butterfat. A Jersey injection now would improve the quality of the milk in my churns later on.

'Why don't you come up to Brenchwood Hall and see Hercules again for yourself?' Margaret was gushing on. 'Then you could make up your mind whether you think he'd do. I'm sure you'll adore him and he'll be so much better for your cows than that horrid A.I.'

I had been refusing her invitations with the excuse of pressure of work ever since my narrow escape at the edge of the pond. But this was work. I'd not seen the bull since July and he could well have grown enough to manage the smaller of my cows. Yet I could not help wondering whether her offer was to provide the stimulus which she evidently considered essential for my cows, or perhaps for herself.

However, in the end I thanked her and agreed to have Hercules for a month or so. We could offer him lodgings in a loose box where, I assured her, he would be most comfortable. I didn't add that it was the only loose box I had and was mainly reserved as a maternity wing cum sick bay. But as the only cow left to calve now was Popsi, when her time came they could swap places and young Hercules could spend a night or two tied up in the cowshed. It would probably do him good to see how the other half lived.

Pete and I cycled the two miles or so up to Brenchwood Hall to fetch Hercules. He had not grown as much as I had expected, although he was probably of average height for his breed at his age. But what he lacked in stature he certainly made up for in aggressiveness, which was something Margaret had forgotten to mention.

Perhaps she wasn't aware of it. The actual work on her hobby farm was left to her 'man', Percy Follen. He was a wiry little chap of perhaps sixty, with sparse thin hairs on his arms and curling up up from his collarless shirt, like those left on a chicken after plucking. Whenever I saw him I had an urge to singe him. He lived in the gardener's cottage and while his wife 'did' for Margaret in the house, Percy had his hands full with the Jerseys, the two horses kept for riding and the lazy grey mare, Dolly. In addition to this, poor old Percy was the general handyman about Brenchwood Hall, painter, decorator, car cleaner, lawn mower and gardener. He had also been responsible for knocking up the diving board and landing stage on the pond. As Margaret continually referred to him as 'my man', sometimes I wondered whether there were also extra-mural duties she called upon him to perform from time to time. But no, Percy was kept so busy that I doubted whether he'd have energy enough left for that at his age.

Percy introduced us to Hercules over the top of the half-heck door of his loose box. 'He's a mite frisky,' he said.

Hercules slowly dipped his back so that the root of his tail bulged upwards, while at the other end he seemed to be squaring his shoulders. He was standing with his back half towards us and had obviously failed to realise that strangers had come until Percy spoke. Now he was trying to look important and behave like an old bull. So far he could only see us with one eye and he rolled this round slowly, twitched his ears and huffed. Then he looked right round. He turned to face us, but rather too quickly to be in keeping with his dignified act. He lifted his head and curled up his nose as though we smelt repulsive. His face was dark brown with a touch of fawn highlighting his large, liquid eyes and he had the characteristic light fawn circle around his black nose. His shiny copper ring was still too big for him and it dangled from his nostrils and failed to rise up and cock-a-snoot at us like that of an old bull when he curled his nose.

'Still,' Percy went on, 'all young bulls be frisky, b'aint 'em, eh? Eh?' He was poking a calloused finger into Pete's ribs and a hideous row of yellow false teeth dropped uncontrollably as he smiled. I wondered why he didn't give them a good scrub.

He nipped through the door, clicked his tongue a few times and had his forefinger through Hercules' ring before the young bull had time to come out of his act and take evasive action. 'But he be all right really,' Percy continued, grinning at Hercules, 'b'ain't yer, me beauty?'

Hercules flicked his ears back, rolled his eyes and looked non-plussed. He gave a tentative pull backwards, found it hurt and the tip of his tongue gently explored his smarting nostril.

Percy led him to the door. He reached up, unhooked a short rope attached by a swivel to a spring clip and fixed this on the bull's ring in place of his finger. He handed me the end of the rope and un-bolted the bottom half of the door. 'There 'e be, then. Off yer go!' He gave Hercules a smart smack on his rump as he walked out of the door after me, which made him snort and glare at me as though I'd done it. Just as I was feeling keenly conscious of the need to foster friendly relations with the creature.

Margaret had been hovering in the cobbled yard. Were we sure we could manage? Wouldn't it be better if she brought him in the horse box behind the car? I wondered if she was regretting her offer to lend me the bull. Or perhaps she thought I'd cheated by arriving to collect him with Pete as a chaperon. But I needed him to push my bike back.

Carefully I assured her that we'd be fine and I waved my thanks. 'Just you be a good boy now, Hercules,' she called down the drive after us. A couple of moments later she added: 'Do your stuff.' And I know I detected a trace of desperation in her voice.

By the time we reached Maywood, Hercules had a bloody nose. It was his own fault. He would not realise that I'd pull him up short every time he tried to bunt me up the backside. Percy had trained him to walk to the rope, but I was a stranger. He was simply dying to try out his sharp horns on the seat of my trousers, much to Pete's amusement as he brought up the rear, wheeling the two bikes. For a while Hercules would walk quietly and I let the rope go slack so as not to yank at his nose unduly. Then the temptation of me walking in front of him, and within range, was too much for him and he would whisk his tail, lower his head and charge. And when I side-stepped and pulled him up short on his ring, while Pete shouted 'Olé', he would shake his head, look hurt and shove his tongue up each nostril in turn. Even after he tasted the blood he never learnt.

Percy had given me instructions that Hercules was to be exer-cised every day. He was not to be left standing in the soft straw and dung of a loose box and only let out to serve a cow. That way a bull became bad tempered and I knew Hercules required no more encouragement in that direction. He was to be taken for a walk along the hard road every day so that he remained used to being

135

handled—and to keep his feet trim. Percy reckoned there were few worse sights on a farm than a bull with twisted, overgrown hooves through months of standing in spongey dung. I agreed with him.

I relayed these instructions to Bert as he hung over the door sizing up Hercules. And I suggested that taking the bull for a walk every day would be just the job for him. He could spend half an hour at it every morning after milking, when he returned from breakfast. I'd been expecting an objection and was surprised at his ready acceptance.

'Aye, I don't mind,' he said, without looking up. He was holding his hand out and Hercules was giving it an exploratory lick. Evidently they were establishing a useful rapport.

The snow still lay on the fields but had melted from the lane. The next morning Bert got through his share of the chores with splendid speed so that he could take the bull out. And for the next three days he and Hercules took their morning walk like a couple of buddies. Evidently Hercules was still nursing a sore nose after our walk from Brenchwood Hall. He followed quietly as Bert led him up the lane as far as his home and proudly showed him off to his father and mother. Leading a bull was something of an achievement. Old Jack had never done it. And although he was only a little bull he was very fierce and you had to know how to handle him. I could just imagine young Bert telling the tale.

Each morning the walk took a little longer and on the fourth day Bert returned alone. He was looking decidedly dishevelled as he sloped into the cowshed to find me. There was mud on his cap and face, his hands were plastered, his flannel shirt had bunched up into a heap under his braces and he was crying. It took me a patient ten minutes to find out what had happened. It would have taken less time if Pete had only kept quiet, instead of wringing renewed sobs out of his brother, by calling him a silly little sod, and telling him it served him right for being such a cocky little bugger.

Apparently he and Hercules were on such splendid terms and had reached such a high degree of understanding, that Bert had decided the bull could be trusted to walk without a lead. So he had unclipped the rope. And for a time Hercules had followed him down the lane as though he was still being led. But soon Bert discovered that the bull was gaining on him, and with no rope to flick, and words of command ignored, he found himself forced to walk faster and faster to keep his distance. Hercules began to snort, to swish his tail, to prance, to shake his head. And Bert began to run. The lonely narrow lane stretched before him and the safety of the farm seemed a hundred miles away. Only the gate into a meadow offered an escape from the now charging Hercules. Bert swerved and threw himself at it, plunging through the snow-capped mud to clasp at the top rail, scrabbling with his mud-clogged boots for a footing on the lower bars. Desperately he climbed for the leap to safety, but the agile little bull had spotted his manoeuvre and altered course accordingly. So that just as Bert was poised to clear the gate, Hercules arrived in the nick of time and neatly tossed him over. Bert rubbed his backside ruefully as he told me.

We found Hercules celebrating his victory with a triumphant attack on the hay rick. We heard him before we saw him. The bellowing and snorting could be heard in the cowshed and were causing interested and alert looks from all the cows. And when we saw him he was pawing at the ground, throwing back lumps of hay and mud, while his head was heaving at the hay in an attempt to topple the stack. He heard our shouts and looked round, inquisitve, hay seeds littered like confetti over his head and shoulders. He looked at the sticks we were brandishing, decided they were of no consequence and renewed his attack on the hay. Only now he was itching all over and was using the rick as a giant back scratcher. Instead of charging it he was throwing his body against it while he hoicked out lumps with his horns and bellowed with satisfaction. By the time we'd driven him away and down into his loose box, there was more mess around the hay rick than even Colonel had ever made.

I found Bert wreaking his revenge on Hercules that same evening. We'd agreed that he shouldn't let the bull get the better of him and for this reason he should go on looking after him and exercising him as before. With Pete out of the way I'd given him a little lecture saying that I hoped he'd learnt his lesson, that he could never really trust a bull, particularly a Jersey, and that he should treat him with respect but let him know who was boss.

Which advice he took seriously. He went off jauntily enough just before milking time with an armful of hay and some sticks of kale. It should have only taken him a minute or two to push the food into the loose box and return to the cowshed. When, after ten minutes he'd still not returned, I began to get worried about him. Horrid visions appeared in which Hercules had him cornered and was goring him. I hurried across the yard. Rounding the corner to the loose box I was relieved to see Bert standing outside. His back was towards me.

The top door was shut and the bottom one was half open. Bert was standing behind it. The bundle of hay was on the ground beside him and the juicy leaves of kale were placed temptingly just outside the door. Hercules was hungry and particularly partial to kale. But every time his head ventured slowly out from under the top door, and his tongue curled to hook the kale, Bert rapped him smartly over the nose with a stick and sent him wincing backwards.

'Buggered if I don't teach 'im who's boss,' was all he would say to me.

11

NONE OF THE COWS had actually seen Hercules as yet. But they had smelt him and they had heard him. I detected a definite air of expectancy in the cowshed and there was no doubt they all knew there was a fella around.

Lotty was the first to claim an introduction. As soon as I walked through the dark morning into the cowshed, and the lamplight fell on her, I suspected she had come on heat. She was always a keen observer and a stickler for routine. But this morning her head was more erect than usual, her ears flicked at every sound and she didn't pounce on her corn with her usual relish. It was obvious there was something else on her mind and when she only gave half her usual amount of milk I was certain.

'Lotty's bulling,' I said, as I stood up from milking her.

'I'll tip young Hercules the wink when I feed him,' said Bert. He and the bull were on better terms again. They had reached a state of mutual respect. Or perhaps it was armed neutrality.

I'd been wondering about Hercules as I'd been milking. Lotty was a big cow and I doubted whether he would manage her. Probably it would be better to ring up for the artificial inseminator to call and this had to be done before ten o'clock to be certain of a visit the same day. I told the boys what I thought.

'Cor, e'll manage 'er. Easy!' Bert declared.

'Course 'e will,' Pete agreed. 'Her don't want no bloody A.I., do yer, Lotty?' He walked over to her and slapped her on the rump. She raised her tall horns high and swished her tail.

Bert came over and joined us. 'Hercules'll soon slip you a length, old gal. 'E'll be a fast worker, I'll lay. 'E'll give yer summat to look surprised about, that 'e will.'

Lotty appeared to be listening intently while we discussed her love life. In the end she could stand the suspense no longer and shuffled forward to pee.

'Go on,' Pete urged me, 'let Hercules have a go. That's what 'ees here for.'

'Go on,' Bert echoed, 'let's see what 'e can do.'

'Okay,' I agreed, 'we'll see if he can manage her. If not, I'll ring the A.I.'

After breakfast we slipped Lotty's chain to drive her into the yard. But before we had a chance to get her out of the shed the sight of the other cows' rumps, standing in an inviting line, was too much for her. With a moan of pleasure she mounted the luckless Bluebell with a lesbian leap. In a field this would be fair play. Bluebell could run forward to dislodge her and then turn and mount Lotty herself. And Lotty would stand still beneath her and find at least some of the pleasure she was seeking. But to be mounted in a cowshed! And by the vicious Lotty! Bluebell was horrified and she bellowed and bucked in great alarm, tugging at her chain so that I thought she'd wrench it from its socket. I'd never seen the timid Bluebell so upset. Even after we managed to knock Lotty off her back she quivered with anxiety.

Lotty was beside herself with excitement. Sometimes a cow will hardly show a heat and it may only last for a few hours of discreet concealment. Often it is hard to spot her, sometimes impossible if she is tied in a cowshed. There may be just the slightest fall in her milk yield, insignificant unless you know she is due for a heat. Or perhaps an alertness that is only faintly more noticeable than usual and easily missed. Even with free access to other cows in a field, or a yard, she may fail to form a satisfactory relationship with another cow and a few half-hearted attempts at mounting may be all that is seen. But to another cow a heat can be a rip-roaring affair. It is an event to be bellowed about and enjoyed. It is a day of frenzy and utter abandon when she works herself up into a muck sweat with one or two others who have agreed to partner her. Or perhaps they haven't agreed but have been forced into a day long lesbian relationship by persistent importuning. And sometimes the most unlikely cows partner each other. Cows that usually have nothing to do with each other will suddenly become frantic friends for a day and then avoid one another like the plague once the heat is over.

Lotty bellowed for all to hear as she scuttled out of the cowshed. We drove her into the yard and Elsie, Doris and Brutus forsook the hay rack in the bullock lodge and bounded across to see what all the commotion was about. We had barred their access into the yard so they thrust their heads over the rails, front row spectators blowing hot snorts of enthusiasm into the morning air. Brutus, in particular, responded to the new smell he sensed by curling up his little nose and uttering a high pitched moo. He seemed to surprise himself because his face straightened, his ears dropped and he turned to Elsie and Doris as much as to say: 'Was that me?' I made a mental note to get the vet to him before he made any more discoveries about his burgeoning body.

Bert led Hercules into the yard and let him loose. The little bull swaggered towards Lotty to introduce himself. He was little more than half her size but, from the way he was marching through the straw, he had all the confidence of an old bull instead of one who was about to attempt to break his virginity. Lotty had been having a few words over the rails with Brutus and had just dismissed him with a hoick of her horns when she heard Hercules approach. She turned to look at him, raising her head as though she couldn't believe that this was the bull whose smell she had caught and whose bellowings had sent such shivers of excitement through the cowshed.

Hercules stopped short. 'He's afraid of 'er horns,' said Pete. He had settled himself comfortably on the rails to watch the performance, safely out of the way of any possible attack.

But Hercules was showing no fear. Instead he was starting his seduction of Lotty by raising his head, wrinkling his nose and snorting to acquaint himself better with the interesting odour of ovulation. He had to be quite certain in his own mind about this before embarking on more positive steps. Evidently he was satisfied because now he lowered his head and turned it halfway away from Lotty, straining his body rather as a muscle man turns to flex his biceps and display the bulges in his body.

Lotty watched this performance and it seemed as though she was trying to make up her mind whether to take it seriously or not. To a comfortably proportioned matron such as she, the spectacle of this little fellow taking off an old bull was puzzling. He looked all wrong. Yet he smelt right. But she didn't hesitate for long. Whatever he was, the fire in her loins was overpowering her. It just had to be quenched. At least here was a fellow creature and she was free to get at him.

Hercules was obviously taken aback by her precipitate action. He was barely halfway through what he believed to be the dignified approach when Lotty was on him, riding him like a great mountain, thrusting down on his rump with her wide belly, her udder rising and swaying behind him. He tried to shake her off, plunging forward and swaying sideways, but she was right over him, gripping him with her front legs, holding him powerless while her orgasm coursed through her. He staggered under her weight and thrusting.

'Her'll break 'im,' Bert called out, with concern. 'Break 'is bloody back if 'er don't get orf 'im.'

'Course 'er won't,' sneered Pete. 'Her's only telling him ter get on with it and cut out the fancy stuff.'

'Well why don't 'er give 'im a chance, then? Won't be fit fer nothing in a minute, that 'e won't.'

Lotty dismounted and stood squarely in the straw, her belly heaving, her tail curved to one side while her secretions clung to it in thin transparent loops. Now she was content to wait, holding her position, expecting to feel the weight and the thrust of the bull.

But Hercules took a few moments to recover. He seemed uncertain as to what had happened, undecided as to whether the attack he'd been subjected to was an accepted method of fore play. He took a couple of steps away from Lotty, found he was still in one piece, shook his head, flexed his muscles and rolled one eye at her. He ambled round behind her and licked slowly at her secretions. Then he curled his nose, held his head high so that his mouth was half open and turned his face towards us as though we should appreciate what a terrible smell it was.

'Get on with it, for Chrissake,' I urged him, 'can't you see she's waiting for you?' He seemed to be taking a long time for a young bull. Obviously Lotty's onslaught had thoroughly unnerved him.

But now he was ready. With an excited little grunt he reared up at the high rump in front of him.

Bert was watching intently. 'Higher, yer fool, higher,' he called out. 'Look at 'im, 'ees shovin' it into 'er udder.'

'He can't reach, not nohow,' Pete decided.

Hercules was trying his best. He was thrashing about and even appeared to be rising on tip-toe in an effort to enter. I felt like picking him up by the back legs to help him. If it had been possible

I would have done. But it was obviously useless. Lotty was too tall for him and was standing slightly uphill from him which made it worse.

I muttered it was hopeless. She was much too big a cow for him to start on.

'He'll make it,' Bert said, 'Only wants ter be a bit taller, that's all. Wants an apple box ter stand on, then 'eed reach.'

Hercules had given up and dismounted. He was looking slightly puzzled, as though he was quite sure there should be more to it than that and wondering just where he'd gone wrong. He started to lick Lotty again and she marked time with her hind legs and seemed prepared to await his pleasure.

Bert's suggestion of an apple box made me wonder. If only we could manoeuvre Lotty to some lower ground so that Hercules stood above her, he might just be able to manage her. Now we'd got this far it seemed worth an extra try. I looked around for a suitable place and was surprised to see that other spectators had joined us. Henry, the cat, had appeared and was gazing at us from under the rails outside the yard. He was sitting bolt upright on the bank on the other side of the pond. He was looking pretty smug and I wondered whether he'd been watching Hercules' abortive attempt and laughing to himself. He was obviously very interested because he was even taking no notice of Mrs P. P. She was beyond him, standing on one leg and warming the other one, swearing quietly at him and probably daring him to face her. They were both on a rise in the ground, which then dipped towards the pond. It seemed to be the ideal launching pad for Hercules—if we could get Lotty to stand between him and the pond.

We started to drive her. At first she went quietly, slowly swaying across the yard as though she was still expecting Hercules to mount. But when she realised she was on her own, her head shot up and she turned to face us, bellowing her disapproval. I thought she was going to charge past us and I brandished my stick at her while Pete assured her, in unctuous tones, that we were only trying to help her. But it took a sharp tap on her nose to convince her and screwing up her eyes she turned and charged off out of the yard, with her udder swaying from side to side and firing squirts of milk from all four barrels at the extremity of each swing.

Pete nipped through the rails to head her off. Soon he had her careering into the bottom yard where she came to a heaving halt, trapped in the corner where the spile fence dipped down and entered the pond. Henry had been quick to spot that his position was soon to be overrun. With a dozen long strides and a leap he'd taken refuge on a wall, shaking a front paw and then fiercely preening his whiskers before settling down to glower at the agitated Lotty. Mrs P. P. hadn't been so fortunate. Because of her advancing years she'd been slow to sense the danger. She'd been too occupied with warming her foot and threatening Henry so that when he fled she swelled with victory, quite unaware of Lotty bearing down on her. It was only when the sex-crazy cow was almost on her that she shot into the air with a frantic fluttering, made an undignified belly landing and floundered across the yard with a horrified squawking. To add to her humiliation, a young cockerel, one of her own foster brood, paused in his gleaning, raised his head high, blinked a red eye and took off after her, turning her flight into a love dash. He overtook her, trod her rapidly, walked over her and raised himself to his full height while he flapped his wings and looked pleased with himself.

Bert had captured the dazed Hercules. When Lotty departed he stood looking perplexed, uncertain of the next move expected of him but obviously quite sure of a feeling of frustration. He was quivering slightly and his shining new penis seemed uncertain whether to pop out or disappear. He bellowed with a high pitched moo as Bert led him around to the lower yard.

I had joined Pete and we were keeping Lotty cornered, poised on the edge of the pond in the dip in the ground. We were standing one either side of her. Her ears were flicking wildly to and fro as she listened to Hercules and every time she tried to swing round to charge to him, we brandished our sticks to keep her facing the pond.

'Lead her right up to him,' I called out to Bert. 'Don't let him go 'til he's right behind her.'

Pete was watching apprehensively as the bull approached the ground slightly above us. 'Don't start messing about now, Hercules. Get stuck up before 'er turns on yer,' he advised him.

Bert fumbled with the clip on the bull's ring. Hercules had spotted his chance and was prancing slightly, making urgent little grunts of excitement.

As soon as he was free he threw himself on Lotty, searching and thrusting with lengthening and gleaming enthusiasm. Soon he felt the place and with uncontrolled excitement he heaved upwards. But as he thrust, his back feet shot from under him down the snowy slope and he whipped over in a backward somersault, landing flat on his back with a sickening thud.

For a few moments he lay there, motionless, and I thought, God, he's killed himself. However am I going to explain this to Margaret? His legs were rigid in the air. The only moving thing was his fiery penis, twitching and retreating as though it was trying to hide in shame. His eyes were shut, his mouth half-open and his tongue was lolling out. He'd knocked himself out for the count.

As I walked towards him, wondering what to do, he shook his head and rolled over on to his side. For a few seconds he lay there and his eyes were rolling round as he wondered where the hell he was and what had hit him. Then he reared up, shook his head and got to his feet, looking at us without seeing and with his ears flopping. He staggered off across the yard and Henry looked down at him with great interest – and perhaps a tinge of admiration for somebody who had managed a backward somersault on the job.

Pete and Bert were helpless with laughter so I took the bull's lead from Bert and caught up with Hercules. He was still dazed as I clipped the lead on his ring, led him across to the fence and tied him there to regain his senses.

Lotty had turned round and was wondering what had happened. This time she had every reason to give us her surprised look. And we were wondering what had happened to Lotty.

'D'you think he managed her, or not?' I asked.

'No!' Pete was certain. 'He never got in 'er. Look, 'er ain't arched 'er back.'

Bert straightened his cap and thrust his hands behind his back. 'They don't always arch up.'

'What?' Pete exclaimed, 'with a shove like 'e gave 'er, 'er would've arched up right enough. If 'eed have gorne in. But 'e didn't.'

'How d'you know? I reckon 'e did,' Bert persisted.

'Stands ter reason 'e didn't. If 'eed have gorne in 'eed have torn 'iself when 'e went over backwards like that.' Pete spat to add weight to his argument.

'Well, 'e must've gorne somewhere . . . 'e started orf all right,' Bert added, lamely.

'Up in the bloody air, that's where 'e went.' Pete began to laugh again. 'Up and bloody over and knocked 'iself out on the job.'

Now Bert was laughing again. 'That's what yer calls a flyin' fuck. A champion flyin' fucker, that's what 'e is.' And Bert slapped his leg and doubled up with laughter, obviously relieved that his charge had at least achieved some distinction.

Well over an hour had gone by in our attempts to mate Lotty. It was now after ten o'clock and too late to 'phone for the artificial inseminator to call that day. I'd been told it was still possible to inseminate a cow several hours after she would no longer stand for a bull. Probably it would still be possible to do Lotty the next morning, and if I rang now I'd be sure of a visit then. But I wanted to make quite sure of getting her in calf this time round and it seemed too chancy to wait until the following day and hope she would still conceive to A.I. We were already into January and I wanted to get as many of the cows as possible in calf that month. Then they would all calve down in October and be at maximum milk production when the price rose to its highest over the winter months.

So I decided that Lotty would have to pay a visit to Charlie Dunnell's bull after all. Anyway, it seemed a shame to disappoint her after her hours of frustration with Hercules. While Bert took charge of the bull again, leading him back to his loose box to ruminate over his failure and recover from his shock, Pete and I drove Lotty the mile and a half along the lane, one in front and one behind, to the farm down in the next valley known as Frog's Hole.

It was one of the bigger farms in the neighbourhood and boasted such fine things as a Dutch barn and concrete in the yards. And there was a modern cowshed with an asbestos roof, tubular yokes for tying the cows instead of clumsy chains, and a shiny, hissing, pulsating milking machine. All the niceties I would have liked to lighten the work load at Maywood in place of my antiquated, if picturesque, buildings and my makeshift modernisations. But Charlie Dunnell came from a line of farmers who had lived at Frog's Hole for generations. If there had ever been a mortgage it was long since paid off so that money was available for capital improvements such as a new cowshed, and the like. And his herd of blood red Sussex cattle had been fostered over the years so that now only the best heifers were kept as replacements and there was a surplus of quality to sell profitably each year. As with all farmers, times had been hard for Charlie in the hungry Thirties, but with low overheads, fat land and a simple way of life, he had paid his way through to the outbreak of war. Then he was poised to take full advantage of the agricultural revolution which swept the production of the farms to unheard of heights over the next decades.

Yet in spite of his obvious prosperity the memories of hard times died hard and Charlie Dunnell husbanded his money as carefully as he did his crops and stock. Not for him the luxury of a dog and stick and gun life around his farm, with others to do the hard graft for him. He worked the place himself, with only his daughter, Alice, to help him. With a full range of labour saving machinery he only needed to call in casual labour at the busy times of hay and corn harvest.

With a daughter for his only child, Charlie was the last of the line. Maybe he wished that Alice had been born a boy for that reason. He never said; so nobody knew. Certainly he couldn't have wished for her to be a boy from the point of view of capacity for work. She did as much, and more than many a man.

She appeared from a loose box as we drove the still excited Lotty up the drive into the farmyard. She wore a man's tweed jacket that was through at the elbows and fitted her like a sack, and a pair of dark brown corduroy trousers, flecked with cows' hairs and stuffed into a large pair of wellies. Her head was bare, her brown hair in a shingle cut and there was down on her weathered cheeks and the faint promise of a moustache.

She stood in the middle of the yard awaiting our arrival, at ease with a pitchfork like a sentry with a rifle. 'Waatcher!' she called, 'got a customer for ol' Roger, have yer?' Her voice was low pitched and her laugh that followed rasped like a bronchial wheeze. 'How you, Pete? Ain't seen you since buggered if I know when. Nor ol' Jack neither, come to that. How's ol' Jack? Ain't seen 'im since when he helped last harvest. Helped! Well! Can't really call it helped, can us, eh Pete?' And she laughed again and her thick eyebrows shot up. For a glimpse she looked almost feminine as her eyes lit up. 'Whoa there, gal, whoa!' She held out her pitchfork and Lotty stopped and looked at her enquiringly. 'Find ol' Roger for yer in a minute, that us will. And how you, Dave? How's it down Maywood then? Made a good start, eh? Heard as how there's more churns up the end of your lane than ever ol' Checky had. We hears things, yer know. Ha! Ha! We hears things. Whoa there, gal, whoa there!' She rambled on, not listening for any replies, holding out her arms and pitchfork to keep Lotty cornered.

Lotty needed time to make up her mind about Alice and these new surroundings. It had been a long walk. Now and then she had run, swinging her udder and spraying the hedgerows with milk when she thought there was just a chance of diving in front of Pete. And that had made her hot, and in a lather, and her dung had come loose with all the excitement and her tail had caught it and flicked it all over her body so that Pete said she looked like a speckled shit heap. I must say I was rather ashamed of her appearance and mumbled something to that effect when Alice paused for breath.

'Yes, yes, gets 'emselves into a state 'em do. Right old state what with the walk and all. You should see 'em in summer! My God, you should see 'em when the grass loosens 'em and squirts out of 'em. Can't even see their ol' fannies fer shit sometimes when 'em gets here. Still, ol' Roger don't mind a bit o' shit. One thing about 'im, 'e don't mind that. He still gets on with 'em, shit or no shit.'

I made the mistake of catching Pete's eye. The snigger he was trying so hard to suppress burst out of him and he put his hand to his face and spluttered into it.

'Got a cold then, Pete? Got a cold have yer, boy? Wanna lay orf that courtin' this snowy weather. Ha! Ha! Wanna keep aside the fire o' nights instead of out in the snow. Still, ain't much cop tellin' you boys that, I'll lay. Randy young buggers the lot o' you. Whoa there, gal, steady, steady, whoa there.'

Charlie Dunnell rounded the corner; cord breeches, gaiters, boots and a barrel for a belly, over which was stretched a khaki pullover, with holes showing the white and stripes of his flannel shirt beneath. He was a big man, with heavy jowls, little tufts of black hair on his cheekbones and bushy eyebrows specked with white. The black hair beneath the rim of his cap was turning white and sprouted down low on his bull neck.

'Morning, Mr Dunnell,' I said. For some reason he was a man whom few people addressed by his Christian name.

He nodded his head, taciturn as his daughter was garrulous. He stood looking Lotty up and down with his heavy hands clasped behind his back. Presently he said: 'Is her clean?'

I knew he was referring to her inside and not her dung-spattered outside. 'Oh yes, she's fine.'

'Ain't got any whites?'

I assured him that I'd never seen any discharge.

'Her looks a fair milker,' he conceded, 'four or five gallon there,

I'll lay, when her's fresh calved.' He nodded and ran a huge and calloused hand with a rasp over his chin.

He looked at me for the first time. 'Seven and a kick, right? That's what it'll cost ye, seven and a tanner. If 'e don't get 'er in calf this time, then the next go's free. Can't say fairer than that now, can I?'

I agreed, handed him the money and Lotty gave a bellow of impatience. Or perhaps she was objecting to the price. Perhaps she wanted to see what she was getting for seven shillings and sixpence, to make sure it wasn't another little squirt like Hercules.

Dunnell pocketed the money in his roomy breeches and turned to his daughter. 'Offer 'er to him then, Alice, offer 'er to him, gal,' and with a nod to me he moved off about his business. Alice shouldered her pitchfork and strode off to fetch the bull.

Roger, the bull, had already got wind of Lotty's arrival and was calling a greeting from somewhere in the depths of the buildings. There was a ring of authority in his call, which started deep down and rose to end on a high shout. Lotty found the suspense unbearable. She tossed her head, swished her filthy tail and dived past us with a bellow as she tried to get to the bull herself. She made a hurried circuit of the yard, but the three gates had all been shut so that the best she could do was to stop and bellow over each one in turn just to make sure the bull heard her.

Alice opened a gate and led the bull into the yard. He was a massive, lumbering ton of thick neck, deep wide body on four short and sturdy legs. He was so huge it seemed that walking would be about as much as he could manage and he waddled like a big man with an overpowering gut. When Alice let go of him he stood four square and looked at Lotty with little interest, but his ring flicked up over his broad, wet nose as he caught the smell of her. Lotty needed time to size him up so she went through her usual routine of threatening gestures with her tall horns.

Alice smacked the bull on his fat rump. 'C'mon, Roger, don't hang about. Get on with it.'

He took a couple of dumpy paces forward, raised his head and curled his nose again. Lotty dared him to come any closer. Then she changed her mind, advanced towards him with her head erect and made a lunge to leap on him. Years of practice had taught Roger how to deal with this opening gambit, whether it was the uncontrollable urge of a shy and nimble heifer or the deliberate demand of a sex-crazy cow. Either could prove equally exhausting to deal with unless he nipped these advances in the bud and took control of the situation himself. And with surprising agility and a deft shuffle he was round before Lotty could get a foothold, ramming his huge rump against her head as she landed back on the ground, juxtaposed to steady her and stimulate himself with a languid lick under her tail. He moved with the aplomb of a true professional.

He succeeded in quietening Lotty but was in no mood to hurry. He gave her an occasional lick and raised his head and curled his upper lip as he looked round at us. Which was all too much for Lotty. As usual she signified her anticipation by having a good pee.

Alice became impatient. 'C'mon, Roger, fer Chrissake. You'm like an old bloke fumblin' round 'cos 'ees past it. Dunno what's come over you lately, buggered if I do.' She jabbed him in the ribs with the handle of her pitchfork.

Roger responded with an urgent, high-pitched grunt. He moved round quickly, reared high and plonked his huge weight on Lotty. He positioned himself momentarily and thrust just once and deeply.

Alice was bending down watching closely. She stood up with a jerk as Roger crashed back to the ground.

'Better let 'im have other go,' she decided. 'Silly old sod. Didn't get it right, I'll lay.'

'Looked okay to me,' I said, innocently.

'No, can't be sure, that we can't,' Alice declared. 'Let 'im have another go. Let 'im do 'er again. Too heavy for 'em, that's what 'ees getting. Weighs 'em down. Makes 'em squat. Then 'e don't get it right. Gets the wrong place, silly ol' sod. Let 'im have another go, I say. Make sure of 'er like.'

And the next time there was no doubt in anyone's mind, least of all Lotty's. She arched her back, closed her eyes, and when we drove her home she was walking on cloud nine.

12

'I SUPPOSE YOU wouldn't like to lend me some of your Land Army gear?' I asked Jean, one evening a few days later.

'I beg your pardon?' She looked at me quizzically. 'Are you sure you're feeling all right?'

'Perfectly. It's just for my interpretation of one of Mum's quaint ideas, that's all. She's persuaded me it's my duty to take part in the annual village concert on Saturday week.'

'*You*? Oh no! That I must see.' Jean's peal of laughter split the quiet night. 'But what's my Land Army gear got to do with it?'

'Well, you see, I've got to do a comic song. It's a time filler really, one of those front of the curtain acts while they bump about behind changing the scenery. It seems they're stuck for somebody to cover up for them while they get ready for a Women's Institute sketch. It's a spot none of the usual village soloists will touch with a barge-pole. Apart from the noise going on behind, you're quite likely to get rammed up the rear for your trouble. But, of course, dear old Mum has to pipe up and say she's sure I wouldn't mind doing something. Trouble is she brought us up to perform at village concerts from an early age.'

'And the clothes?'

'Well now, *I* was thinking of doing a Farmer Giles act, you know, a smock and a beard and a bit of straw in your mouth and a few urr's and arr's. But Mum reckoned that was too corny and why didn't I dress up as a land girl?'

'And do what?' Jean was looking at me guardedly.

'Sing a song about life in the Land Army. She's already started

writing the words to go to the tune of "John Brown's Body". She's
going to accompany me on the piano and she spent all last evening
bashing out the tune to her terrible words. All about milking lovely
cows and feeding them with hay. So I thought up a first verse
instead about fending off a randy cowman with a milking stool.
But she didn't think that was quite proper and refused to play
when I started to sing it. Never mind, I expect we'll reach a compromise in the end. So, what about the clothes?'

'If you think they'll fit.'

'Oh I expect we can make them. If the dungarees are a bit short I
can stuff them into wellies, the hat with its badge will be okay and
that only leaves the green jumper. Of course, I could never hope to
fill that like you do, but with a bit of padding . . .'

And that led to a kiss, which seemed to end that topic of conversation for the evening.

Preparations went ahead. Mother and I concocted the song
between us. We thought it was tolerably amusing and, with a few
props and actions, would keep the audience quiet during the stage
setting. I wasn't altogether happy about standing up and making a
fool of myself, but Mother's enthusiasm was as infectious as ever
so that by the time of the dress rehearsal on the Friday I was quite
keen.

Especially after Jean had been to work on my face and figure.
She stood back to admire her handiwork. 'There, you really do
look gorgeous.'

'Oh yes,' Mother agreed, *quite* like a girl.'

'I hope it's good enough to fool my friends,' I said. I had been
careful to keep very quiet about it and had made Mother promise
not to let on to Pete and Bert.

'But I expect everyone will recognise you,' Mother said, gaily.
'Besides, that's half the fun of village concerts, when everybody
knows who's who.'

And the song, which I sang wandering on with a bucket and
milking stool and sitting down with the appropriate actions, raised
a few titters from those watching at the dress rehearsal. So I felt
slightly more confident as I drove down to the village hall with
Mother and Jean on the Saturday night.

The hall was filling rapidly as we joined the people thronging the
doorway. We cast our shillings into the saucer on the card table
just inside — audience and performers were expected to contribute
alike, under the mournful eye of Mr Boorland, the builder — and

we greeted the Vicar. He was a broad man, with steel grey hair, horn-rimmed glasses and moist lips, which he dabbed at regularly with a folded handkerchief because, poor man, his saliva tended to overflow with much talking. He really needed a bib to cope with a long sermon.

'Ah, so glad, so glad,' he greeted us. 'All ready to perform, I hope.' He was chief usher and compere combined.

As he moved away to greet other arrivals, I noticed a tall contraption against the back wall of the hall. One table was perched upon another and two chairs on top of that, and the whole lot was festooned with electric wires, sprouting from what looked like three old fashioned, chromium plated car headlights. And poised on the very top was Harry Ongley, the village handyman, pencil behind his ear, range of screwdrivers in his top pocket, sweating profusely as he tinkered with his invention.

He certainly hadn't been there yesterday at the dress rehearsal. And I wondered at this innovation as I turned to follow Mother and Jean towards the stage and the door beside it leading to the cramped, communal dressing room in the wings.

Already all the village and his family seemed to be there as I pushed my way along the narrow aisle between them. I spotted the great white dome of Ernie Carter's capless head, his brother Fred, sitting firmly under his trilby, their wives and all their children and they took up a whole row between them. Boney Jackson, the blacksmith, tall, upright and gaunt, best suited and shaved for the occasion, but already showing a five o'clock shadow. Beside him his stern wife, Chapel, looking smug because he was with her and this was one Saturday night when she wouldn't be forced to lock him out, banishing him to yet another night in the smithy for rolling home drunk and disorderly. And there was Percy Follen, wispy whiskers curling up for air from under his best collar, and his comfortable wife with her apple cheeks and halo hat, and their fat married daughter, up from Hythe with her two brats for the weekend to enjoy the concert, mainly because Margaret Featherstone-Kelsey was the organiser and star of the show. And Bill Checksfield was winking a cornflower-blue eye at me, proud of the white chrysanthemum in his buttonhole, blowing sparks from the yellow hole in his moustache while his tall wife nodded primly. There was Charlie Dunnell, square and severe in the front row, and with him was his tiny wife and their daughter, Alice, who was wearing a dress and actually looked like a woman. Even old Jack was there, still in his cap and raincoat and sucking his pipe, but Mildred was bright and beaming beside him, with a red ribbon clasping her jet black hair.

And they were all staring up at the red curtains, watching them as they bulged and heaved, as if they were waiting to open a great, mysterious parcel.

As I turned to shut the door behind me, I took a last look across the hall. And the village youths had decided that now was the time to make an entrance. They were thronging the back, grouping themselves beneath Harry Ongley's contraption while he warned them loudly from above to stand clear. As I shut the door I saw Pete's scrubbed and shining face, and a moment later I caught the smirk from Bert as our eyes met and I disappeared. Oh well, they were bound to know sooner or later.

Mother was already swarming with the cast from the W.I. as they buzzed around jars of make-up. She only had a one-line part but that was qualification enough to join the fun. And I found Jean and grabbed her by the hand, leading her through the throng to a comparatively quiet corner. She had to fix my wig, tart up my face and secure her hat at the right angle on my head. I already had the rest of the gear on under my overcoat, so all I had to do was equip myself with a pair of presentable tits.

'It's like a madhouse in here!' She was shaking with laughter as she set about my face.

'Village concerts are always like this at the start.' I was trying to keep a straight face for her to work on. 'It soon starts to thin out as people finish their acts and peel off into the audience to face the critics.'

As well as the W.I., half the primary school seemed to be present, darting around exclaiming at the rouge and lipstick on each others' faces, over excited at the songs and recitations they were to perform. And the church choir were all around, clasping sheets of music, growling into their waistcoats as they tested their voices, spilling out across the stage in trial groupings. In the centre of all was Margaret, the last act, organiser and star of the show, resplendent in long blue satin and a single string of pearls, which leapt and swung from the shelf of her bosom. She was busy organising as usual, sweeping around, searching out the various turns and making sure they all knew the order of appearance.

She spotted us in the corner, waved and waded over. 'Ah, there you are! Wondered where you were. Afraid you might have funked it at the last minute, what? I say, Jean, he does look ducky, doesn't he?' She patted my cheek. 'You'd better be careful of the boys at the back, you know. I'm quite sure they'll all fall for you.' She threw back her head and laughed loudly, setting her pearls swinging. 'Don't forget now. You're after the choir. As soon as they draw the curtains to set the stage for the sketch.'

'Don't remind me,' I groaned to Jean, as Margaret bustled off.

'You'll be okay,' she whispered and kissed me lightly on the cheek. 'I'll be off now. Mustn't miss the show. See you later and I'll keep you a seat. Promise I won't laugh.'

'God, I hope somebody does. I'd hate to do it in deathly silence.'

But she had gone and didn't hear. Already the lights were out in the hall and the vicar was on his feet making the opening announcements. And Harry's spotlights had sprung to life from their pinnacle at the back. Only they were more like searchlights as they jerked about the stage, looking for the vicar. They found him and held him. He was dabbing at his mouth with his handkerchief and now shading his eyes with his programme.

So the concert got going with the usual run of recitals and songs from the children, carefully rehearsed over the weeks and politely received by the audience.

Until a couple of seven-year-olds stood shyly in the centre of the stage. A boy and a girl, clasping hands tightly and blinking into Harry's searchlights, dressed as an old-fashioned Darby and Joan and with their hair powdered white. The audience hushed. The cast crowded the wings to listen. Even the youths at the back went quiet. And in the silence they sang an old, old love song, their voices quavering at first, but gathering strength with each verse until the clear notes and the gentle sight even had grown men dabbing their eyes. And when they finished the audience went wild. They stamped their feet and they clapped and they cheered, while the children bowed as they had been taught and then looked anxiously about them because they didn't know what to do next.

In the end they had to give three encores and I was thankful I didn't have to follow them.

But they warmed up to the show so that songs and dances and even tedious monologues were received with enthusiasm. And almost before I realised it the choir were on stage, bursting their way through 'Devon, Glorious Devon', while Harry worked feverishly, trying to bathe the whole lot in light.

Then the curtains were being drawn and they were coming off stage, clearing their throats and grumbling.

'Bloody searchlights. Fair made I sweat.'

'Got stars in me eyes, I did. Couldn't see old Charlie with his baton, not nohow.'

So that was why it had all sounded a bit ragged. But the applause had been hearty and now Margaret was bearing down on me, gathering up my bucket and milking stool and thrusting them into my arms.

'Off you go now, you're on. Your mother's already at the piano. Good luck!'

Jovially Mother started the introduction from behind the curtains. So I began my calvary walk from the edge of the stage along the narrow path in front of the curtain. Bucket in one hand and milking stool under the other arm, I was halfway through the first verse by the time Harry found me in his searchlights. Chuckles started from the black depths beyond, whistles shrilled from the very back and the perilous path before me disappeared in a galaxy of stars. How I wished he'd turn the cursed things out.

Somehow I reached the centre of the stage, avoiding the sudden bumps and bulges in the curtain as the scene shifters pranced about behind. I was terrified of making a false step and falling off the stage. At the end of the first verse I bent down and set the bucket carefully beside the curtain under the imaginary cow. I stood up. As I held out the stool and drew breath for the second verse, I heard:

'Who's takin' yer home tonight, darlin'?'

I knew it. I knew it. There was no mistaking Pete's voice. It was all I could do to refrain from shouting back a suitable rejoinder.

Fortunately the laughter lasted most of the way through the second verse and now was the time that the song demanded I sat on the stool beside the bucket. With a slow flourish I waved the stool high in front of me and brought it down between my legs to sit on it. And at that very moment there was a jolt from behind the curtain, which caught the bucket fair and square and sent it clattering into the audience.

There was no point in singing the next verse, although Mother was pressing on regardless from behind the curtains. The audience were in hysterics, convinced that it was all part of the act. So I mimed a girl nervously dealing with a fractious cow. And when I bent down to retrieve the bucket being offered to me by a, for once smiling, Charlie Dunnell, I heard Ernie Carter's voice booming above the laughter.

'You got a kicker there, right enough Dave. Old girl.'

And another voice offered: 'When yer coming 'ter milk fer I? I ain't got no kickers as bad as that!'

And another, a younger voice: 'Why don't yer come up my place fer a romp in the hay instead?'

Well at least they were enjoying themselves as the laughter and remarks went on. And it was halfway through the last verse before I caught Mother up and stood up with the bucket and stool. Then I nipped to safety through the curtains. But the clapping and cheering continued and I had to go back and sing the last verse again.

The dressing room was almost empty now. The W.I. were moving smoothly into action as I rubbed the make-up from my face and removed my bosoms. I combed my hair, put on my overcoat and slipped out under cover of darkness to find Jean in the audience.

'Not much like the rehearsal,' she whispered, 'much funnier.'

'That's the last time I get involved in capers like that,' I vowed. But I was feeling quite pleased with myself.

'Oh no, I always knew you were a clown.' She laughed and squeezed my hand.

Now there was only Margaret's performance left to come. There was a hushing and an expectant shuffling as Harry brought all three beams to bear on her, shimmering centre stage. She was basking in the limelight, smiling and sparkling and suddenly I realised that she was responsible for hiring Harry. This was what it was all about.

It was quite obvious that Margaret had established a well-loved repertoire of songs at village concerts over the years. In no time she had us applauding, joining in choruses, following her every movement as she swept about the stage, hands clasped, arms suddenly thrown wide, pearls flying. And before long the audience were calling the tunes as they remembered old favourites and Margaret gleefully obliged.

But the end had to come sometime. She held up her arms for silence: 'And now, to finish, your favourite and mine, Cherry Ripe.'

The pianist suggested the key and soon Margaret was leaning forward, singing to us confidentially about the ripe cherries and the full and fair ones who came to buy. And I hoped Ernie Carter was paying attention.

And soon there is a couplet in the song which goes:

'If so be you ask me where,
They do grow, I answer THERE.'

This was the crescendo Margaret had been leading up to, and on the word THERE, she flung her arm towards the wings, setting her pearls leaping. And Harry had been prepared for this gesture. He swerved all three searchlights across with gusto to look for the cherries. Which was all too much for his contraption. The top chair toppled. Harry made a grab for it. The beams of light played drunkenly across the ceiling and went out in a horrible crash.

In the stunned silence that followed, Margaret was still singing delicately in the darkness:

'Where the sunbeams sweetly smile,
There's the land of Cherry Isle.'

Somebody found the switch for the main lights. When they came on everybody started to laugh and clap. And Margaret was still singing so we all joined in with her to finish the song.

13

POPSI WAS THE only cow left to calve that winter. She was a Canadian Holstein, nearly all white but with a black patch on her forehead and curling white eyelashes over pink-rimmed eyes, which made her look pretty and rather delicate. The calf she was carrying was by artificial insemination, and great play had been made of this fact by the auctioneer when I bought her, as he tried to raise the bidding by a few extra pounds. So we had been looking forward to this birth with more than usual interest.

She was tied in the cowshed along with the other cows as she waited her time. And when, one morning, I noticed that she was springing, we moved her out to the loose box to change places with Hercules. Which delighted the little bull, particularly as he was feeling very pleased with himself and wanted to show off. The day before he'd broken his virginity with a rapid and very accomplished coupling with the petite Bambi. And he had spent the next hour boasting about it over the door of the loose box. Now he could bore the cows with his prowess in person.

Popsi walked to the loose box with the awkward gait of a cow close to calving. The ligaments of the pelvis had slackened and caused her to walk straddle-legged. I knew she couldn't be long. Cows seldom lasted longer than a day before calving after reaching this stage. So every time I passed near the loose box during the course of the day's work, I took an anxious peep over the door to see how she was progressing. And every time I was greeted with a placid stare, with maybe a momentary pause in chewing her cud while she wondered at my concern.

By the time the boys were ready to go home after the evening milking, Popsi had still not calved. But when I went to give her a last armful of hay and I walked behind her, I noticed the shining side of her water bag as it started to protrude from her vulva. Now she wouldn't be long and I went in to tea confident that I should have another calf before bedtime.

But three hours later she had made no more progress and it was obvious she wasn't going to manage on her own. When I went into the loose box and hung up the hurricane lamp, she rolled her eyes at me and heaved to move the calf. Her belly bulged up, her tail stood out straight behind her and I saw one soft hoof of the calf stab out. Then it slid back into the vulva as Popsi relaxed and only the little tip protruded.

Assuring her that I'd be back to give her a hand very soon, I left her in the dark again while I went to fetch a bucket of hot water, disinfectant, soap and towel. And I wanted a length of slim rope as well.

Mother watched me with concern as I filled the bucket at the sink. 'Are you sure you can manage on your own? Don't you think you ought to call the vet?'

'I can manage. I've calved a cow before, you know. I expect she just wants a helping pull, that's all.' I tried to sound more confident than I felt. 'But I do wish they didn't always choose night-time to give birth.'

'Yes, tiresome old things.' She came and stood beside me at the sink. 'Would you like me to come and help you? I don't suppose I'd be much use, but I could always hold something. Or just give you moral support.'

'No, honestly, I shall be okay. You don't want to come out in the cold. If I do get stuck I can always get the boys down to give me a pull.'

She stood at the door and watched me as I disappeared across the yard. 'Take care, now,' she called after my dancing shadow.

When I walked back into the loose box, Popsi watched me with interest as I took off my jacket and rolled my sleeves high above my elbows. I thought about taking off my shirt altogether but decided the night was too cold for just a vest. It didn't matter if my shirt got dirty. Popsi seemed to forget that she was meant to be calving as she looked on while I lathered the soap on my arm. But when it was her turn and I started to wash off and soap her vulva, she began to heave again and the almost transparent hoof of the calf pushed out towards me.

I rubbed some more soap on my arm. I put my hand on the hoof of the calf and traced the slimy leg back inside Popsi to find the other foot. As I worked my arm into her so she thrust back against me as she tried to push the calf out. Inside her it was like a hot, wet, heaving cavern, filled from floor to ceiling with the seemingly massive bulk of the calf. I found the chest and ran my hand round trying to locate the other foot. And the head seemed to be nowhere within reach. Evidently the calf was lying with one foot forward and the other one tucked back with the head. I struggled to push farther into the cow, finding the neck of the calf and reaching desperately to recognise some part of the head in the hot darkness. I was almost up to my armpit and it seemed hopeless as the roof of the cavern pressed my searching hand down against the slippery calf.

'Whoa, don't push, don't push!' I implored her. 'You'll wear us both but if you keep pushing like that. I've got to get it straight first and how the hell can I if you keep pushing like mad?'

At the sound of my voice, Popsi shuffled round slightly and lowed quietly. I withdrew my arm and stripped off my shirt so that I could reach inside her to the very limit of my arm. I wondered whether to go and fetch Pete. But no, he couldn't help me straighten the calf. Only one person at a time could do that and my reach was longer than his anyway. Yet I knew I could do with some of the moral support Mother had offered. It would help to combat the sense of desperation I was beginning to feel. Popsi was doing all she knew to relieve herself of the pain and discomfort of the calf and I was doing all I could to help her. But it seemed a physical impossibility and we were fighting against each other, which made it worse.

My head was resting on her rump and her hairs were rough against my cheek as I thrust and stretched in one determined effort to locate the head. Then I touched an ear and the flabby feeling sent a surge of encouragement through me. I gripped it and pulled it round slightly so that I was able to walk my fingers over an eye and down the nose until, with a final lunge, I slid the palm of my hand over the nose and fastened my fingers into the jaw. Slowly I brought the head round until it was in line with the one protruding foot and ready for the nose dive into the straw-covered world.

Popsi heaved and I felt a thrill of excitement as the head of the calf moved forwards slightly under my arm. Now I could reach round and feel the shoulder of the trailing foot and, with careful manipulation I brought the leg forward, bending it and pulling it until I had a hold on the soft hoof and could ease it forward to join the other one, now hanging outside the vulva.

All the time I'd been expecting Popsi to go down. But she remained standing and I was glad I'd been able to straighten the calf while she was still fresh and before the uterus contracted on me. And now she was ready to calve on her own. But the calf was a big one and it seemed impossible that it could slide out as Popsi heaved. Each time she tried the feet barely moved forward on their downward journey.

I couldn't get a grip on the slippery feet, so I fastened the ends of the rope I'd brought around each leg, just above the hoof. Then I took the strain, leaning backwards and pulling downwards, waiting to heave on the rope when Popsi pushed. She was getting anxious and she shuffled her back legs and flicked her tail so that it whipped wet and cold on my bare shoulders and neck. I wished I had someone with me to hold it still.

She became quiet for a moment. As the urge gripped her again she moaned and her belly lifted and tightened as she strained. I pulled with all my strength, leaning back so that my whole weight was on the ropes. But nothing more than another inch or two of legs appeared and it seemed as though the head could never find room to be born.

'Come on, gal,' I urged her, 'Now's the time to push. You've got to be worse before you're better, so get it over with. Come on now, one great big push from you and and a pull from me.'

And time after time she tried to shift the calf while I pulled until the ropes bit into my knuckles. It was hopeless. The calf was huge and I knew I'd have to get help.

Just then I heard a movement outside. I looked round and Mother was standing in the doorway, her coat clasped round her and wearing a woolly beret, obviously jammed on as an afterthought and slipping at a saucy angle. 'Are you all right? Can I help? Ooh, aren't you cold without your shirt on?'

I smiled with the relief I felt at seeing her. But I said: 'You shouldn't have come out here on your own. You could've tripped over something in the dark.'

'Rubbish! I'm not *that* doddery. Besides, I've got my torch.' She came inside, switching it on and flashing it at me. Then her face clouded: 'Poor old Popsi. Can't you manage to have your baby?'

Popsi shuffled round to stare at her, crossly swishing her tail over the calf's feet.

'It's too big,' I sighed. '*I* can't manage her, not on my own. *Why* do I have to be blessed with such awkward creatures?'

'Oh, come along now! Sometimes births take ages. I'm quite sure Popsi's doing her best.'

'So am I, but we don't seem to be getting anywhere. I've never felt such a big calf.'

'Don't you think you ought to send for the vet?'

'No, it's coming the right way. All it needs is brute force to get it out. No point in wasting money on getting the vet just to help pull.'

'Would you like me to help you pull?' she asked. But there wasn't the usual confidence in her voice.

'No, gracious no,' I reached for my shirt and started to pull it on. 'Tell you what, though. Can you stay here with her while I go and get Pete?'

'Of course I can.' As I was putting on my jacket, she said: 'You won't be long, will you? I don't know what to do if anything happens.'

I laughed. 'It won't. Practise one of your Talks on her. She'd like that. It'd keep her mind off her troubles.'

'Go on with you,' she said. As I went out of the door she turned to Popsi and I heard her say: 'Never mind, old lady, I'm *sure* you'll soon feel better.'

I rode off on my bike to fetch Pete. And when I reached the cottage and explained about Popsi, old Jack insisted on coming as well. 'There be a few wrinkles I know 'bout calvin' a cow,' he said, with some importance, as he put his pipe into his slack mouth and reached for his coat and cap. 'But of course, mind yer, I ain't had no 'sperience o' they artful semination ones. I expect that calf be dead by now,' he added, mournfully.

Pete and I left him to come on his own while we rode. Mother was warming her hands over the hurricane lamp when we joined her in the loose box. 'She's still the same,' she greeted us.

'Evenin' Missus.' Pete scratched at his beret awkwardly.

'Hello, Pete. What a pity to drag you away from the fire.'

'Can't be helped. I don't mind.' He laughed and kicked at the straw.

Popsi peered round at us, winding a twist of hay into her

mouth. Mother said: 'She seems to have forgotten about her calf. She's been much more interested in the hay.'

'We'll soon get her mind back on the job in hand,' I said, pulling off my coat again.

The rope was still dangling in a loop from the calf's legs and now I cut it in half. We tied the ends to pieces of wood to make pulling easier. Pete and I stood shoulder to shoulder, each of us taking the strain on a rope.

Popsi heaved. 'Pull now,' I yelled. 'Downwards, pull!'

But only the legs of the calf stretched out as we pulled. It was as though the pelvis was gripping the calf like a vice, refusing to open enough to let it slide through.

'It's just got to come,' I said, taking a fresh grip on the handle of the rope. 'The calf's lying right. It's big, that's all. But it's just got to come.' I tried to sound more confident than I felt.

'What about its feet?' Mother wanted to know. 'Are you quite sure it's all right to pull on its feet like that? I'm sure you must be hurting it.'

'Nonsense. Anyway, we've got to pull like this because there's no other way.'

Jack shuffled into the loose box, hands behind his back and lifting his coat tails, a drop of saliva suspended from the bowl of his pipe. 'Won't 'er come?' he asked.

'Don't bloody look like it, do it?' Pete countered.

The old man nodded and grunted at Mother and walked towards the cow. His coat tails fell away as he brought his hands up to place them on her rump. His fingers were thin and grey with nails curved like claws and black with dirt. He pulled up his sleeves to the elbows, gripped Popsi's tail with one hand and prepared to work the other hand inside her.

'Hey!' I called, 'hold on a minute. There's a bucket of water and disinfectant over there—and some soap. Better use that first. Anyway, you needn't bother, the calf's coming the right way. There's no need to feel.'

He looked up at me with bewilderment from under his large cap. His pipe gurgled as he drew on it and he took it from his mouth and shook it. 'Don't want soap and water fer to clean yer hands. Them juices in the cow'll clean 'em quick enough. Nothin' like the innards of a cow calving, or sheep lambing come to that, ter clean your hands. They juices be powerful strong. Kill any dirt, 'em will, stronger than all yer disinfectants.' He poked his forefinger into the bowl of his pipe and raked away at the ashes before shaking them out on the straw.

Popsi was heaving half-heartedly and I motioned to Pete to take the strain on the rope again. But Jack waved his pipe at us. 'Let 'er bide a while,' he advised, 'p'raps 'er'll loosen up if yer let 'er bide.' He struck a match and the soggy remnants of tobacco crackled as he drew on them. The strong smoke curled around the rim of his cap and he slotted the box of matches back into his waistcoat pocket.

'Ain't yer never cobbed a finger in a cow or a sheep?' he asked.

I'd no idea what he meant and was really too anxious to get on and help Popsi to care about his question. I wished he hadn't come and I turned to look at Pete as though it was up to him to do something about his father. But he just shrugged and shook his head.

'You know,' Jack went on, 'when you've got a festerin' finger or a dirty cut. Fair cleans 'em out it do if you puts 'em in a calving cow or a lambing ewe. Powerful them juices be 'cos they'm protectin' the calf, ain't 'em?' He gurgled at his pipe again and shook his head slowly. 'No, never used no disinfectant, nor soap, nor water to calve a cow, that I ain't.'

Pete sensed I was becoming exasperated. 'Give us a hand here, Jack, for Chrissake. Catch 'old them legs while we has the ropes. Us needs a bloody good pull, not a lot o' natterin'.'

Meekly the old man did as he was told. He stood in front of us, his hands gripping the calf's legs and his pipe gurgling and stinking as the spittle doused the embers. Popsi heaved and we pulled while Jack muttered about the evils of 'artful semination' and how he'd always said no good would come of interfering with nature in that way. And for a time it seemed as though he was right. The huge calf was jammed tight as it tried to slide through the pelvis.

We eased up and waited for a minute or so. I felt inside Popsi again just to make sure. There was the nose, tucked well between the top of the legs, and the crown of the head rose up in a hard, hot mass beyond the pelvis. Surely there was room for it to come through. There must be room! 'Come on, Popsi, let's have one more real try.' I slapped her hard on the rump.

Now she moaned and heaved and we all pulled and in a moment the white nose of the calf appeared with its tongue peeping out of its mouth.

'Her's comin',' Jack grunted, 'steady now, let 'un come steady. Don't want ter tear the cow.'

We waited, taking the strain on the calf while Popsi made another effort and the head and shoulders of the calf came away. We took the weight in our arms but it hung there, trapped by its hips in the pelvis, a wet, white bundle with a patch of black on its back disappearing into the vulva. I wiped the mucus from its nostrils and it shook its head, opening its eyes and blinking its long, curling lashes. Popsi sighed and sank to her knees and then her belly, stretching her hind leg so that her full udder stuck up like an inflated balloon.

We eased the calf to the floor and now we had to kneel to work at releasing it. We were getting little or no help from Popsi. She had made her huge effort, the final push that caused the moan of pain as the head and shoulders squeezed through the pelvis. The rest of the calf should have come away in a rush after that, a wet floundering heap in the straw waiting for her to turn to and lick. But it hadn't happened that way. The pain was still there. The yawning pelvis was aching as it gripped the hips of the calf while the uterus contracted to expel the last of its burden. So Popsi had lain down. She was exhausted with her efforts, dismayed that nothing had come of them except the gaping pain which no amount of heaving could shift.

'Oh dear, poor, poor Popsi,' Mother said, with a sigh. 'You've been trying *so* hard. I *wish* I could help you.' She was holding the lamp above us and now she looked at me. 'Why is it stuck? Are you sure it won't come?'

'Big hips,' I sighed. 'I've heard this happens with A.I. calves sometimes. They use such colossal bulls.'

Even Jack sensed the distress Popsi was suffering. He shed his long coat and joined us on the floor, clasping the calf round its chest. 'Twist it,' he said, 'twist the bugger so's its hips come level.'

We rolled the calf as best we could, trying to rotate the part gripped by the taut vulva. But all we seemed able to do was to move the head and shoulders so that the body corkscrewed while the hips held fast. Try as we might there seemed no way of moving the calf however we manipulated it and pulled.

Jack sat back on his heels and pushed his cap to the back of his head. 'Buggered if it'll shift. Old Dunnell told I 'e had one like this once. Said 'e had ter use a block an' tackle ter shift 'un. Fixed it up to a post in the yard. Pulled on the calf an' dragged the cow clean across the floor, 'till 'er jammed in the doorway and the calf came away. Calf were dead,' he sniffed.

'You're bloody cheerful, I must say,' I told him. 'We don't want a block and tackle. We'll pull this away between us in a minute, once she gets her strength back and starts to try again. Let her have a rest and then we'll see. If the head and shoulders have come, the rest *must* come directly. Must do.'

Pete was looking as worried as I felt. He lifted the calf's head on to his knees. 'He's still alive. Bloody great thing, ain't he? Must be a bull calf by the size of 'is head.'

'Sure he's a bull calf,' I sighed. 'All this bloody trouble and he'll fetch thirty bob at the market next Tuesday because nobody wants him except for veal. Couldn't have been a ruddy heifer, could it?'

We knelt in silence round the half-born calf. Popsi had stretched right out and now her head had gone flat on the floor. The one eye visible was open wide and rolling and the heavy breath from her nostrils was quivering the straw. Her belly rose and fell rapidly and two teats from her distended udder stuck up like stubby fingers.

Mother held the lamp higher and peered about. 'Oh dear, I wish there was something we could do. Don't you think you ought really to call the vet?'

'No, I don't,' I said, loudly. 'It'd be an hour at least before he got here. Anyway, we'll soon have the calf out.' I tried to sound confident. It was the only way.

She thought for a moment. 'D'you think it would be any good if I helped to pull? I don't mind helping. Every little helps.' She gave a small laugh.

'You're helping fine with the lamp,' I smiled up at her. 'We wouldn't be able to see a thing otherwise.'

Jack's pipe was still in his mouth and now he took it out and sent a squirt of nicotine-laced saliva past Popsi's back and said: 'Can't leave 'er too long like this, us can't. Give up, 'er will, if 'er lays back like that too long. Always gives up if their heads go down, that they do.'

'Right!' I said, 'let's have another go then. All got a good grip? Take the strain and pull like hell when she heaves.'

Pete was behind me pulling on the ropes, Jack had the calf by its neck and I was sitting on the ground with my arms round its chest, my knees up and my feet pressing into Popsi's rump. 'Hey up! Popsi! Come on now! One big try!'

She responded to my shouts with a great heave and a moan. Her head came up, her belly filled and we grunted and tugged on the wet calf. Suddenly it moved and with a slosh its hips and hind legs came away, sliding out on to the straw. Its slimy tail slapped feebly in the sudden freedom.

'Good old Popsi!' Pete was laughing with relief as he untied the ropes from the calf's feet. 'Buggered if I didn't think you'd had it. Good old Popsi, gal!' He lifted the calf by the chest and dragged it round to Popsi's head. 'Here you are, ol' gal. Here 'e be. Take a lick at 'im. I'll lay that'll make you feel better.'

For a while Popsi lay still, her head thrust back on the floor and she took no notice as Pete pushed the calf's head against her nose. But soon she reared up and in a moment she was staggering to her feet. With long, rasping licks her tongue combed the mucus from the calf's coat. As he struggled to sit up and take notice so she bowled him about with her strong and eager tongue. She licked over his head as he shook it, under his chin knocking him backwards, along his back pressing him down, searching under his tail as he reared upwards and sending him sprawling again. It was too good a sight to miss only a few short minutes after what had seemed to be a hopeless situation.

So we just stood and watched. Finally the calf got to his feet, seeming to stand on tip-toe as he tried out his neat, translucent hooves before giving a little skip and thrusting his nose into Popsi's dewlap. She raked him with another lick and he wobbled along beside her belly, finding her bulging udder and bunting at it. Already the milk had started to weep in thin trickles, falling like waving threads of silk into the straw. Soon the calf fastened on a teat and sucked at it noisily while his tail quivered and wriggled with excitement.

Popsi gave a final lick at his tail. Then she straightened her neck, her ears dropped slightly, her eyes half-closed and her expression was one of huge contentment.

Usually we removed the calves at birth because it was the kindest way and upset the cows the least. But Popsi had fought so hard for her calf I just didn't have the heart to take him away from her that night. And by the time we left her, to go across to the kitchen for well-earned cups of cocoa, she was lying comfortably in the straw with her calf dry and warm beside her.

The following morning I was up earlier than usual. I was anxious to see that all was well with Popsi after her ordeal and that the afterbirth was coming away as it should. And I knew that I must take the calf away without further delay. I'd woken up in the night and cursed myself for a soft-hearted fool in not removing him immediately. Now Popsi would take more notice of her loss and could well hang on to her milk in protest. So I armed myself with a bowl of corn to distract her attention while I spirited the calf away.

I opened the door of the loose box and Popsi stared at me as the lamplight shone in on her. I saw in a moment that she had cleansed because she was in the process of eating her placenta. It was a revolting sight on an empty, early morning stomach and it was all I could do to stop retching. Hurriedly I hung up the lamp and clawed the rubbery frond from her jaws, dragging it in a half-chewed skein from deep in her throat and letting it fall back quivering like a jelly on the floor. I called her a primitive quadruped as I buried my fingers into the heavy mass in the straw and lifted it, trailing globules like ripe damsons buried in red seaweed, and dumped it outside the door. Bert could bury it in the midden later and before Skinny had a chance to happen by and have it for breakfast.

Popsi watched me with interest. She had only been clearing up as her nature dictated and perhaps she was disappointed I'd robbed her of her meal. Not all cows bothered to eat their placenta. Maybe it was only when they were nervous, or had suffered a rough calving. But it seemed all wrong when one did start to eat it. Far worse than a pig devouring hers, or a dog, or a cat. They were carnivorous and because their teeth and stomachs were designed for meat it wasn't so bad. But a cow winding in a long ribbon of intestinal garbage, only to regurgitate it later and chew it with her cud, and when it could still be seen imperfectly digested in her dung, that didn't seem right. It had given rise to old wives' tales about the harmful effects it could have. Some said it caused a cow to go prematurely dry. Others that she would go down with milk fever.

Which is just what did happen to the luckless Popsi. We had kept her in the loose box for another twenty-four hours and she had spent the first day bellowing for her calf, and listening to his intermittent answers from across the yard. But this had not affected her milk and when I'd gone to her with bucket and stool that evening, the thick, yellow colostrum had come copiously as I milked out enough to feed the calf.

By the following morning she had ended her loud mourning

for the calf and we cleaned out the loose box, littered it with fresh straw and drove Popsi to the cowshed to change places with Hercules once again. The other cows greeted her with solemn stares, obviously content to have her back among them again in place of the bumptious little bull. He'd been nothing but a fidget, continually cocking his head and rattling his chain, convinced there must be a cow somewhere who was desperate for him, if only he could be free to make a tour of inspection.

Popsi was showing every sign of being a marvellous milker. Her udder was still hard and swollen so that even when milking was finished it felt as though the pliable teats were rooted in a cake-hard casing. Already she was filling a bucket at each sitting without milking her right out, and when she got into her stride I was confidently expecting her to break all records.

I showed her to Jean with pride. She was a regular visitor now. Whenever her journey home from work took her even vaguely in the direction of Maywood, she would make a detour and come for the evening.

'Poor, dear Popsi,' Mother told her as we sat by the fire, *'what* a time we had with her.' She had just finished her own enthralling account of the calving, skirting skillfully around the actual details which were too delicate to mention in general conversation. It was an account which, I knew, would be polished and repeated whenever the opportunity arose. It would probably form the central illustration of a new Talk. Perhaps an Animal Talk. Surely a worthy successor to the famous Flower Talk.

'I think it was jolly good of you to go out there at all, Mrs C.,' Jean said.

'I wouldn't have missed it for anything.' Mother's eyes sparkled. Then she looked into the fire with a small smile. 'I'd have gone anywhere just to see her joy when she licked her calf.'

'And I suppose you've taken it away from her now.' Jean looked at me, accusingly.

'Afraid so,' I said, 'can't be sentimental. Got to make a living from the brutes.'

'I know you have to, darling,' Mother sighed. 'But still, it does seem cruel.'

I stood up quickly and grasped Jean by the hands. 'Tell you what! Come on out and look at Popsi for yourself. See if you really think she's pining for her calf.' I pulled her to her feet.

Jean laughed. 'If you insist. I suppose it's time I was going, anyway.' She bent down and kissed Mother on the cheek. 'Goodnight, Mrs C. Thanks for another super tea. I wish I didn't have to go. But he wants to throw me out.'

'Back into the dragon's lair,' I said, with a snarl.

'How *is* Mrs Wilkes?' Mother asked, brightly.

'Don't ask,' Jean frowned. She took a deep breath. 'Still, I couldn't care less now. I sweep in like Lady Muck and ignore her remarks.' She waved her arm royally in front of her.

'But I'm sure she means well, my dear,' Mother said, as she stood up stiffly to see us off.

We walked into the rich warmth of the cowshed and the placid company of the cows. I lit the hurricane lamp and there were slow, quiet movements as heads turned and eyes rolled.

'Sorry, girls,' Jean said, 'didn't mean to wake you all up. Blame him.' She put her arm round me and squeezed as I led her towards Popsi.

'There she is,' I said, 'right as rain. Forgotten all about her calf and the trouble she had.'

She was lying down and she stood up as I spoke. She stretched slowly, showing off her bulging udder. Then she slowly turned her head and blinked her curling, white eyelashes at us.

I stood the lamp down and walked up to her. 'Look at the milk she's got,' I said, running my hand over the hot folds of her udder, 'it'll be fit to go in the churn tomorrow.'

I stood back and put my arm around Jean again. 'She's given gallons of colostrum already,' I enthused, 'Skinny and Fatso have been beside themselves, wallowing in their short bonanza. They'll miss it when there's no more tomorrow.'

'I expect they will,' she said, absently, and looking up at me.

'And old Henry,' I went on, 'he's been drinking it 'til he's sick of it. I dread to think what it's been doing for his hormones.'

She didn't laugh. She didn't even reply at once. Instead she turned to face me and slowly put her arms around my neck. 'Oh, I *do* love you so much,' she whispered.

My heart raced as I held her close to me. 'And I love you too,' was my lame reply.

From the moment I saw Popsi the following morning I was almost certain she'd gone down with milk fever. Her legs were stretched out and she'd gone over on her side. Her head had fallen back and was lolling against the partition between her and Daisy so that the chain was pulling into the folds of her neck. Already her belly had started to blow up because, in this position, she was unable to belch the gases that continuously bubbled in her. There was no time to be lost. It was a job for the vet and I hurried back indoors to 'phone him.

Pete and Bert had arrived by the time I returned. They were standing over Popsi looking startled.

'I know,' I said, before they could speak. 'I've 'phoned for the vet. Give me a hand to see if we can prop her up a bit.'

We pulled her head up and managed to unfasten her chain. We heaved behind her trying to roll her upright. 'You, Bert,' I said as we strained, 'go and get a bag of corn. See if we can wedge it behind her to keep her up.'

It was an almost impossible task. Her legs had gone rigid so that they acted as pivots instead of folding under her to let her roll. We heaved and pushed and grunted and all we succeeded in doing was to prop her head forward with the bag as a pillow so that at least she wasn't flat out. But I knew she wasn't upright enough to belch and I just hoped the vet arrived before she blew up enough to squeeze off her breathing.

'What's up with her?' Pete wanted to know.

'Milk fever. It comes on sudden like this with some heavy milkers.'

''Cos 'er had a bad time calvin' I suppose.' Bert was nodding sagely and had thrust his hands behind his back.

'No, nothing to do with that,' I said, sharply. 'Lack of calcium, that's what it is. Suddenly making all that milk draws the calcium from her blood before she can replace it. And that makes her go down and rigid and she blows up like that because she can't belch. Good job she's on winter grub and not out to grass. At least she won't blow up so fast.' I hoped I was right. 'There's nothing we can do now 'till the vet comes so we'd better get on with milking the others.'

We went about our work in silence, each of us casting anxious glances at the unfortunate Popsi as we passed by.

'D'you reckon you'll have ter knife 'er if 'e don't come soon?' Pete asked, after a long groan of distress from Popsi.

'Dunno,' I replied. 'Never done that. Still, she's not bad enough for that yet. I reckon she's got a long time to go. She'll be as right as rain as soon as the vet gets some calcium into her.'

'Remember when ol' Jack knifed our cow?' Bert squeaked, with a grin. It was the first cheerful note of the morning. 'Remember? Do yer, Pete?' He got up and walked over to look down on Popsi. 'Whoossssh, it went. And stink! Christ, fair knocked I back, it did.' He reeled convincingly.

'When was that?' I asked. If Jack really knew how to puncture a blown cow it was good news. I'd never even seen it done. I knew more or less what to do, but the thought of it scared me.

'Summer 'fore last,' Pete said. 'Ol' Dunnell had some red clover in that field next our place. Come ever so thick it did after he'd hayed it and our ol' cow, Polly, broke into it.'

Bert laughed. 'Jack helped 'er, you mean. Said Dunnell wouldn't do nothing with the second crop o' clover. Said it were a pity to waste it when it could be makin' milk. So 'e pulled some spiles out of the hedge, 'e did.'

'And ol' Polly walked through and blew up like a bloody great balloon in no time,' Pete continued the story. 'Fit ter bust, 'er were and ol' Jack went runnin' round in circles, flappin' his coat and tryin' ter get 'er to walk it orf.' He laughed at the memory.

'And Mum comes out with the carving knife and told 'im ter knife her,' Bert butted in, excitedly. 'Said 'er would die else. And that's what 'e did. The knife bounced orf 'er the first time. Then 'e used two hands and in it went and whoosssh when 'e twisted the handle. Went on and on comin', it did, whistlin' out of 'er and stinkin'.'

'But it cured 'er,' Pete said. 'Went down like a tyre, 'er did. And the knife hole closed up and you couldn't even find it.'

'Lucky,' I remarked. 'There's a proper instrument for that really. Trocar and canular, they call it. Like a dagger with a case round it. When you plunge it in you can draw it out and leave the case in the hole for the gases to escape through.'

'The carvin' knife worked all right with Polly,' Bert said, with a sniff. 'Shall I go and get ol' Jack ter fetch it down.' He peered down at Popsi when she groaned again. 'Her tongue's come out now. Don't arf sound bad.'

Poor old Popsi was having a rough time. Her tongue was lolling out, her eyes had closed and she seemed to be unconscious. Surely the vet would be here before long. He'd said he would come right away and it was only eight miles. He knew better than I how urgent it was with milk fever. Where the hell was he? Five minutes for getting his clothes on, assuming he wasn't already dressed. No, give him ten; fifteen minutes at the most for the drive out. That's twenty-five. It was half an hour since I'd 'phoned, so where was he? Perhaps his car wouldn't start. Perhaps he was still flogging a cold engine while the wretched Popsi gasped her last. Thoughts ticked through my head like heart beats.

'There's a car now,' Pete called.

In a moment it sloshed to a halt outside, the door banged and Paul Hastings loped into the cowshed with a broad grin. He was tall and gangling, with a long lock of hair flopping down over his forehead and a striped college scarf wrapped twice round his neck.

'You're all looking very solemn,' he greeted us. He looked down at Popsi. 'Having a rough time of it, is she?'

'Good job you're here,' I said. 'She's blowing up like mad. I was beginning to think I'd have to stick her.'

He laughed. 'She's got a fair way to go yet, I'd say. Still, we'll soon have her right. Third calver, is she? Heavy milker? When did she calve?' The questions were rhetorical because diagnosis was simple.

'Three days ago. Hell of a time we had with her. Bleeding great calf. A.I. job.'

'Hang on the hips, did it? They usually do from the big Friesian bulls they use. We've had several real brutes just lately.' While he was talking he unwound his scarf and draped it over the end of the partition above Popsi. He began to assemble his apparatus, corking a long, thin tube into a bottle of calcium solution and giving it to me to hold. He rummaged in his box and pulled out a length of thin cord which he draped round his neck. Then he opened a metal box, carefully extracted a stubby intravenous needle from the surgical spirit and put the bulbous end between his lips.

He motioned to me to follow with the bottle while he stepped over Popsi's prostrate legs and squatted down beside her head. He passed the cord under her neck, pushed the end through a loop, pulled it tight and held it with his left hand while he prodded at the vein with his right finger, testing it as it began to swell. When he was satisfied of the exact position, he took the needle from his lips and jabbed it into the bulging vein. Immediately the blood began to flow through the needle. He released the cord and took the bottle from me. He up-ended the bottle and when the solution was trickling freely through the tube, he plugged it over the needle.

He stood upright and held the bottle high. Popsi was flat out, unaware of what was going on. Peter and Bert were watching intently, silent and with their mouths half-open.

Paul caught my eye and winked. 'Abracadabra!' he said. He turned to the boys. 'Now you'll see the magic recovery of a half-dead cow.'

They smiled uncertainly, not sure whether he was fooling. Pete scratched his head through his beret and kept his eyes fixed on the raised bottle. Bert sniffed, waited for a moment or two and then kicked Popsi gently on her rump. When there was no response, he said: 'Her never 'eard yer,' and gave a little cackle. Paul smiled.

The solution drained out of the bottle and silently entered the vein. There was little more than an inch left in the bottle when Popsi's front leg moved. The only eye that was visible opened and the curling white lashes flicked hesitantly. Before the bottle had a chance to empty completely, Paul knelt down and disconnected the tube. He removed the needle and held his finger on the vein for a while.

'Right', he said, standing up, 'now let's see how she feels. Come on, you lads, get behind her and give her a push.' He grasped her front legs and now he could bend them under her and soon we had her sitting upright, propped there by the bag of corn. Her eyes were still unseeing and her head lolled unsteadily. There was a rumble deep down inside her and it quivered up, vibrating her dewlap as it broke up into her throat. It was closely followed by another and yet another satisfying belch. I felt relieved as though I'd done it myself.

'I'll lay that makes you feel better, ol' gal.' Pete was holding one of her ears and looking into her eye. But she was still dazed and unable to take in what was going on.

'I'll give her another bottle,' Paul said, producing a full one from his box and connecting up the tubing. This time he just jabbed the needle into her shoulder and started the solution flowing.

It took longer to empty now that it wasn't going directly into a vein and Paul handed the bottle to Pete. Now Popsi's ears flicked and her eyes rolled as full consciousness returned to her. By the time the solution had drained from the bottle, and Paul had removed the needle and pummelled the spot, she had shuffled her legs more firmly under her and was almost fully alert.

'That should do her,' Paul said as he returned his apparatus to the box. 'She should be up in an hour or so. No ill-effects, we hope.'

I thanked him with great relief. As he fastened his box and prepared to carry it to the car, I remembered Brutus. 'Oh, by the way, to save a special journey, could you castrate a yearling for me? He's only just across the yard.'

'Sure,' he said. He smiled and suddenly made a lunge at Bert, grabbing him by the collar. 'What about this yearling? Want him done as well? He looks as though he's just about ready to start riding.'

'Yea!' Pete called with enthusiasm and a wide grin, 'I'll give yer a hand with the little bugger.'

Bert squealed and fought, lashing out with his arms and kicking until Paul released him, pulling his cap down over his eyes as he did so. Bert shook himself, settled his cap back on his head and pulled his shirt forward. 'Huh! Take a better bloke than you ter hold I down.' And he gave a cackle as he made sure he kept out of everyone's reach.

Brutus eyed us warily as we let ourselves into the bullock lodge. Before we were inside, some instinct told him we were after him for he backed away from us while Elsie and Doris stood still, watching delicately. Paul had produced a pair of nose clips and I held these, ready to spring them into Brutus' nostrils so that we could tie him up. I offered him my empty hand as I advanced towards him and for a moment he was inquisitive and stopped his retreat. With a quick dab I buried my finger and thumb in his nostrils and squeezed tight, preventing him from moving. I fixed the clip in place of my fingers and while the others pushed I led him into the corner and tied the clip up to the hay rack so that his head was stretched up and firmly anchored.

'Nicely done,' Paul said, 'I've had a few rodeos in an open lodge like this, when you don't get 'em first time. Now we'll just tie his legs and you, Pete, grab his tail and push it straight up over his back. Hold it there, mind, and he won't be able to move.'

He soaked a wad of cotton wool in antiseptic, took a scalpel from the surgical spirit and held it in his teeth as he advanced towards the luckless Brutus. The bulging scrotum filled his hand as he swabbed it with antiseptic. He took the scalpel and made a quick incision towards the bottom of the scrotum. Brutus made no sign of feeling anything. With a deft movement Paul worked the shining testicle into his hand and pulled it backwards.

'Ouch!' Pete said as he watched and Paul grinned as he parted the cord and held up the testicle. It lay in the palm of his hand, pinkish white, smooth and marked with blue veins like a piece of polished marble.

He handed it to Bert. 'Hold that. And mind you don't drop it in the straw, whatever you do.' He spoke sternly.

Bert took it carefully, as though it was something precious. Soon Paul had removed the other one and given that to him to hold as well and he stood there, with his hands in supplication before him, gazing down with curiosity at the glistening, warm testicles and their trailing tails.

We released Brutus. He shook his head in disbelief, swished his tail and his scrotum cringed away, wrinkling up from the drop of blood that hung from it. He walked off with no sign of pain and joined Elsie and Doris at the far end of the lodge.

'He'll be fine,' Paul assured me as he shut his box. 'There are no flies to bother him at this time of year and he should heal up in no time. But just keep an eye on him, all the same.'

He turned to Bert, still standing and offering the testicles. Paul raised his hands with fingers outstretched. 'Ah! Delicious!' He smacked his lips. 'Just right for my breakfast!'

Bert had been smiling as Paul approached and now his mouth dropped and his nose wrinkled. 'You ain't going' ter *eat* 'em, be yer?' His tone was of utter disgust.

'Of course I am! There's nothing nicer sliced up and fried with eggs and bacon. Mind you, they want stewing first or they're too tough. But young ones like these, ah, *magnifique!*' He put the tips of his fingers to his mouth and kissed them away. Then he picked up the testicles with exaggerated delicacy from Bert's outstretched hands, placed them together in his left hand and wagged his finger up and down as he instructed the boy. 'Now you must soak them in salt water for an hour and then wash them and pull off all the mucky bits. Then simmer them gently in milk for another hour, take them out and press them between two plates. Slice them up, cover each slice with nicely seasoned flour, egg and breadcrumbs and pop them in to fry with the eggs and bacon. Absolutely delicious, I can assure you.'

Bert's look of disgust didn't change. 'Yer won't get I ter eat no bollocks fer breakfast,' he said as he turned away and spat with conviction into the straw.

And always after that the boys no longer referred to an animal's testicles as balls, or bollocks, or knackers. They always called them 'the vet's breakfast'.

14

THE SNOW WHICH had fallen after Christmas clung to the fields into February. It crowded in dollops beneath the hedgerows, mostly from where it had drifted but piled higher as the chill wind searched among the branches and sent lodged lumps plopping to the ground. Bill Checksfield said that more snow was bound to fall because snow that hung around without melting was waiting for a mate.

The first lambs were due to be born in about a fortnight and Checky was anxious to get the snow over and done with before they arrived. He came cycling out from the village nearly every day. I'd find his bike propped up against the gate in the top field and see him plodding among the ewes, crunching in the hoof-packed snow which was littered with strands of frozen-in hay, peppered with piles of black droppings and stained with yellow patches where hot urine had bitten in, revealing a penny-sized patch of grass like the dark centre of a festering boil. Checky walked among the ewes, searching for signs of swelling udders, strapping his arms vigorously across his chest and then blowing into the black, woollen gloves that stretched in holes over his thick fingers. If I was busy I'd leave him to it and postpone my own visit to the sheep. He'd soon come searching for me if he found anything amiss.

One morning it turned much colder. I could feel it before I got out of bed and when I stretched across and lit the candle, the yellow flame shone on the frost patterns decorating each window pane with its own exclusive work of art. The water was frozen solid in the glass on the table and I leapt out of bed and huddled into my clothes with chattering teeth. Down in the kitchen I awoke the glimmer of life still in the kitchener, raking the bars into a storm of white ashes and blowing on the slithers of morning wood until they flared and the flames licked at the logs and carefully chosen lumps of coal I'd poised above them. And when the kettle boiled, spattering and sending angry drops slithering across the stove, and the tea was made, I stood with my hands cupped round the mug, sipping and peering through the steam and the dripping window out into the cold yard. The patches of snow, which had been slowly slipping into icicles down the roofs of the buildings, were just visible like low clouds. And right outside the window, where the lamplight shone along the yard fence and over the well head, the night mists had been gathered and crystallised into a sparkling coating of jewels.

Outside the air stabbed into my nostrils like needles, freezing each hair rigid as it flowed by, and plunged into my lungs so that I gasped it out again in a puff of vapour. As I walked across to the cowshed the lamplight fell on familiar things, the gate, the fence, the cast iron pig trough propped against the wall. But now they were all silver-dipped and shining. Even the odd stones lying about the yard sparkled in the glancing light like out-crop diamonds. The lane glistened darkly and as soon as I stepped on it my foot slithered. So I walked along the snowy verge, beside the thick hedge where every last twig had its own coating of rime.

Even in the familiar warmth of the cowshed the hot breath showed in the lamplight and when I went into the dairy the tap was frozen. As the drinking bowls were taken off an extension of the same pipe, there was no water to come into them when thirsty cows pressed their noses against the levers to start the flow.

No wonder my arrival had been greeted with stares of unusual interest. I soon found that the bowls had been polished by the rasping tongues searching the cold metal for water. With each cow needing three or four gallons of water for each gallon of milk she produced, I was faced with an unexpected problem. It's only when you haven't got it that you realise how much you take water through a pipe for granted. Not that the lack of water in the dairy mattered so much. It was so cold that the milk needn't go through the cooler and we could get round the washing up by using the kitchen sink.

But you can't scrub round the needs of cows. When they're thirsty they don't let you forget. They stare at you accusingly.

They shove their tongues up their nostrils to remind you again. They low quietly and when you still ignore them they raise their heads and shout. Try telling them you have to find the blowlamp. That it takes time to thaw a pipe and prayers that it won't have burst. Try telling them that anyway there isn't time to do all that now because first you've got to milk them, to get the churns up the dark and slippery lane before the milk lorry comes along because it won't wait if you're late. They won't believe you're really trying and will hold back half their milk in protest.

Fortunately the distant founder of Maywood Farm knew nothing of piped water and had dug a frost-proof well at the back door and a pond near the farmyard. So after breakfast Bert got the job of breaking the ice on the pond and starting the steady task of humping buckets of water to quench the thirst of the protesting cows. As Pete had helped me to install the water bowls in the first place, he reckoned he knew all about plumbing. He unearthed the ancient, brass blowlamp from the depths of the stable, filled it up and proceeded to pump and prick at it until it was roaring with approval. And I left each of them in his separate pursuit of water while I went off to see to the sheep. Afterwards I wished I'd stayed behind with them.

The road was too slippery for Checky to venture out on his bike so I had the sheep to myself. Over my shoulder I carried a sack of ground oats mixed with chopped swedes and as soon as the ewes saw me they came hurrying towards me. They waddled with their bulging bellies all around me, bleating, getting under my feet, the hard little snowballs on the loose ends of wool rattling like ruffled paper. We walked in a haze of steam. At least they didn't feel the cold. They were bleating because they were greedy. The rack was over half-full of sweet hay, but they knew the contents of my sack was sweeter. They barged one another for a place as I trickled the corn and swedes into the trough. It had been mixed and bagged the night before and already there was a faint smell of fermentation and wine. The ewes gobbled it up quickly and earnestly, displaying their red-raddled rumps in still lines so that I was able to walk quietly behind them and make sure there were no signs of lambing yet.

They were all in fine fettle. A raw morning didn't bother them under their thick, greasy coats. I left them licking the last traces of corn from the troughs and decided to tramp the long way home. The tinkling morning was too good to miss. Let the hurry and worry of a frozen farmstead wait for another hour while I wandered across to the far corner and climbed the gate into the unbroken white of Gill Field.

I followed the hedge, sometimes plunging in almost to the tops of my wellies when the snow filled a dingle and levelled it with the rest of the field. The hedge broadened into a shaw and the slender trees were frozen into silence, except for the briefest flurry when an overloaded bough shed its rime in a white whisper to the ground. Now the snow was criss-crossed with the loping lines of rabbit runs and here and there they had scrabbled in search of blades of grass. And they had gnawed mouthfuls from the feet of the trees, yellowy white gashes in the grey bark and browning at the edges like bitten apples. Down through the shaw I listened to my footsteps cracking unseen twigs beneath the snow. Suddenly a brown flutter ended in a robin, perched on two pins buried in frost. He was so close I could see his chest heaving and he looked at me as though I should tell him what had become of the rich pickings of his little kingdom. So I shook out the remnants from the empty corn sack to give him something to be going on with.

The broad pond at the end of the shaw was a sheet of shining darkness. I followed the forlorn footsteps of a moorhen, through the stark rushes and on to the ringing ice. It cracked with a long heave that echoed into the depths and was answered by a series of tinkles round the edge. But it was firm and I walked out over it, looking down into it and seeing the bubbles caught and frozen in clusters when they had risen as the fat tench stirred lazily in their comfortable beds of mud.

At the other side of the pond Banky Meadow drifted down in a gentle slope to the stream that formed the boundary of the farm on that side. It was hidden under a slender ribbon of trees, twisting through the valley. I wondered whether it had been cold enough to freeze the running water and I set off down to see. I had only gone a short distance when a movement in the snow caught my eye. It was way down beside the stream and something was bustling about without going anywhere. I walked faster, hurrying as best I could in the snow. At first I thought it was a rabbit in a trap. But there was more movement than the hopeless jerks of a rabbit trying to free a gripped leg. Anyway nobody would set a trap to catch a rabbit at random in the snow. Then I saw it was a pheasant and it was behaving in the most peculiar manner. It was flopping around, its head lolling from side to side, scurrying in clumsy circles and repeatedly clawing at its head, first with one foot and then the other. It was a cock bird, his russet and speckled plumage all the brighter against the snow, and as I came closer I saw that the shining green feathers on his head were flecked with blood from his vivid wattles.

He took no notice of me. Which was strange because few game-birds have hearing like a pheasant and his bright eye can spot a movement a field away. But this one was too preoccupied with his troubles. He was too far gone to bother about me and as I came up to him he flopped helplessly to the ground as though he was completely fuddled. His head kept weaving from side to side as he fell, first on one side and then the other, and his free leg would scratch vainly at his face and beak. And the beaten snow around him was spattered with blood as though it had been sprinkled with a handful of holly berries.

Here was a welcome and free dinner and I caught him up and put him him out of misery. He flapped his wings for a moment and then he was still. I held him up by the neck to see if I could discover what had been the trouble. All around his beak, eyes and wattles the skin was torn and then I saw a strand of horse hair protruding from his mouth. Puzzled, I pulled at it. But it was firmly anchored down his throat. Obviously he had swallowed it somehow and had driven himself to distraction trying to hoick it out.

With a shrug I bundled him into the sack I was carrying, only half-wondering about the horse hair. Then I noticed that the snow by the stream and under the trees was disturbed. Scuff lines of footprints led here and there and disappeared to and fro along the bank. And I saw other strands of horse hair, black threads looping through the snow. I picked one up and found that the end had been threaded through a dried pea and carefully knotted. So that was it. I didn't have to follow the footprints along the bank of the stream to know they would branch off and follow the hedge along the side of Southey Meadow, and up through the little copse leading to the back of Jack's cottage.

As I made my way back to the farm I wondered how many pheasants he had bagged like this. It was worse than the gin trap Pete and Bert had told me he used. At least that killed them outright when they pecked at the corn on it. It was even worse than a similar trick, used by a poacher of my acquaintance in Wiltshire. He used to select a spot near water, in the shelter of a copse, among dead grass and sleeping roots of primroses and wood anemones, a place where he knew a cock pheasant and his harem liked to feed. First he fed them late at night with wheat and a few raisins. And in the morning, when the day was only half-awake, the pheasants flopped down from their perches on the low branches and gobbled up the food with their voracious appetites. So on the second, and again on the third day. But on the next night he buried a fish hook into each raisin and fastened each one with slim, brown line to a stout pole. Now with no fear the pheasants picked up the sweet raisins, swallowing them deep into their crops where the fish hooks gripped, and they were held captive to the pole until the poacher returned to bag them.

As I came near to the farm I could hear voices cutting cleanly through the cold air. There was anxiety in their tones as Pete and Bert argued. I hurried to see beyond the thick hedge across the lane to the cowshed.

'You ought ter have known bloody better,' I heard Pete shout.

'You see'd I do it, you never said nowt,' Bert answered his brother. 'Get up, yer bugger! Get up!' He was screaming and I heard the thwack of a stick on cowhide.

'It's just 'cos you'm a lazy little bugger,' Pete accused him.

I reached the gate and looked over. Down the lane a little way and just below the entrance to the cowshed, Big Tits was sprawled in an awkward heap on the glassy surface. The boys were gesticulating above her.

I leapt over the gate and skidded down towards them, shouting in anger as I asked them what the hell they thought they were playing at.

'It's his fault,' Pete shouted back at me, pointing at Bert and jabbing him in the chest. 'Too fuckin' lazy ter carry the water, that's what. Got fed up with it after 'eed watered four cows.'

'No, I weren't,' Bert screamed back.

'Yes, you was! You said the cows could get their own bleedin' water.'

'*You* never said nowt when I untied Big Tits and drove 'er out. *You* never said mind else 'er'll slip. T'were your fault as well.'

'Oh, belt up, the pair of you,' I yelled. 'How long's she been lying here?'

Pete shrugged. ''Bout ten minutes. Her can't get up. I think 'er back leg's broken.'

As he spoke my stomach sank and I bent down over Big Tits. She was lying with one hind leg doubled unnaturally under her and now and then she was pawing at the slippery lane with a front foot, as though she still had half a mind to try and stand up. But she knew it was useless and too painful. She blew jets of steam from her nostrils and the whites of her eyes showed her alarm. Her huge, flaccid udder spread like a pouf and the heat from it had melted the ice in a fringe of wetness. She must have been in pain from the broken leg she was lying on, but she was unable to move because she relied on the underneath leg to lever her huge body upwards. Her eyes rolled at me with the pathetic fear of a trapped animal. And I knew there was nothing I could do to help her. I had to face the situation with a hard heart.

'So that's the end of her,' I said, as I stood up. 'Because you were both bloody thoughtless. You ought to have known better, Bert. And you ought to have stopped him, Pete.'

They shuffled uncomfortably and looked down at the cow. Presently Pete said: 'Can't us get 'er up, then? P'raps if us all pushed. . . .'

'Don't be daft,' I cut in. 'A cow with a broken leg's no good to anybody. Even if she could stand she couldn't walk and when she went down again she couldn't stand up. And she'll lose all her milk anyway. No, it's the knacker yard for her, worst luck.'

The boys glanced at each other in silence. Neither of them had thought any further than how to get the cow up and back into the cowshed. They had not expected to hear a sentence of death.

'Poor ol' Big Tits,' Pete said, with feeling. He moved closer to her head and bent down to hold one of her horns. 'Poor ol' sod.'

'Get some sacks,' I shouted at him, 'wrap 'em over her. At least we can try and keep the poor old thing warm.'

I went indoors to 'phone the knacker yard.

'What was all the shouting about?' Mother wanted to know.

I told her, briefly, as I slammed through to the 'phone.

When I came back into the kitchen she walked up to me. She gripped my hand with strong fingers. 'Never mind, my son. These things have to happen sometimes. It's all part of life and often it's hard to understand why at the time.'

I pulled my hand away. 'But I *do* mind. So would you mind if you were that poor old devil lying crumpled in the cold. Just lying there because it hurts too much to try and get up. Lying there because you were just thirsty and you trusted a fool when he hurried you to water down an icy road. Lying there because your leg's all twisted and broken and all you can do is wait to be shot.'

She put her arm round me: 'Of course I mind. Believe me I know how you feel. And how she feels. I know she has pain to bear, but she can't know what's got to happen to her.'

My hand crept over her shoulder and I pulled her towards me. I blinked to squeeze away threatening tears. 'Of course she can't know that,' I said, quickly, 'but I do.'

The short open lorry from the knacker yard came creeping down to the farm in the afternoon. Each of us had been listening for it, but nobody had mentioned it as we busied ourselves tearing up strips of sacking and lagging the exposed pipes now that Pete had thawed them. The lorry squeaked to a careful halt. I went out into the lane and as I reached it I glanced back to the cowshed. The door was ajar and Pete and Bert were standing together, peering through as though they were loath to watch and yet felt compelled to do so.

The knacker man leered at me from the lorry, with an oath at the state of the roads. His face was lean and he had a cast in one eye so that I was unsure where to focus as I told him the best place to turn round. I couldn't help wondering which eye he drove by.

I stood beside Big Tits as the lorry backed towards her head. I shouted to the driver to stop when he was near. Bolted to the floor of the lorry behind the cab there was a winch with a steel hawser and the planks on the floor of the lorry were slimy with loose dung. Cow hairs had caught in tufts on the hinges of the tailboard and there was dried blood on the tangle of ropes and clutter in the front corner.

Without a word the driver slid down from the lorry. He held a humane killer and he whistled softly through his teeth as he loaded it and walked towards us. Big Tits watched him and for a second her ears shot forward as he came in front of her. Then they fell back as he gruffly grabbed her nose and, without hesitation, pressed the flared end of the barrel on the flat skull between the eyes. He squeezed the trigger and for a few moments after the report her whole body went tense. Then it quivered and finally subsided and lay still. A tiny trickle of blood oozed from the hole in her head and matted in the hair.

'Give us a hand, will yer?' The drover's voice brought me back from my sad reverie. He had climbed into the lorry and was pushing one of the loading ramps towards me. I lowered each one in turn, side by side in front of the cow as he clipped the top ends in position. He unfastened the hawser and the winch squeaked as it unwound until he had enough to reach and could wind the end round the cow's neck and hook it back on itself.

Slowly and with a creaking the hawser tightened as he turned the large handle of the winch. The ratchet clicked steadily on the cogs and Big Tits' head stretched towards the ramps and her lolling tongue dragged against them. The lorry springs sagged as her deep body started to slide upwards and I had to climb up past her and yank her head round when one horn started to catch on the tail of the lorry. Very steadily her body scraped, flopped and sagged until it filled the floor of the lorry and her nose was pressed up against the drum of the winch. When the ratchet was released the hawser went slack and her head went down. She moaned as though she was returning painfully to life as wind escaped from her.

The knacker man pulled the heavy handle from the winch and flung it into the lorry. He heaved up the ramps from the back, crashed them with a clatter across the cow's feet and slammed up the tailboard. He fished into the top pocket of his jacket, and counted three grubby pound notes into my hand as though he was bestowing a great favour upon me.

15

MORE SNOW HAD fallen by the time the first lambs were born. It came silently during the night, covering the lane and filling the ditches so that the boys had to forsake their bikes and come to work on foot. They arrived in the cowshed, stamping their boots in powder-edged footsteps across the dark concrete and arguing. Bert said there was a foot of snow, easy, and you couldn't go by what was in the land because it scudded off and into the hedgerows. And Pete accused him of exaggerating, of not knowing what a foot was, and bet you there wasn't more than eight inches and he'd wade into the middle of the pig meadow and prove it when he fed the sows.

Skinny and Fatso had gone into hibernation. They were fed up with the snow. It had lain about so long they'd almost forgotten the pleasure of foraging. Confined to their sties, they each built themselves huge nests of chewed straw to burrow in and they slept and snored deeply as their new litters started the first squirmings inside them. Twice a day the rattle of buckets in the cowshed embellished their dreams and gradually became real. They grunted and emerged from their mountains of straw, shaking their heads so that their ears flapped like clapped hands. They dripped short pieces of straw as they stretched, moved over to squelch and shit in the corner and ambled back to rub the sleepy tingle from their skins in a swirl of dust. Then out into their little yards to squeal and shout to make sure everybody remembered it was grub time.

When they had slurped up their meal and licked every trace from the troughs, they tunnelled back into their beds and took no notice as Pete and Bert disagreed loudly about the depth of the snow. The boys measured with their thumbs and fingers and anything else they could think of. In the end I had to hunt out an old ruler and disappoint them both by showing them that only five inches had fallen.

But the snow was deep enough for us to decide to harness Colonel into the cart to take the milk churns to the top road. He was snug in his stable, dozing with his head down, taking his weight on three legs while one hind leg was crooked and balanced on the tip of one hoof. The chickens were crooning around him, pecking at minute seeds of hay and rummaging in his dung for a cooked breakfast. They had fluttered from their perches in the cart shed and dipped their feet into the snowfall outside with long, drawn-out complaints. The stable was the nearest port of call across the white ocean, where there was food and warmth. So they had all gone there, squawking, flapping and half-airborne when their feet dipped drumstick-deep into the snow and they found walking impossible. When Pete and I arrived the old horse jerked awake and stamped his foot and the chickens scattered. One took off past us in high dudgeon, frantically beating her wings on a haphazard course, which ended in a belly flop in the deep snow under the hedge. She sat there, her wings spread out flat on the snow, crooning crossly and her bright eye puzzled at her predicament. And then she beat her way out in a storm of snow and swearing and disappeared, helter-skelter across the top of the snow in the general direction of the cowshed.

When we put the harness on Colonel and tightened the girth, he stretched and raised his tail and farted long and loudly. It smelt of hot hay and fermented corn and warm stables. He stamped his foot again because it itched and the frost nails we had spiked into his shoes scored the brick floor. He backed out of his stall awkwardly because he didn't want to go to work, and he swished his tail angrily and greeted the white morning with a snort of disgust. And when we backed him towards the cart, with the shafts dipping into the snow, he straddled one of them on purpose and made a great commotion of stamping like a frightened colt when we tried to straighten him.

Besides the milk churns there was room on the cart for trusses of hay and a bag of corn and swedes for the sheep. When we drove into the field after unloading the milk, the ewes started towards us, plodding slowly and ploughing into the snow. It still lay on their backs in lumps and decorated their faces with quiffs. But it clung to their bellies like gathering snowballs as they walked so that they soon stopped, panting and bleating as they waited for the cart to reach them. They trailed back behind us to the hay rack and the buried troughs and now the going was easier for them where the snow had been trodden.

We lifted the cold, galvanised iron troughs and banged the snow from them. And we fought to find a place to put them down again because the ewes milled about us wherever we moved, fearless of our shouts, certain that we'd forget to feed them unless they tripped us up. And they pressed around Colonel's legs too and shuffled to and fro under him, but he stood quite still with his head dropping. When we did manage to get the food to them, and they stood eating in a steaming line, there was one missing. I counted them again and so did Pete.

'One must have lambed,' I said. 'Let's see if she's behind the hurdles.'

Beyond the hay rack we'd set up hurdles, plaited with straw and forming a pen where the ewes could shelter from the wind. But it was empty and had only served to trap more snow where it had swirled inside and drifted about. The sheep had left the pen severely alone and the holes in the snow showed they had chosen to sit out the downfall in mid field.

'She'll be around the hedge somewhere. We'll just have to walk round 'til we find her,' I said.

Colonel was waiting for us to turn our backs on him and as soon as we started towards the hedge we heard the rattle of harness and clonk of the cart. I looked round. His head was down, his ears flat and he was scattering the sheep with nostril-quivering snorts to get at the corn.

'Whoa! You sod!' I hurried back. 'For that you can jolly well carry us round the field.'

From the vantage point of the cart it was easier to see into the hollows and we found the ewe in a padded patch of snow where the field dipped to meet the hedge. As I jumped from the cart and walked towards her she faced up to me and stamped her front foot angrily. A lamb tottered beside her, its tight-curled coat wrinkled and yellow and its umbilical cord trailing in the snow. The ewe turned nervously and I saw a second lamb. It was lying flat on the snow behind her, still clammy with mucus and not moving. I walked to it quickly and picked it up. The ewe stamped and blew steam, swearing at me with half a bleat and half a grunt as she tried to make up her mind whether it would be any good bunting me. The lamb was cold and slimy and its head flopped as I lifted it and held it with one hand under its chest. It seemed dead. It hung limply. Yet I was sure there was a sign of warmth against my hand and I lifted its head, opened its jaws with my thumb and forefinger and puffed sharply into its mouth. It made no response. Its eyes were shut in their sockets of womb-pressed wool, its tiny pink tongue was still and there was no sign of a quiver in its black nostrils. But now there was definitely warmth against my hand under its breast and surely I felt a heartbeat? I puffed into its mouth again and again. I knelt down and sat on my heels, taking the lamb on my lap and still holding it on the breast while I worked its left leg in a circular motion to pump vigour into its heart. Its head was in the crook of my right arm and suddenly it stirred, just a faint flicker but enough to tell me that warmth would revive it.

As I stood up I unbuttoned my coat, stuffed the lamb inside and fastened it there. I told Pete to grab the other lamb and call to the ewe to follow. He picked it up under its chest and walked towards the cart. But the ewe stayed behind, searching her patch of snow and bleating anxiously.

I had already caught Colonel's bridle and started to lead him back. I was in a hurry to get the lamb to the warmth of the kitchen and Mother's tender care. I stopped and called back to Pete: 'No, silly, not like that. Hold the lamb by its front feet. Dangle it down in front of the ewe. Let her smell it. Baa like a lamb as you walk away. Go on, baa! baa! baa!'

He made a curious sound and smiled at me shyly. The ewe started to follow in his tracks only to stop, uncertainly, before turning and bustling back to the place she'd chosen.

'Shout higher!' I called. 'You're meant to be a lamb. Baa! baa! baa!' My imitation was reasonably lifelike and the ewe turned and started towards us again.

Pete took up the cry with more confidence, which grew as the ewe beat through the snow after him and flicked her tongue rapidly at the lamb dangling in front of her. So she followed in the broad track Colonel kicked across the field and she licked the lamb with gusto when Pete dumped it down on the trodden snow near the hay rack.

Soon she was surrounded by inquisititve sheep. It was no wonder an animal always chose to be on her own in a far corner to give birth. Her mates, every one of them heavy with her own offspring, behaved as though they had never set eyes on a lamb before. A circle of anxious aunties, puffing and fussing as they strained forward and were held at bay by the agitated mother. Presently the novelty wore off and they moved back to feed. I left Pete to make sure the lamb started to suck before bringing Colonel back home.

I burst into the farm kitchen. There was fug on the windows and steam rising from a pot on the range. Mother was on her hands and knees scrubbing the brick floor. It was a weekly duty at which she slaved, sighing deeply and yet persisting because she always believed that unpleasant tasks were somehow good for her soul. However the cleanliness of the floor was always short lived because she was as bad as I at sloshing in with dirty boots.

'I've got a present for you!' I began to unbutton my coat with delight.

She sat back on her heels and looked up curiously. She smiled as soon as she saw the lamb and got stiffly to her feet. 'Oh, the poor thing. Fancy being born in weather like this. It looks simply frozen.' She stroked its head and her hand was wrinkled from the water. 'Oh dear, is it still alive?'

'Only just. But I think it'll revive by the fire.'

'Let's find something warm for it to lie on. Here, this'll do.' She grabbed her old duffle coat from behind the door and flung it on the floor in front of the fire.

I laid the lamb on it. It lay stretched out with its clumsy legs towards the fire and I bundled the coat up behind it, along its back and propping up its head. It was blinking its eyes and the jolting journey inside my coat had helped to revive it.

'Can you warm some milk? See if you can get it to suck? There's a box of teats in the pantry somewhere, near the bottles of cow medicine, I think. I'll have to leave you to it. I must get back and see if we can improve the lambing pen.'

'Of course I'll look after it. I'd love to.' She bent down, picked up her bucket and shot the contents into the sink. 'The silly old floor can wait,' she added, with a laugh. The lamb was a life.

She reached for a saucepan, poured in some milk and banged it on the range. She hurried off to the pantry in search of a bottle and teat.

'Don't get it too hot,' I called, as I went out of the door. But I knew it would boil over while she prepared the bottle and knelt to nurse the lamb. Milk always boiled over with Mother and she would rush to lift the saucepan with a 'Whoops! Oh, dearie me, too late again.'

For the next two weeks life was hectic. Days and nights seemed to merge into one long rush as lambs came tumbling into the bitter world. The persistent snow seemed to make the ewes anxious. They missed the reassuring sight of grass, the feel of it pressing into their cloven hooves, its earthy smell and the sweet taste of the short tips. The snow was a blanket hiding their familiar world. It clogged their progress when their bellies were already heavy; it dazzled in the fleeting sun and blurred their sight; it robbed the fragrance from the wind. So when a lamb was born and floundered in the snow, the mother was already distracted and unable to devote her whole attention to the job in hand. In the main the first lamb was all right. She would lick it and fuss it to its feet until the urgings of the twin inside her demanded her attention. When that had been born, sometimes she spared it no more than a few cursory licks, leaving it to fend for itself while she returned to her first born who was clamouring for her attention. Her natural instinct to share her attentions equally among her offspring, sometimes even three of them, seemed to desert her. It almost appeared as though she thought it was enough to cope with the snow and that one lamb was really all she could be expected to manage.

So we had to keep as continuous a vigil as possible to revive the lambs which had been deserted. Sometimes a ewe could be persuaded into her responsibilities when the second lamb failed to look after itself. Provided you were on the spot you could rub life into the lamb until it could stand and then hold its nose to the udder to get it to suck. If it was still too bemused to grip the teat, then you had to hold its mouth open and its head within range with one hand, using the other to grope under the wool for the tiny teat. Then squirt the milk into its mouth until it got the general idea. As the ewe seldom took kindly to this persuasion it meant you had to hold her as well, by shoving her head between your knees, gripping until your groin ached and just hoping she didn't bunt upwards as you leant along her back and struggled with the lamb. More often than not this happened at night because darkness added to the ewe's anxiety and the majority of lambs were born then. So the kindly light from the hurricane lamp was essential, adding another dimension to the operation, and more than once it was kicked over and sizzled in the snow, while the wild flame leapt and blackened the glass and went out just as you reached to right it.

The kitchen became a warm nursery to which lambs were hurried for revival. Miracles were wrought at the foot of the black kitchener, beneath the yawning oven door and the red crackle from the bars. Chilled, wet lambs, lives in limbo already drifting into frozen stillness, stirred, snuffled, sucked at the warm milk and bleated piteously. And soon they were tottering about, tangling with the chair legs, jerking with little jumps because suddenly it was good to be alive.

As soon as a lamb recovered I took it back to its mother. She would smell it carefully under its tail as I placed it beside her and give it a quick lick or two when she recognised it as her own. Then I'd make sure it sucked, watch its tail wriggle as it tasted the milk and know that the chances were good it would survive.

Some lambs died. Their cold bodies stiffened in front of the kitchener and we lifted them like cardboard cut-outs and placed them outside the back door to await burial. Sometimes we made use of them in a macabre trick used by shepherds throughout the ages.

Bill Checksfield hated a dead lamb to be a complete loss. Since the first lamb had been born he had plodded out from the village every day on foot, arriving with cheeks red and shining like burnished apples, and had stayed until it was almost dark before starting back on the two-mile walk to his tea. He brought cheese sandwiches and a powerful onion for his midday meal and a bottle of cold tea to wash it down. But it took three days before we could persuade him to eat with us in the warm kitchen, instead of crouching on an apple box in the stable and munching away with Colonel.

'I be come fer to looker the sheep, Mam, not fer to get in your way. Thank you kindly, all the same,' he raised his cap and explained to Mother whenever she asked him to come in and eat with us.

She became concerned. 'But you can't sit out there in the cold, Mr Checksfield. You won't be in our way, really you won't. Do please come in and join us.' When he continued to refuse she told me she was sure it was his wife who was at the back of it. We'd an idea she never really approved of his continued connection with the farm. So Mother reckoned he was acting under orders not to impose on us.

In the end he had to agree to eat with us. It became impossible for him to refuse any longer as the lambs started to arrive in earnest and he had to be in and out of the kitchen anyway. Mother plied him with cups of tea and slowly he felt more at ease as we nursed the lambs. He always took his cap off and hung it carefully on the hook behind the door whenever he came in. And his eyes wrinkled under his heavy white brows and the sparks flew from his cigarette as he worked on the lambs with his calloused hands.

'The old boy's marvellous with the lambs,' Mother said one day. 'He's so gentle and has such patience.' She was smiling gently and there was a rapturous look on her face. So the shock was all the greater when, one morning, she was confronted with a harsher aspect of lambing.

Checky sat back on his heels with a lamb across his lap and pronounced it dead.

Mother looked down with a pained expression. 'Oh no, not *another* one.'

Checky looked up. 'Afraid so, Mam. T'were dead when I brought 'im in, I reckon. Terrible weather this be for lambing, terrible, terrible.'

I had just come in. 'That was her only lamb, which makes it worse. She's got a load of milk too.'

Mother sighed and returned to her work about the house.

'Can't waste a ewe like that,' Checky said, 'milk's too precious to waste this weather.' He looked up and scratched the back of his head – not because it itched but because it was a habit he had whenever he was about to make a suggestion. 'What about them triplets born yesterday?' he asked. 'P'raps us could get her to take one of they.'

'No harm in trying,' I agreed. I pointed to the dead lamb still lying across his lap. 'We could use that skin so's she thinks its hers.'

'That's what I thought.' Checky fumbled in his jacket and produced his pocket knife. He spread the lamb on the floor in front of him, drove the sharp blade under the skin of its belly and ripped it up in a long line to its wrinkled throat. He had just started to tear the skin back, working his knife under it to part it from the cold, dark flesh, when Mother came in.

'Heavens! Whatever are you doing to the poor creature?' She stood quite still, looking down and with her hand cupped against the side of her face.

'We need its skin,' I explained. 'We want to fool its mother into taking on another lamb.'

194

'Surely not like that! If the sheep's lost her only lamb I'm sure she'd love it if you gave her another one. Surely you don't have to mutilate that poor dead creature?'

Checky went on skinning, working a front leg out as though pulling it from a sleeve, tearing the skin from the back and cutting into the base of the slimy tail so that it came away with the skin. 'Trouble is, Mam, nature don't work easy like that. When her leaves a ewe without any lambs, then her don't mean her to have none. When you puts another lamb beside the ewe her can smell it ain't hers. Her bunts at it something terrible and won't have nothing to do with it.' He was working on the hind legs and soon he had freed them both. The body lay dark and shining with white socks on its ungainly legs. 'So we has to fool her by dressin' up the new lamb in her own lamb's skin.' He wiped the blade of his knife on his trousers and snapped it shut. It would be used later to peel and cut up his onion. He got to his feet with a grunt, draped the skin over his arm and held the body with his same hand while he went to the door for his cap. 'Sometimes it works, Mam, sometimes it don't. But all these things be only sent for to try us.'

'I see.' Mother nodded, quietly. 'But I do think it's all rather horrid.'

Checky smiled back at her as he went out of the door. 'It's just part of farmin', Mam. It ain't all sweet and easy.'

We caught one of the triplets and Checky smeared its head with the inside of the skin. He put its front feet through the holes he had left in the skin and tied the flaps under the belly with two pieces of binder twine threaded into holes he pierced in the skin. He was careful to tie the tail so that it followed the line of the live tail and then he held up the lamb to admire his handiwork.

'There's a nice new coat for you,' he laughed. 'That'll keep the cold out, I'll be bound.'

We had the ewe penned off by herself and he leant over the hurdles and placed the lamb beside her, with its head towards her udder. She stamped her foot as she watched him and swung round quickly to face the lamb as soon as she realised it was there. She baa'd softly, curiously, smelling carefully along its back and licking quickly at the place where the tail had been severed.

The lamb made for the swollen udder, fastening on a teat. It couldn't care less that this wasn't its mother. Milk was milk. But before it could get more than a quick taste the ewe moved away, stamping her foot, lowering her head towards the lamb, undecided whether to bunt it or lick it. The right smell was there, yet something made her doubtful. Perhaps it looked wrong with its ragged, dirty coat and its two tails.

So I climbed into the pen and held her by the wool under her throat. The lamb wanted no telling. It made another determined attack on the udder and when the milk flowed its tail lifted and wriggled, tossing the other tail from side to side.

Slowly I released the ewe's head and she stood still. In a moment she looked round, sniffed and licked at the flopping tail. Then she was content to keep the lamb as her own.

16

LITTLE WILLIE LIVED a life of luxury. He stuffed himself and snoozed the hours away in the small sty we had made for him at one end of the stable. Apart from his regular two square meals a day he had any odd scraps that were going, from a cow cabbage to the sweepings from the corn bin. All contributions were gratefully received and he put on weight with surprising speed as he munched his way towards an early death.

Unfortunately pigs are only reared to be killed. Mostly you can wave them goodbye on their way to market after a lively loading into the lorry. You can forget their ultimate destination as you look forward to the cheque. But if you hanker after home-cured bacon (and we certainly did in those hard days of rationing) then you have to harden your heart.

At that time it was still possible to kill a pig on the premises, without having to cart it off to the nearest abbatoir, or the local butcher if he is licensed to kill. You only had to call on Ernie Carter and, for a few shillings, he would come round to the farm to kill and dress your pig. It was just another of the services he offered, along with the hiring out of Bill, the boar, and the other multifarious sidelines on his farm.

Little Willie had to be killed and cured before the warm weather started. So I rang Ernie to make a date and was given instructions as to how to prepare for his visit.

There was a long discussion about the sty and the stable as a suitable place for the slaughter. When he was satisfied he said: 'And you'll need a big tub of hot water too, you know. Big enough to put the pig in. Half an old cider barrel's best. Got one, have yer?'

'Yes, I think so.' I ranged my mind's eye rapidly over the buildings and their contents. 'Yes, I've got an old tub we use for corn sometimes. That'll do, provided it still holds water.'

'Put it in the pond then. Soak 'un in the pond so's it tightens up. Fill it and sink it fer a day or two, that'll do the trick. And how you going' ter heat the water?'

'In the copper? There's one in the backyard. We haven't used it for ages, but it's okay. Must hold twenty gallons, I'd say.'

'Make sure the water's real hot, mind. If it ain't hot the hairs won't come out. Nothin' worse than trying' ter scald a pig and the water ain't hot. Stiffen up 'e will afore ever 'ees done. Then it's a bugger.'

'But what about burning him with straw?' I asked. 'The last time I helped kill a pig the chap burnt the hairs off with straw. We laid him on an iron gate and lit a fire under him. Seems easier to me than messing about with tubs of hot water.'

Ernie listened. Then there was a pause and I heard him sucking his teeth before he said: 'Now I'll tell you something, Dave. I don't like that way, not nohow. Dirty and stinkin' it is and when you've finished you've still got ter clean 'im up. Least *I* think yer have to wash 'im. But I know one dirty devil wot'll just brush it orf with a handful of straw and hang it up all charred to dress it. And you know who I'm talkin' of, I'll bet a bob.'

I did indeed. There was competition in the pig sticking business and Ernie's local rival was Boney Jackson, the blacksmith. Boney lived by fire and perhaps that was why he preferred to singe the hairs from the pigs he killed. He'd tried to land the job of killing Little Willie the last time I had taken Colonel down to be shod. Colonel had been one of Boney's customers for so long that his shoes were bespoke and there was always a new set hanging from a special nail in the firelit corner of the dark smithy. But there was always time for a chat while the shoes were heated, and while the smoke from the burning hoof had wafted up and Boney had blown it from his face as he bent to fit the shoe, he had asked about killing Little Willie. Perhaps the rising smoke had reminded him and he had spoken as though he had taken it for granted he would be asked. I think he was more interested in the trimmings of offal he would take away with him than the actual money for the job. Meat was severely rationed at the time and Boney always looked as though he could do with a square meal. He was as thin as a rasher of bacon himself. But I had decided that Ernie's reputation as a slaughterman seemed the better and I had to prevaricate rapidly so as not to offend Boney.

Little Willie was snoring comfortably, oblivious that the last hour of his life was ticking away as Ernie drove down to the farm. He always snored loudly, just as he'd always wheezed as he walked, and I could hear him clearly as I walked past the stable to greet Ernie. At least ignorance was bliss, I thought.

Ernie was out of his car and all I could see was his ample backside as he burrowed under the open lid of the boot. He had discarded his check jacket and donned his torn white overall, and when he straightened up the tails of it rested like crumpled rags on his protruding backside. Certainly *he* didn't look as though he needed any extra meat to keep going. When he turned round he held an assortment of wicked looking knives, a saw, a chopper and a scrubbing brush. He smiled and his teeth crowded to be noticed. 'Here I be, then, all armed and ready.'

'Fine. And we're all ready for you. The tub's in the stable and the water's bubbling in the copper. The boys'll bucket it up whenever you say.'

'Us better watch points first,' he said as he came towards me and we walked into the stable. We had cleared the stall next to the sty, swept the bricks clean and the tub was waiting expectantly under a beam from which, all being well, the washed and lifeless body of the pig would soon be hanging.

Pete and Bert had joined us, buckets jangling over their arms as they crowded in to make sure they were missing nothing. They had been looking forward to Ernie's visit. They well knew that some of the pig would be coming their way once it was cured and smoked.

Little Willie awoke with a start as we looked over into his sty. Immediately he was suspicious, leaping from his bed and peering up at us and grunting as he wanted to know what we were up to. He well knew there was no food in the offing in spite of the sound of buckets.

Ernie cleared his throat as he looked down at him. 'There's one thing I got ter tell you.' He raised his cap and stroked his bald head, returning the boys' smiles with a wiggle of his eyebrows that sent creases like ladders climbing up his forehead. 'I've forgotten ter bring me 'uman killer. Still, no matter, the ol' pig ain't very big and us can soon stun 'im afore I sticks 'im.'

'Don't you think you ought to go back for it?' I asked. 'We ought to do the job properly.'

He laughed loudly. 'Cor, bless yer, us'll do the job properly all right. Same as us allus done afore they made them guns compuls'ry. Got an axe, ain't yer?'

I nodded. It was buried in a log in the woodshed.

'Now I'm going' ter tell you.' He held up one finger. 'One good sharp blow with the back of the axe between the eyes and that'll stun 'im as good as the 'uman killer. Always used to pole-axe 'em, us did. Always pole-axed 'em in my young days. Still got a pole-axe I have, somewhere up home. But an ordinary axe'll do as well. Only got ter knock 'im silly long enough ter get the knife in.'

Little Willie's head was on one side. He was listening intently as Ernie jabbed his finger at him for emphasis.

I sent Bert to fetch the axe and suggested it was time to fill the tub with the boiling water.

'That's it,' Ernie agreed, with a grin, 'have it all ready so's we can pop 'im in as soon as 'ees bled. And we'll want some buckets of cold too, mind,' he called after the boys as they went chuckling and rattling off.

We prepared to catch the pig. Now I've said that the sty was only a makeshift, built with boards and corrugated iron across the top half of a stall. It never had a door and all of us were agile enough to leap over whenever it was necessary to get inside. Understandably the portly Ernie was unable to enter in this way, and as we would soon have to drag the pig out, I began to dismantle the barricade by prising a way through.

Little Willie watched me carefully, with his backside jammed firmly in the corner, unsure of both the stranger and the unusual activity. He grunted gruffly as the nails holding the corrugated iron sheets screeched when I levered them out, and his head peered forward when the end of the sheet came free and opened up a small gap into the outside world. The runt of a litter learns cunning at an early age. He has to, in order to survive among his boisterous brothers and sisters, and he is always suspicious and forever has his eye on the main chance.

Which is why Willie acted as he did. The situation was already developing in a disturbing way that he didn't understand and there seemed no point in hanging about. So, as soon as he spotted the gap in the barricade he charged at it, squealing as he thrust through and huffing with victory when he burst past us in the stable, his hooves scrabbling to get a grip on the brick floor. He shot out of the door and suddenly stopped as he plunged into the snow outside, wondering what the devil he'd stepped into. Although he had never seen it before, he only stopped for a moment's inspection as our shouts of dismay goaded him into desperate escape.

We all gave chase. Pete was advancing on the stable with the first two buckets of water as Willie rushed out, and he left them steaming in the snow while he took off after the pig as he bundled by. At the same time Bert emerged from the woodshed, brandishing the axe as he leapt into action because Willie was making straight towards him across the bottom yard. With a snort of disgust at finding Bert in his path, the pig veered off towards the pond, wheezing terribly as he skirted the edge and plunged off up towards the bullock lodge. He shot under the rails into the yard and now galloped to try and make faster progress through the soft straw under the startled gazes of Elsie, Doris and Brutus.

By now Skinny and Fatso had stirred from their slumbers at the sound of all the snorting and commotion. They tumbled out into their yards, leapt into view with their trotters on the wall and shouted out what I could only presume were words of encouragement and advice to Little Willie. He was making for the meadow, through the open gate and ploughing into the snow, steaming and snorting like an overburdened goods engine.

'Head him off!' I bellowed from the bullock lodge to Pete, who had given chase across the snow.

Ernie was beaming in the bottom yard, which was as far as he intended to go in the chase. 'Bet yer a bob the pig beats 'im to the wood,' he called out.

And he was right. It was like a race in slow motion through the snow as Little Willie made for one of the weak spots in the hedge with unerring memory. He reached it with a gasp, rooted at it and puffed through into the wood with open-mouthed exhaustion. Pete flung himself after him and I doubled back through the stack-plat to the lane, ran up it and crossed into the wood in the hope of heading the pig off and driving him back down into the meadow.

I could hear him wheezing away in the white stillness as I made to cut him off. Running through snow is like running in a dream and although you try hard you never seem to get very far. Fortunately Willie found the same difficulty and because of the weeks of stuffing himself in the sty without exercise, he was sadly out of training. Besides, it must have been much harder for him on four short legs, plunging in belly-deep in places. So he stopped and I followed through the trees to the sound of his panting.

Pete reached him first and I came down on them as they faced each other across ten yards of snow and trees. 'Come on, yer little sod,' Pete held out his hand invitingly, 'may as well give up. Yu'm too bloody puffed to go any farther.'

Willie wheezed and watched him carefully. He was playing for time, desperately trying to get his breath back, almost like a floored boxer mouthing the count and preparing to jump up at the last second as Pete slowly advanced towards him. 'Ain't no good yer trying' to get away. Your time's up matey. Besides, I'm lookin' forward to a rasher or two orf of you, so let's have yer.'

I was creeping down on Willie from behind, as quietly as falling snowflakes as I made towards a grab at his back leg. I signalled to Pete to stop his advance and tried to make him understand that he should go on talking to keep the pig's attention. He understood me all right and proceeded to inform Little Willie just what I was up to. The pig grunted back at him as though he didn't believe a word of it. 'Go on with you, pull the other one,' he seemed to be saying. And when I threw myself forward and grasped his hind leg he squealed with disbelief.

Bert brought a rope and we slipped it through Willie's jaws and tightened it over his snout, passing the loose end round him behind his front legs and half-hitching it over his back. He squealed continuously as we dragged him back to the stable while Skinny and Fatso watched in stunned silence, unable to believe that a pig who had actually reached the sanctuary of the wood had been foolish enough to get himself caught so soon. Usually it was worth at least a couple of days of freedom, if you felt like a break.

Ernie was waiting for us in the stable. 'You're a one for havin' animals break out, Dave, to be sure,' he chided me. 'What with old Colonel and them sows, you'll be grazin' over the whole parish afore you've done.'

'They like to enjoy themselves,' I laughed. 'And they all come home in the end, you know.' I heaved Willie forward to fasten the rope securely into a ring set into the partition beside the tub. He knew when he was beaten and he stood quite still, wheezing and gasping as though he had a bad attack of bronchitis. His bright eyes darted and swivelled as he watched the steaming water being poured into the tub.

When all was ready Ernie grabbed the axe and addressed Willie's skull like a golfer preparing to drive. It crashed down with a dull thud and the pig's legs crumpled under him. In a moment Ernie had dropped the axe and taken his knife and he cut a gash down the throat and buried the blade inside until he severed the jugular vein. The blood spurted out, surging on to the floor and flooding under the kicking body, the legs working like pump handles to drive every last drop from the veins.

'That's 'im dead and bled,' Ernie said, with satisfaction. 'Into the tub with 'im now, afore 'e gets cold. Come on, you boys, grab hold. Now us'll give 'im a nice hot bath.'

By the time we had curled him round inside the tub Little Willie really looked very comfortable. His eyes were shut and he seemed to be grinning as the steam rose and the water sloshed in red ripples between his lounging legs.

Ernie puffed and grunted as he worked, scrubbing and scraping, sluffing off the hairs and twisting and turning the pig until he had explored every last crevice with his knife or brush and removed the hairs from them all. He drove meat hooks behind the tendons of the hind trotters and we hoisted him up and hung him upside down from the beam.

'Cor!' Bert exclaimed, 'he's all white now. And 'e used ter be a black pig with a white stripe. Can't even see where 'is white stripe went now.'

'Big, ain't 'e?' Pete said. 'Don't arf look big strung up there. Never thought 'e was as big as that to see 'im in his sty. Never think 'ees the same little sod wot was always getting left behind.'

Bert laughed, 'Wonder what ol' Skinny'd say if 'er could see 'im now.'

'Wouldn't recognise 'im,' Pete replied. 'Why, 'er never even knowed it was 'im when 'er see 'im just now.'

They chatted on, remarking and exclaiming as Ernie dressed the pig, removing the offal and laying it carefully on the table we had set up.

He heaved a double handful of intestines into the tub. 'Come on, you boys, here's a job for yer. You can clean out some o' these guts fer sausage skins.' He took a strand of intestine and pulled it between his thumb and forefinger, squeezing all the gunge out of it and leaving an empty skin coiling behind him on the floor like a starved snake. 'That's it, like that. Then wash the skins out in a clean bucket o' water and there 'em be, all ready fer fillin' with sausage meat.' He turned to me. 'I got a sausage machine up home, wot I bought from ol' Fullerton's bankrupt sale. You can bring up all the odd bits of meat and fat and I'll mince 'em and run 'em through the skins for yer.' He was still wallowing away in the tub, getting Pete and Bert started on the yards of intestine. 'Nothin' like a nice home-made sausage, me boys, specially when it's been hung up ter smoke along o' the bacon. They don't want long in the smoke, mind, and then you can hang 'em in the kitchen and they'll keep a month or more. Just cut some orf and pop 'em in the pan for breakfast as you wants 'em. Always have 'em, I do. You bring the bits up, Dave, and I'll make 'em for yer and I'll keep back a couple o' pounds for me trouble. Suit you, eh?'

I agreed, but he never heard me as he went on talking.

'You wants half lean meat and half fat for good sausages, mind. And some herbs and some salt, and a sprinklin' o' breadcrumbs to soak the fat and there's a proper sausage for yer. Not like them dry ol' things they sell as sausages these days. Terrible, they be. Ain't no meat to 'em.'

He stood up once he was satisfied the boys were doing the job properly. They hadn't really been listening to him and were chattering and giggling as they made lewd play with the skins. Bert was poking his finger into an empty skin. He nudged his brother. 'Do for a frenchie, wouldn't it?'

'Don't be daft.'

'It would that. Tie a knot in the end.' He giggled and demonstrated.

Ernie had started cutting the pig in half down its spine. He looked down, scowling. 'What you know 'bout them things?'

Bert looked up, belligerently. 'I seen 'em, ain't I?'

'Boy your age seen 'em. Lor, what's the world comin' to? Where you seen 'em, then?'

'In the hop garden. Them ol' women wot was there last hop pickin' had one. Blowin' it up and lettin' it go, they was. Shootin' all over the place, it were. Said they found it by the hedge. I reckon Pete left it there. Did yer, Pete?'

Pete dropped his handful of guts and grabbed his brother by the throat. For a moment I thought Bert was bound to join the intestines and bloody water and gunge in the tub. But he fought back and managed to stay clear until the giggling tussle ended as abruptly as it had begun.

Ernie started working on the pig again. 'Don't wanna use them things,' he advised, seriously. 'Why, 'tis like goin' ter bed with yer socks on.'

He finished chopping and the pig hung in two halves from the beam. 'That's it, then,' he said, wiping the blade. 'That's me done. Let 'im hang 'til tomorrow and then cut 'im up like I showed yer. Got your salt ready for the brine?'

I nodded and told him I had a box of salt blocks.

'Now I'm goin' ter tell you,' he went on. 'Same tub'll do. Clean it out and put in some cold water and enough salt as it takes ter float a potato. Then pop the joints and the sides in and let 'em soak for a fortnight. Then they'll be ready for ter smoke.' He continued cleaning his knives and he pointed one at me. 'And oak sawdust, mind. Make sure 'tis oak sawdust what you use for ter smoke 'im. Ol' Bourne down the sawmills will let you have some. Make sure 'tis oak. Tell 'im what it's for, 'e'll know. None o' that ol' elm or pine rubbish. Oak's the stuff for ter give it flavour.'

A few minutes later he was on his way down to his car, tools in one hand and a lump of liver in the other. And as he drove away I promised to bring up the ingredients for the sausages after I had cut up the pig the next day.

A month later Little Willie hung in golden joints from the hooks in the beams in the kitchen. Dealing with the hams, the fore-ends and the sides had been comparatively easy, setting them to soak in the brine, floating around like slimy icebergs. And when it came to smoking them, the privy proved to be the ideal place where they could hang, while the smoke from the smouldering sawdust on the floor curled up and penetrated, undisturbed by draughts in the small room. We cleaned it all out and captured Mrs P.P. when she strolled in to roost, and she protested violently as I carried her over to the cart shed and pushed her up on a beam by herself. It was too dark for her to see to fly down, so she had to stay there that night. But she spent her days over the next two weeks, prowling up and down outside the bog, swearing at the firmly fastened door while the hams and the bacon quietly matured in the thick fog within.

But if this had been straightforward, operation offal in the kitchen had been more complicated. For three long days Mother seemed to be fighting a running battle with quantities of skirt and fleed, liver and lights, trotters, cheeks, bones and ears, which glistened and quivered in basins and bowls on the shelves in the pantry. They all had to be dealt with straight away. There was no 'fridge or deep freeze where they could be cast out of sight and mind until time and inclination ripened together to tackle them.

So Mother sought an ally in Mrs Beeton and I would find her pacing the kitchen, book in hand and specs on her nose, reading aloud and going into the pantry to prod at the various parts of the pig for which Mrs Beeton detailed delicious recipes. Or she would be distressed, searching frantically and had I seen her specs? They must be somewhere because she knew she'd had them when she was reading up about fleed cakes. Now she was ready to tackle the liver and make the pate and the sausage and the specs must be somewhere. They can't have just disappeared. She had a habit of flinging her glasses down wherever she happened to be when she finished using them. Which could be anywhere and getting her to retrace her movements didn't always provide the clue to their whereabouts. Except once I followed the trail into the pantry and found them sitting on a shelf, silently staring down at Little Willie's ears.

As well as the fleed cakes and the pate, the rendered lard and the liver sausage, she made huge amounts of brawn, pressing every available pudding basin into service and leaving them to set. And later, smiling with bright cheeks, her tousled hair flopping, she upended each basin and shook it, bidding the brawn 'come out, come out,' as she set a range of quivering mountains across the table. There was far too much for us to eat and so she stowed various goodies in her bicycle basket and pedalled off full tilt to deliver them to those she thought to be in need.

I smoked the sausages Ernie made and they hung in shrivelled, brown skeins from the ceiling, beside the sides of bacon. Mother stood on a chair to cut down the number she needed and when she pricked them and threw them in the breakfast pan, they swelled up and sizzled and gave off a mouth-watering aroma, which reached me across the yard as I came in from the cowshed. And when they came to an end, there were the thick rashers of bacon, cut from the sides with a knife, curling and crisping and spitting on the black range.

Little Willie certainly did us proud and I gave thanks to him over many a glorious breakfast and a summer ham salad.

Spring

17

FOR OVER TWO months the cowl on the oast house had been hunched against the north wind, never swinging more than a degree or two in either direction. Then the snow slipped from the steep slope of the conical roof and landed in solid lumps, blocking Henry's way in and out through the ventilation holes at the foot of the roundel. He was trapped inside for two days while we wondered what had become of him, when he failed to turn up for his milk and his usual prowl around the cowshed and the yards.

'He's gorne to find 'isself a bit.' Bert dismissed the cat's absence with a shrug.

I felt sure he wouldn't go far afield in the snow and said so.

'Course 'ees cleared orf,' Pete said. 'He ain't had none for ages. 'Tis gettin' towards spring and 'ees been cat-a-wallin' round here something shockin' lately. Ain't you 'eard 'im? He'll be back in a day or two, you mark my words, skinny and stinkin' and full of 'isself.'

We left it at that. But Henry had no intention of remaining out of sight and out of mind. As I walked up the lane the following day I heard him calling. Not his usual strident voice but a rather plaintive request for help, coming from the oast house. I went inside and searched for him, thinking he must have got himself trapped somehow. But although I could still hear his cry, it was fainter and didn't seem to be coming from inside at all.

I walked outside again. Then I saw him. He was right up under the cowl, pacing precariously around the rim, obviously feeling very cold and sorry for himself. However he managed to scramble up there inside the sloping roof I shall never know. But manage it he did in his bid for freedom. But it was quite certain he couldn't get down again, either inside or out. He kept looking down the steep tiles, squatting and tentatively testing the slippery slope with an outstretched paw.

'So that's where you are! How the hell did you get up there?' I walked to the foot of the roundel and it was then I saw his escape holes had been blocked by the avalanches.

At the sound of my voice he renewed his pleading with greater urgency and he lifted his tail and rubbed himself against the edge of the cowl. Obviously he had been watching the comings and goings on the farm from his eyrie and pleading his case for several lonely hours. Now he was delighted at final recognition.

I found a ladder and raised it inside the roundel, from the drying floor to the cowl. And I climbed and poked my head up through the open rim to the inside of the tall cowl. Quietly I invited him to come down as I tried to gather him into my arms. But he seemed convinced that I was bent on casting him to his death. He dug in his claws and held tight to the rim of the roof, growling ominously. It developed into a flurry of swearing from both of us before I had him clinging desperately to my shoulder on the downward journey. He growled all the way down, his tail waving wildly, and three rungs from the bottom he leapt ungratefully from my embrace and flew to freedom through the open door.

By the time I reached the cowshed he was already at the dairy, gliding lovingly against the door post and purring as though I was the greatest pal he had.

A day or two later the wind came from the south and in a matter of hours roofs were dripping, ditches gurgling and the ice on the pond in the yard broke away from the bank and floated like a sunken island. The snow shrank from the fields leaving the grass bright and glistening, stretching up and shimmering to show how much it had grown while it had been hidden. It was amazing the growth it had made and Jack was at pains to remind us that he always *had* said a coating of snow was as good as a sprinkle of dung. Just as, throughout the summer, he constantly told us his recipe for growing good hops was a shower of rain once a week and a shower of shit on Sundays.

Before March was out the spring had arrived, soft-footed and sparkling, a flower-filled apology for the clinging winter. The underwood trees in the wood, that had huddled and whispered with snow, now fluttered with new green and the ancient oaks elbowed head and shoulders above them to display grey branches bursting with yellow curls. Clusters of primroses appeared everywhere, scattered like stars along the banks and nodding in luxuriant clusters among the trees, while dog violets peeped through the grass with faint blue faces. Waxy leaves of Lord-and-Ladies rose like green arrows through the hedge banks, spotted with purple and unrolling shyly to expose themselves, each one turning out to be a rampant Lord with not a Lady in sight to admire them. White anemones crept delicately into the woods, turning their purple collars to the slightest breeze and the bold, yellow king-cups stared up with plump, shiny faces from the wet patches beside the ponds. Birds flashed about in a frenzy of activity, proclaiming their territorial rights until the wood could hold no more echoes and the robin, who had despaired of his little kingdom in the snow-filled copse, now burst out with a song like falling spatters of water.

The cows smelt the new grass and blew at their hay with contempt. They didn't want to know when we told them the ground was still too wet and they would only stodge more precious grass than they ate. They had been eagerly awaiting the spring and now it had come it was time to be shot of the stuffy cowshed and the dull, dry food. Their milk yield dropped by two gallons in a single day, just to let me know how they felt about it. So we turned them out. But only for an hour at first to stop them making pigs of themselves and blowing.

They trod carefully out of the cowshed and once they were outside they swayed off up the lane with increasing speed, like a bunch of women barging to the sales for bargains. We had been careful to loose Lotty first and she led the way into the meadow, lowering her head and blowing at the ruts in the gateway, snatching at the first tuft of grass that grew alone at the edge of the drying mud. She moved on into the grass, excitement mounting with every quivering movement, tearing with her tongue, winding it back for another grab, blowing, tail swishing, speed increasing until she kicked up her hind legs with joy and went bucking across the meadow, driving the winter stiffness from her joints.

Soon they were all following her example, each one expressing her delight in her own particular way as they fanned out across the field. Daisy was a swaying brown rumba and Bambi a daintily prancing fawn; Popsi flashed her white flanks, careering in a crazy circle, while Laura, Blackie, Myrtle and Florrie formed their own quartet of capricious capers. And the shy Bluebell followed at a distance, biting at the grass and giving little jumps for joy because she couldn't really resist it and perhaps, just this once, it wouldn't upset her milk yield. As I watched them I sadly missed the lumbering Big Tits and wondered how she would have brought her great udder into the swing of things.

When they settled down to serious eating I thought how scruffy they looked. During the long winter months in the cowshed we had kept the dung from caking on them and in the dim light they always looked presentable against the bright straw bedding. But out here in the sun, in the green spring-cleaned meadow, they looked dusty and dirty with dung-stained legs and ragged tails and no bloom on their coats. No wonder they had objected to staying in the cowshed any longer. They had milked well. Now they deserved the first fruits of spring and I knew it would only be a matter of a week or so before they all appeared in new spring outfits.

I could hear Pete and Bert talking and laughing, bass broom scrubbing, pails clanking and water sloshing as they made the most of cleaning a cow-free shed. I had left them to it while I had the pleasure of leaning on the gate in the sunshine and watching the cows, just to make sure that none of them started to blow up with the strong spring grass. There was a load of work crying out to be done all over the farm and half of me was itching to get on with it. But the other half kept me clinging to the gate, watching the cows because I wanted to and revelling in their enjoyment.

I heard a car drive down the lane and I only turned to look when it stopped behind me. Jean leaned from the window and called to me: 'Slacking again, I see! Nothing better to do than dream over a gate?'

'Hello! I wasn't expecting you.' I kissed her through the window and she tasted as fresh as spring. She wore a pale green shirt with the sleeves rolled high and the neck was unbuttoned so that I looked down to swelling softness. 'You look good enough to eat,' I growled. As I finished speaking there was an indignant yapping from in the van. 'Hello-ello, and who are you?' I asked.

'Well, as a matter of fact,' Jean began, 'that's why I made a detour here to see you.' She reached back, grabbed the puppy by the scruff of the neck and hauled it over on to her lap. It was golden as a sunset, quivered as it looked up at me with large brown eyes and darted quick licks under Jean's chin for reassurance.

'Yours?' I asked.

'No, yours! You keep saying you must get a dog so I've brought you one.' She cuddled the puppy and nuzzled her cheek against it. 'You do like her, don't you?'

'Her? A bitch?'

'Uh-huh. Isn't she sweet? Pure Golden Retriever. She was the last of a litter on a farm I went to, the only one they couldn't find a home for. They managed to sell all the others, five guineas each they said they got for them. When I said I knew someone who might have this one, they gave her to me. As she's a lady I've called her Sadie, you know, "Sadie was a lady?" 'She laughed and looked up at me under questioning eyebrows. 'You *do* like her, don't you? Of course I know you really want a dog, but you'll be able to breed some wizard puppies from this one when she grows up.'

She propped Sadie up on her haunches and threw back her head to admire her. The puppy shivered and whimpered, looking up at me without knowing what to do with her ears. Jean turned her eyes up to me without moving her head and the beginnings of a smile dimpled her cheeks.

I shrugged. 'What can I say, with two girls trying to persuade me?'

Jean hugged Sadie, opened the door of the van and got out still clutching her. 'Good, I knew you couldn't resist her. Now we'll take her in and show her to your mother. I know she'll love her.'

And Mother did. She fussed over her and fed her the best of everything. She made a bed for her in the kitchen and went down to her if she heard her whimpering in the night. She scolded her whenever she made a puddle and forgave her long before she finished mopping it up. And she had no control over her whatsoever.

Sadie set about enjoying her new life at Maywood as soon as she arrived. She wanted to make friends with every creature and was often puzzled when her lively displays of affection were not always reciprocated. In fact they seldom were and from the very first she fell foul of Mrs P.P.

The old hen had been strolling across the yard, pecking at anything that looked like food and watching us from the corner of her eye as we arrived carrying Sadie. And when Jean dashed off to leave, late for her work and waving 'see you tomorrow', Mrs P.P.

had found a warm patch of sun, out of the wind against the wall beside the back door. She was resting gently, her crop full and puffed up so that her beak nestled in the feathers and she had a job to keep her eyes open.

Of course she was a sitting target. Sadie, all legs and waving tail, bounded out of the back door on her first journey of discovery. She caught wind of the old hen before she'd gone a dozen yards. She stopped in her tracks, turned, and with tail going wild and ears pricked forward as best she could, she hurried towards the crouching bundle of feathers, her retriever instinct telling her to investigate.

For a few tense seconds Mrs P.P. remained motionless. She watched the puppy but couldn't believe she would dare to approach *her*, the undisputed boss of the backyard. But when it became obvious that her position was to be challenged, she rose slowly to her most important height, raised the feathers on her neck into a shaggy brown ruff and delivered a vicious peck right on Sadie's exploring nose. The puppy squealed, pulled her tail between her legs and scurried back to cower beneath the kitchen table, yelping with horror. Mrs P.P. settled back to enjoy the sun, crooning crossly.

Sadie was to get her own back on Mrs P.P. eventually. Meanwhile she treated her with great respect, giving her a wide berth, holding her head away and looking out of the corner of her eye as she growled her dislike. But the other chickens were fair game. They, poor fools, scattered whenever she bounded towards them and provided fine, fluttering targets for her to retrieve. The cockerels lost a great deal of their dignity as they were forced from their strutting postures into long-legged escape. And the hens became thoroughly confused, wondering who was chasing whom and ending up by squatting because it was easier to submit to the copulation they expected than get tired out with running. And Sadie would pounce with glee when one stopped in her path, grab it by the neck in her soft jaws and heave it across the yard to the back door with a fine show of importance. If I happened to be around she got a cuff and abuse for her performance and would look at me apologetically, feathers sticking to her tongue and wondering where she'd gone wrong. So she used to try to retrieve to Mother whenever she could because then all she got was: ''Urr! Drop it, you naughty girl,' and there was the chance of a fine tussle, with a bit of side-stepping and playful growling, before she would let Mother take the chicken and send her squawking back to join her mates.

By some miracle of nature she never harmed any of her captives, apart from depriving them of a few feathers and giving them the shock of being dragged off by a slobbering grip round the neck, just when they'd been expecting a peck and a pounce from a cock.

With the cows it was a very different story. When Sadie first appeared in the meadow, straggling along behind me as she learnt to walk on a lead, they bore down on her with a frightening commotion as soon as they spotted her. She cowered against me while they formed a blowing circle, stretching their necks down and creeping forwards as they tried to make up their minds about her. She sat bolt upright, ears back and the whites of her eyes flashing as she looked from one staring face to the other.

'They're only cows,' I assured her. 'They won't hurt you. They're only trying to be friends,' I lied.

She replied to my voice with a quiver and Daisy gave an extra loud snort and took another step forward. This was more than Sadie could stand, and she gave a single, staccato yap, which sent the cows backing away in perplexity. And she was quick to spot her advantage, making a little dash to the end of the lead and barking boldly. The cows tossed their heads, 'so, just another dog' and turned to go about their business.

Henry sized up the new arrival from the tops of walls and fences for the first few days. He sat hunched up, watching her scurrying movements through the yards and buildings. He saw her taste the water in the pond, lapping noisily while her feet sank into the mud and the water rose to her belly. He watched her sample a piebald lump of chicken dung, have a quick bark at Brutus under the rails of the bullock lodge and scarper with her tail between her legs when he charged. When he lost sight of her, Henry stretched up and flowed down the wall, across the yard and up to the roof of the pig sties in one lazy movement. He sat bolt upright and looked down disapprovingly as Sadie snuffled about the midden, paddling paw-deep in the ooze beside it, scrambling on to it and rolling in it because the rich smell excited her. She tumbled down again and had a long, hard stare at Skinny and Fatso as they grazed across the meadow, both very pregnant now and moving solemnly. Some instinct warned her against pushing under the gate to go and have a word with them and instead she turned, sniffing the air because she caught a whiff of Henry, perched high above and glaring down at her. She barked up at him but he just blinked his superiority.

This study of Sadie's movements went on for several days, whenever Henry chose to visit the farmyard. He introduced himself to her slowly, making quite sure she noticed him, but keeping just out of reach whenever she jumped up to where he was sitting and snuffled at him. Once, when she almost unseated him, he gave her a sharp one-two which sent her yelping across the yard. But gradually they got to know each other without engaging in any set battles. They never became bosom pals. There was just a polite passing of the time of day whenever they met, a ritual sniff under the tail, and off they went their separate ways.

As Sadie grew up, so her fears of Mrs P.P. became less. They were forced to share the same backyard and gradually Sadie became bolder, walking nearer to the old hen in passing, sometimes even standing to face her and waving her tail slowly as she tried to make up her mind if it would be safe to take a step closer. Sometimes she became so exasperated that she lowered her head between her paws, starting to prance and to bark as she tried to pluck up courage to move to the attack.

But Mrs P.P. always stood her ground. She knew better than to back away. She had seen what happened to the other foolish hens who allowed themselves to get caught and anyway she had already established her position. She need do no more than raise her ruff, swear a little and fix the bitch with her beady eyes.

Probably this state of affairs would have gone on indefinitely if Mrs P.P. had not had a bit of bad luck. Just as she was facing up to a passing, prancing, barking attack from Sadie, I happened to startle her by swooping into the yard on my bike. And Sadie immediately presumed this was a flank attack from an ally and moved in, while the concentration vanished from Mrs P.P.'s stare.

She was bound to retreat. Away she went, cackling alarmingly, rolling as she ran and with Sadie in hot pursuit. She swept up beside the pond and as Sadie took a snap at her and feathers flew, she rose into the air with a frantic flapping. This was the first time I had ever seen her really airborne and she was so startled at her achievement that she lost all sense of direction and was forced to ditch in the pond. She landed with a great bow wave and already I was wondering how the devil I was going to rescue her without actually diving in myself.

Sadie had gone mad. She was rushing up and down the bank, barking wildly and splashing into the water, but only daring to go in tit-deep.

And as the water stilled around her, Mrs P.P. regained all her customary composure. She sailed the ripples like a galleon, apparently enjoying the cruise, looking from side to side as she moved sedately across the water and landed on the other side.

18

THE COWS RESPONDED to the spring grass with a welcome increase in their milk yield. Soon they were lying out day and night and when we brought them into the shed for milking, the air filled with the sweet smell of clover and regurgitated grass. They belched contentedly, their udders were hot and heavy and their dung ran from them and flew about like bursting fireworks when it hit the concrete floor.

I had decided to have the cows tuberculin tested. In those days, if you could establish a T.T. herd, in which all cows and young stock were tested and proved free of tuberculosis twice a year, and your dairy and cowshed conformed to prescribed standards of design and cleanliness, then it was worth another fourpence a gallon on the price you received for your milk. It was well worth having a go at, particularly as stock from a registered T.T. herd also commanded a higher price in the special sales reserved for such animals.

So I filled in all the forms, had the buildings passed as suitable and received notification as to when to have the cows and young stock tied up and ready for the vet to carry out the testing.

The cows didn't take too kindly to the idea. Paul Hastings was coming at ten o'clock and this meant they only had a couple of hours in the meadow after morning milking before we had to drive them back to the shed again. And cows dislike having their routine upset. When it was time for milking one of us had only to go to the gate and call and the cows would already be on the alert and amble off down to the cowshed by themselves, each to her own stall and wait to be tied up. But asking them to come in again at any other time created a great deal of confusion.

We tried to drive them and they looked at us as though we were mad, doubling back on their tracks whenever possible. It took brandished sticks and threatening shouts to keep them moving with reluctant steps towards the gateway. As usual they all waited for Lotty to go first and she sauntered into the gateway and immediately turned on them all, scattering them with threatening gestures. She refused to move on through the gate however loudly we shouted and swore at her until, in the end, Bert had to drive her off on her own, keeping her moving in the lead.

By the time we had them all tied up they were thoroughly suspicious. Lotty bellowed once and peed and Daisy had a kick at thin air because she couldn't think of any other way to show annoyance at losing good eating time. The other cows shuffled about uneasily and when Paul arrived and breezed into the cowshed, they flicked their ears and eyed him anxiously.

He greeted us jovially, clipping a belt around his waist from which two automatic syringes hung like silver six-shooters. He had stripped off his pullover and now stood with his shirt unbuttoned and a notebook, a pair of curved scissors and some calipers protruding from his top pocket.

'Right! This won't take long.' He handed me the notebook. 'Will you write down each cow's name and age as we come to her, followed by the two numbers I shout out? Then Pete can work with me and hold any cow by the nose if she proves awkward.'

'What I got ter do, then?' Bert wanted to know, cheekily.

'Shut up and keep out of the way or I'll test you too.' Paul flicked a syringe from his belt and advanced towards Bert, who laughed and put up his hands in mock surrender, while Pete urged Paul to prick the little bugger just to keep him quiet.

Paul started at the far end of the shed. He moved up to Blackie's head and clipped the hair in two small patches on the side of her neck. With the calipers he measured the thickness of the skin in each place and called the numbers out to me. First with one automatic syringe and then the other, he injected a regulated amount of each type of tuberculin, avian into the top patch and bovine below. By the comparison of any swellings that may occur, when he measured them on his return in two days time, he could tell whether any cow had reacted to the test.

He worked quickly, pushing up between each cow, clipping,

measuring and injecting, and running his hand down her back as he moved round behind her to get to the next one. The cows waiting their turn were watching every move, rolling their eyes and flicking their ears each time he called out the numbers. He was getting through them famously and each cow was behaving herself and keeping still so that Pete had nothing to do.

Paul finished Bambi and she shook her head and rattled her chain as though to say: 'That wasn't so bad, after all.'

He moved up to Bluebell and she shuffled her back legs nervously as he clipped at the hair on her neck. Her ears went back and she jerked slightly as he clicked each syringe and she felt the slight prick.

'Only one to go,' he said, looking at Lotty as she turned to stare at him. 'And you can keep those horns to yourself, old girl.' He was trying to outstare her as he ran his hand down Bluebell's back to pass round behind her. He was so busy staring at Lotty that he didn't notice Bluebell's slowly raising tail. And just as he passed behind her, and I shouted 'Look out!' she shat and coughed at the same time. A hot streak of dung shot out with great force and hit Paul slap in the chest.

He swore with feeling and turned to face me, bending forwards with his arms held away from his sides. The dung trickled warmly down inside his shirt, bulging it out as it gathered to seep inside his trousers. I had to laugh and in a moment a smile crept over his dung-spattered face and he joined in.

'I've had ever so many near misses,' he said, ruefully, wiping the dung from his face with the back of his hand, 'but that's the first time I've really caught a packet.'

'You certainly got it fair and square, I must say,' I laughed. 'I should think the best thing we can do is to hose you down.'

Pete and Bert gathered round and watched with concern as he undid the lower buttons of his shirt, pulled it gingerly from his trousers and deposited a dollop of dung at his feet.

'Buggered if you didn't arf cop it,' Bert said, seriously. And I think he really did feel sorry for Paul.

'Well the best thing you can do is get me a bucket of water and I'll start with that,' Paul replied.

But he ended up in the bath indoors. And when he departed he was wearing a change of my clothing while his own sat in a soggy heap in the boot of his car.

He returned mine to me when he came back two days later to

read the results of the tuberculin test. And fortunately there were no reactors. I was the pleased possessor of a T.T. herd, worth an extra seven shillings a day in the milk they were producing.

As the cows chewed their way through one meadow and moved on to the next, so we drove the ewes and lambs in to follow them. They liked to eat behind the cows. They nibbled and trimmed the ragged ends of grass and set about the dark green patches around the cow pats with relish. It is strange how grazing animals will clear up behind each other and yet leave the surrounds of their own dung severely alone.

It took a long time to drive the ewes and lambs along the lane. The families just would not stick together. There was a continuous coming and going as lambs got lost, bleating, running and quivering, trying to locate a mother's call among the throaty chorus. And just as there was general reunion and rejoicing as they all started to move forward again while we urged them from behind, another lamb would decide it was feed time and bunt at its mother ferociously until she stopped. The others piled up behind her and there was chaos again.

Most days Bill Checksfield cycled out to look at the flock. And he insisted on presiding over the tailing and castrating of the lambs. In no time at all, as it seemed, the lambs had grown sturdy from the timid toddlers fighting for life in the snow. Now they were cheeky, full of energy, warring gangs of woolly daredevils, racing, chasing, jumping and driving their mothers to distraction. It seemed a pity to have to deprive them of their wriggling tails, which tossed and flew in the crazy games. But tails got plastered with dung and dung attracted the blow-flies.

In the spring and summer blow-flies were a buzzing menace to the sheep. What better place for them to jettison their eggs than in the warm, dung-moist wool around the sheep's backside? Even though we 'dagged' the ewes before the early grass made them loose in spring, clipping the wool away around their rectums so that their dung could pass freely to the ground and they presented a less tempting nest to the searching blow-fly, some still got struck. We looked for the signs every day; for the ewe that walked and screwed her hips suddenly; for the one that tossed her head to one side and bit at the air; for the tell-tale wet patch in the wool. And we penned them in the corner and waded amongst them to catch those that had been struck by the blow-fly and drag them to the outside to deal with them. If you were lucky you caught the trouble in its early stages, when the maggots were small and still squirming on the surface. A quick dollop of Jeyes solution and a scratch with the rim of a penny sent them flying in all directions to die in the grass. But more often than not the ewe only told you of her trouble when she began to feel pain. By then the maggots had burrowed deep and grown fat. They had worked their way under the skin and mined squirming tunnels into the flesh, with a stench of decay. Now the treatment took longer and the ewe struggled, kicked and flicked her lips with her tongue as you probed to clean out and dress the wound, leaving a bare patch, bereft of wool, spoiling the fleece and a target for sucking, irritating flies.

So it was better to deprive the lambs of their tails and reduce the area of attack from the blow-fly.

We erected a pen of hurdles in the corner of the meadow and drove the ewes and lambs inside. We found stones and wood and soon we had a bright fire burning a few yards away. Over the make-shift hob we placed wedge-shaped tailing irons, that Boney Jackson made and sold as a sideline, and left them to grow red hot.

Checky had managed to borrow some bloodless castrators. They were like extra large pincers, shining chromium and with black handle grips. They were so designed that when they were in position and squeezed, they squashed the cord leading from each testicle without breaking the skin of the scrotum. It was a much quicker and cleaner way of castrating than cutting out each testicle, but not completely foolproof. Sometimes a cord survived and then you had a rig, prancing and riding and getting up to mischief.

I tested the irons from the fire and they seared into a log and sent a column of blue smoke hissing upwards. I pushed them back among the crackling flames and we were ready to begin.

Checky rolled himself a fag and held his head back as he lit it from a burning stick. He opened and shut the castrators, chuckling and blowing sparks as he advanced towards Pete.

Pete backed away. 'Now then, don't mess about. You ain't safe with them things!'

'Better start catchin' the lambs then,' Checky said, 'save me tryin' 'em out on you.'

The boys grabbed a lamb each and brought them over, bleating in their arms. Checky and I stood behind an upturned apple box on which I had placed a flat sheet of iron to serve as an operating table. Bert came first, grappling awkwardly with the lamb.

'Sit it on the box and grab hold of its hind legs.' It was surprising how big the lamb had grown. It was bleating and struggling, pushing its head up under Bert's chin as he bent forward and dumped its backside on the box. 'That's it,' I told him, 'now hold its hind legs tight and pull them up out of the way. Fine. . . . It's a ram. . . . You go first, Checky.'

The old man coughed and blew along his fag as he bent forward and grabbed the woolly scrotum with his thick fingers. He pulled at it until he was sure the testicles were down and held them firmly in the palm of his hand as he worked the jaws of the castrators behind, so that they gripped the top of the scrotum between his fingers and the belly. Slowly he squeezed them shut and they bit into the cord with a squeak. He continued squeezing until the final pressure locked the handles. He released them and slid the jaws over to bite into the other cord. When he had finished he fumbled along the red weals he'd left to satisfy himself that each cord was flattened

He straightened his back slowly and nodded to me. 'That'll stop 'im ramming. Should do, anyway. But I never do feel sure o' these pinchers. 'Tain't like seeing the bollocks come right out. Then you'm sure.'

I pulled an iron from the fire. 'You'll find they'll work all right. So will this iron, I'll bet.' I held the lamb's tail flat on the metal sheet so that the inside was facing upwards. The wool ended a little way from the root and there was an area of soft, white skin leading up to the rectum, which was pinching shut like pink, pursed lips. 'Hold him tight now,' I warned, as I pushed the red hot iron on to the skin and pressed down as it severed its way through and the tail came away. The smoke of burning flesh mixed with the acrid stench of smouldering wool and caught in my throat. The lamb had remained quiet and only its little tongue darted out and licked its nose as it stared at me. Maybe it just felt numb. Or perhaps we had shocked it into silence.

Bert started to release it. 'Wait! Hold on a tick,' I said. As he moved the lamb a spurt of blood shot out from the stump of the tail, curving and splashing down on the box. I held the iron against it until it sealed. Then Bert let the lamb go and it took off across the meadow with a frantic bleating, stopped when it realised it was all on its own and came back to join in the general chorus of complaint.

We worked our way steadily through the lambs and the pile of tails grew in a slithering heap beside the box. The lambs milled around outside the pen still holding their mothers, telling of their ordeal in a unison of grievance. Some of their tails had bled through the cauterization. The blood had dripped and congealed in the wool of their hind legs before clotting over. All being well, healthy scabs would form on all the stubs and drop off naturally in time, leaving clean, pink ends curtained in wool.

The ewes became tired of answering their lambs. Now and then a deep voice joined in with the high pitched hubbub, but for the most part they took the opportunity of catching up on cud chewing, so that when one did baa it gurgled like a deep throated gargle. They stamped, jostled, flicked their ears and rolled their eyes, but their jaws went non-stop from side to side.

When we had finished and let the ewes out there was pandemonium. Lambs darted about, often making for the first udder within diving distance. But each ewe knew her own lambs in an instant and sneak thieves were ruthlessly discarded with a quick side step and a bunt up the backside. But when they did sort themselves out, the ewes with twins were nearly lifted off their feet as udders were attacked from both sides. And as the lambs dropped to their knees and the milk flowed, it looked as though they found it easier to wriggle a stub than a long tail.

Summer

19

BY THE MIDDLE of June the fields of grass we had saved for hay were ready for cutting. Between one visit to the fields and the next, less than a week later, the grass had rushed up as fiercefully and forcefully as weeds. Tall stems of ryegrass, cocksfoot, timothy and fescue jostled and shone with washed green and the tiny tassels of brown flowers clung and quivered from the forming seeds. Below them was a damp jungle of twisted leaves and creeping vetches in trails of bright blue. Bursting heads of purple clover rose from broad leaves, pushing up with the stems of buttercups on which the occasional, waxy flower remained. And when I took a few paces into the grass and bent down to part the jungle, then I found the small heads of the Kent wild white clover, and the bright yellow trefoil, with little tints of red as though it had been spattered with blood.

Already the bolder farmers had started to cut their hay, judging the wind and the swirl of the clouds and deciding they could rely on a string of fine days ahead. I prepared to follow their example, sharpening the knives of the mower and feeding the old cogs with oil. I began to try to wind life into the racalcitrant old tractor.

I was sweating at the heavy starting handle, taking a breather every now and then to alter the choke a fraction, or fiddle with the notches of the throttle as I tried to persuade the thing to fire. It had seen better days but I doubt whether it had ever been a first-time starter. I often wondered how many back-breaking hours had been spent in goading it into action. There was never any apparent reason why it should not start. It just seemed to glower at me and expect me to exert my fair share of toil before it would play its part.

Even on this warm, June afternoon it was proving as stubborn as ever.

I sat down on one of the front wheels to regain my breath after a particularly energetic twirl at the starting handle. And I heard the smooth purr of Margaret's Humber as it came gliding down the lane. She saw me as she drove by and waved gaily before pulling up. She was out of the car before I had started down the lane towards her. She was wearing a sleeveless, button through dress with precious little underneath it, judging by the way every part of her appeared to be bouncing as she came striding to meet me.

'Hello! Jolly glad I found you here,' she greeted me. 'Thought I was going to have to search you out across the farm. Too hot for that.' She laughed comfortably.

'I'm just on my way to start cutting the hay, as a matter of fact, as soon as the tractor and I reach agreement.'

'That's just what I've come to see you about. How did you guess?' She laid her hand on my arm and squeezed gently. I found myself tending to draw away as she went on: 'I'd like us to get together over the haymaking.' She sounded as though she was hatching an assignation. 'Pool our resources, what? You could bring your tractor and mower to cut my grass. Then your waggons and Colonel and the boys when the hay's ready to carry. And you can have my man, Percy, and Dolly and the waggon to help you with yours. You know how expert Percy is at building a hay rick and, of course, I'll come along and help as well. I simply adore helping with the hay.' She laughed and swung her arms as though she was using a pitchfork. The button holding her dress above her bosom threatened to give. 'Many hands make light work, what? What d'you say?'

'Okay. Fine. Sounds a good idea.' I had twice as much hay to carry as she did. The arrangement suited me very well and would enable us to speed up the job considerably. 'What about old Jack?' I asked. 'He always reckons to be one of the gang at hay and corn harvest. He'll have to come and I suppose it'd be best if we each paid him according to the hours he put in for each of us.'

Her face fell and she sighed. 'Oh dear, do we really have to have that terrible old reprobate?'

I shrugged. 'He's not so bad. But we do really need four on the waggons, two pitching and one loading in the field while the fourth unloads at the rick. That leaves Percy to build the rick and you could help by pitching the hay across to him. So we need Jack to make up the four. We really need a full gang. Saves so much time and time's precious when the weather's right. I know he's slow and cunning. But we make him load the waggons and we keep pitching hay at him, so he has to work or else fall off.

She smiled at that. Then she said: 'But Percy finds it rather difficult to get on with him. We had Jack up to help us last year, you know, and all last winter Percy was blaming him because there were so few pheasants and partridge about. Poor Percy does so love to go shooting in the winter and there was really very little for him to shoot *at*, poor dear. Only rabbits and really one gets rather tired of rabbits. Percy's convinced Jack took the opportunity of spying out the land while he was with us.'

I laughed. 'Really? I didn't think he got all the way over to your place poaching.'

'Well, of course, one must be fair, mustn't one? And Percy's never actually *seen* him. But you know how it is, "give a dog a bad name" and all that.'

'More likely the bad weather thinned the birds out last winter. Jack's okay really.' I laughed. 'I have to get on with him anyway, being the boys' father.'

She nodded and clasped her hands behind her back. The top button took the strain again. 'Well, I suppose Percy will just have to put up with him. Oh, by the way, how much do you pay Jack for working for you?'

'The going rate. One and fourpence halfpenny an hour, I think it is.'

'Yes, that's what I thought. But d'you know what he charged me last year? One and sixpence! And when I questioned him about it he said he always charged one and six an hour for his time because it was easier reckoning.'

I laughed loudly. 'The old devil! You've got to hand it to him!' I turned back towards the tractor, anxious to get on with the work and escape any more suggestions. 'Anyway, that's settled then. It's a good idea and it'll help speed up the haymaking all round. Now I really must get on or we'll waste all this lovely weather. Mother's in the garden if you want to see her. She's still trying to produce order out of chaos.'

Margaret laughed. 'Oh well, I'll just go and have a quick word or two with her.' She waved and went and I felt a trifle guilty at burdening Mother.

The cutting of the grass went well. The mower was a horse-drawn model, converted to work behind a tractor by the substitution of a short drawbar in place of the shafts, and an alteration to the lifting gear so that it could be operated from the tractor when turning at the corners. An old iron seat stuck up at the back of the mower and two fifty-six pound weights were lashed to this in place of a driver's backside, so that the drive wheel gripped and the knife bed ran level without the fingers digging into the ground. It chattered along, the fingers thrusting under the thick mat of grass and the long knife flashing to and fro between them, toppling the tall stems so that they fell in level lines in a haze of pollen and shearing through the bottom so that it shivered up and curled over like a thick, green fleece.

As I droned round and round the field, leaving the neat swathes shining and starting to shimmer in the hot sun, I wondered at the havoc I was causing among the creatures that had found a home in the quiet, green jungle. Sometimes the little dry bundle of a field mouse's nest was left lying like an onion on the swathe, and I imagined the hurry and scurry as suddenly their whole damp, dark world changed into an open baking prairie. Rabbits waited and watched, clinging to the cover, breaking new trails as they pushed into the diminishing jungle, only to find it came to an abrupt end with a long run to the cover of the nearest hedge, a run impeded by the shimmering swathes and open to the eyes of all their enemies. Before the field was completely cut they had to take the plunge, leaping and swerving to safety, legs a whirl, tails flashing white signals in the sunlight. They were lucky because there was nobody there to shoot them.

But one was out of luck. He listened to the circling roar of the tractor and each time it came close to him he crouched out of sight in the cover and waited for it to pass. But he never reckoned on the chattering knife, protruding from the deafening roar, and in an instant it sliced off his four legs and he was on the swathe, scrambling to run and finding he couldn't move far on bleeding stubs. I stopped the tractor and went to catch him and he squealed with terror because he couldn't get away and he knew I was going to kill him.

We were lucky with the weather. The hay dried well and old Colonel had to work hard pulling the hay turner. For the first two or three rounds of a field he stepped out with a will, with Bert perched high on the seat, flapping the reins and shouting encouragement above the rattle of the spinning tines as they gathered the swathes into airy rows of fluffed up hay. But gradually Colonel's pace became slower and slower and shouts and threats and slaps with the reins had no effect. In the end Bert was forced from his seat and when he grabbed the old horse by the bridle and led him along the rows, he responded and plodded along just fast enough to make the turner work. I suppose he didn't see why he should walk while Bert rode.

When Percy arrived from Brenchwood Hall leading the grey mare, Dolly, hitched to a waggon, Colonel was forced to take a more lively interest in the haymaking. Dolly was a particularly randy mare. She seemed to spend her whole life only just off the boil and was whipped into a heat at the first swish of another horse's tail. Although Colonel was an old gelding, with bones projecting gauntly and a dusting of white over face and muzzle, cut in the first flush of his distant youth and probably with never a thought of sex entering his old head since, Dolly found him extremely attractive.

We had started on the first hayfield, pitching great fluffy fork-fulls up to Jack on the waggon. Colonel stood in the shafts with his head bowed, occasionally flicking his ears and swishing his tail at the flies, leaning slowly on the traces and moving on a few yards at a time when we clicked him forward between the rows. The boys took a great delight in trying to drown their father in hay, pitching it at him from both sides, calling up to him: 'Here's one fer the middle, Jack,' or again, 'Wants some on the front corner, Jack,' or, 'You ain't arf drawin' it in on the arse end,' and the little old man would stamp up and down the load, trying to create some sort of order in the piles of hay flowing up to him, desperately hoping to make the load secure because he knew the ridicule he would receive if the hay fell off on the bumpy route to the stack-plat.

Dolly caught sight of Colonel the moment she came into the field, with the empty wagon rattling behind her. She whinnied a greeting, delighted to see him as he raised his head and looked round, blowing a half-hearted acknowledgment through quivering nostrils. Percy was leading her and she came forward at a brisk walk, her head high so that he had to stretch to hold her bridle and her tail was swishing with excitement.

'Whoa, me old beauty, hold hard, hold hard.' Percy tried to control her as he drew alongside our waggon.

'That ol' sod hossin' again, is 'er?' Jack wanted to know from the top of the load.

'It's ol' Colonel set 'er orf, I do believe,' Percy exclaimed as he tried to quieten the mare. 'Allus the same 'er is when 'er spots another horse.' He was talking to me and had ignored Jack.

'Must want 'er eyes testin' if ol' Colonel excites her,' Pete observed.

Percy turned to me. 'The Madam's arrived,' and I knew he was referring to Margaret and not Dolly. 'Shall us take the full load back now and make a start with the rick?'

We flung a rope over the load and Jack slithered down it, walking away a short distance and gazing up at his handiwork as we pulled the rope tight and fastened it.

Bert watched him. 'He thinks 'ees done a good job. Lucky if that lot gets down to the stack-plat without comin' orf,' he decided.

'You boys don't give him a chance the way you pitch up at him,' I suggested.

'Got ter keep the ol' bugger workin', Pete laughed from behind the load.

Dolly was standing a few yards away from Colonel, blowing and nodding her head, continuously rattling her bit. I don't know what she had been saying to him, but it must have been very complimentary because the old horse strained forward quite eagerly when I held his bridle and clicked my tongue. And he pulled the heavy waggon across the field and down to the farm as though he had shed ten years.

Margaret was waiting to greet us in the stack-plat. She was wearing a pair of pale blue, pleated shorts, fortunely of a generous cut, a sleeveless blouse filled to the limit and a huge straw hat. Her legs were bare except for ankle socks under her sandals and I wondered how she would react to the first bunch of thistles that came her way, hidden in a heap of hay.

'Here comes the first load of summer,' she greeted me, with a large red smile as I led Colonel, puffing and snorting into the stack-plat. 'Isn't this weather simply splendid?' She came over and patted the horse's neck. 'We'll soon have all the hay made in fine style if this keeps up, don't you think? I say, poor old Colonel, you *are* whacked, aren't you?'

'He's no fool,' I said, 'he knows he's got to keep a load of hay rolling once he starts for home. It's easier to take it at a rush than a plod. Now he know's he's got a nice long breather while we unload.' I was pulling the rope off the load and coiling it. Soon I climbed the ladder and sank knee-deep in the hay. 'All ready below?' I called and sent the first forkful sailing down in the direction of Margaret's wide hat.

We had already formed the foot of the rick with old brushwood and straw to keep the hay from spoiling when the ground became wet. Now Percy began to build on the foundation, a stalk of hay in his mouth, cap pushed back and the long muscles bulging along his arms. Each movement was easy and flowing as he rolled and levered the hay into position with his pitchfork, caressing it and coaxing it as he slowly worked his way round and round as the loads came in, forming the rick into the classic shape from the narrow base, swelling outwards and upwards to the eaves and then drawing in up the steep roof to the ridge. His easy, seemingly effortless movements were in sharp contrast to Margaret's labour. She tried very hard. She prodded into the hay I pitched to her, straining and heaving to get it across to Percy. Whereas he held his pitchfork lightly, twisting and lifting so that it was just an extension of his hands and his body remained upright, she gripped hers as though she was about to charge, burying it deep into the hay, using her whole large body to lift a large load and coming away with a jerk and a tuft on the end of her fork and a loud laugh. But she improved as time passed and loved every sweating moment of it.

On the first day Margaret brought a picnic tea for us all. She called it her treat and she kept looking forward to it throughout the labours of the afternoon. She consulted her watch, wondering when we should knock off every time an empty waggon was drawn away and a full one took its place, while I climbed up on it and the endless hay came tumbling towards her again. Towards milking time Percy and I gave in to her and she hurried down the ladder, deciding we should eat in the hayfield and Percy was sent to bring the food from the back of the Humber.

He came with outstretched arms, clasping the huge basket and Margaret spread a cloth on the ground and detailed where each of us should sit around it. She unpacked triangular sandwiches of lettuce, cucumber, egg and tomato, cut and decrusted with loving care by Percy's wife, and which she decorated with sprigs of parsley as she laid them out. There was a bowl of stray lettuce leaves, a plate of rock buns and several bottles of ready-diluted lemonade. It was all so formal that Pete thought it only right he should eat with delicate bites and a crooked little finger. Bert sniffed and chewed with his mouth open, smirking behind his hand at the primness of it all whenever he caught Pete's eye. Jack looked at no one, opened his mouth like a cod and devoured complete sandwiches one after the other. Margaret sat cross-legged, thighs bulging, beaming at us all from under her huge hat, assuring us what fun it all was, how much we all deserved it after our hard work and urging us to eat up because she didn't want to take any back home. Not that there was any fear of that. It took more than neat sandwiches and rock buns to satisfy appetites and when Margaret swished off home, waving and calling that she would help again tomorrow, Bert turned to Pete with a cackle, wondering aloud what their Mum had got for their tea. At least Pete had the grace to call him an ungrateful, greedy sod.

It was during haymaking that milking the cows was a real curse. Every moment of the dry, hot days was precious in the laborious struggle to gather the hay while the weather stayed fine. I be-grudged the time taken in the cowshed. We always had to break off just when the hay was best for carrying, when it was hot and lively before the evening dew began to dampen the crackle and soon the airy pitchfork loads became leaden. But we were slaves to the cows. It was for them that we laboured with the hay anyway. But they gathered at the gate and bellowed across to us when we were late and Bert would be sent off grumbling to make a start, with the assurance that we would join him soon. It was then that Margaret and Percy left us each day to return to the Hall because Percy also had milking to do. And I know Margaret had had enough by that time and was only too anxious to bathe the blisters on her hands and put soothing cream on the scratches on her legs. But she came every day without fail. And although she ended up wearing gloves and slacks, she stuck it to the bitter end and I'm sure she lost several pounds in the process.

Jean came to help us in the evenings, driving straight from work and joining us in the fields. It was then that we pitched high loads on the waggons, filling them until the hay became too damp to handle, and riding on them back to the stack-plat, to be unloaded in the morning while the dew was drying in the field.

This was the best time. The soft evenings when we sat beneath the towering rick, easing our aching limbs and feeling the glow of relaxation and the happiness of work accomplished and friendly faces.

The horses were unhitched and unharnessed, their bellies full of stolen hay as they walked off side by side, tails swishing at the flies that never rested and they went off to graze and laze through the warm summer night.

We had cool cider in a stone jar and sandwiches, thick chunks of new bread clasping slices of home-cured ham, lying in a heap in a white cloth between us. Rose came down the lane in search of Pete because it was courting time. She joined us with a shy, 'I don't mind' when invited and she sat down coyly and Pete pretended not to notice her although she sat right beside him. She said, 'I don't mind' again when Jean offered her a sandwich and again when I suggested she had a mug of cider. She had grown out of last year's summer frock and her breasts stretched to greet me as she reached for the mug. Pete was lounging back against the hay rick, his beret far back on his head, his strong teeth biting into a sandwich and his eyes hungrily following the curve of her thigh.

We talked lazily, quietly and once Bert giggled with a tale to tell about Dolly. It had to do with her heat and the cider made him talk even though the girls were there. The mare had kept swishing her tail, jerking the waggon instead of moving it steadily along the rows. Jack had fallen down on the load and sworn at her and Bert had prodded her rump with the handle of his pitchfork. Which had made her raise her tail expectantly and so he'd satisfied her by sliding the handle into her. She'd worked better after that.

Pete exploded and blew out breadcrumbs. Jack muttered into his third mug of cider. The drink was smouldering pleasantly in his thin belly. He had only half heard his son's rude tale but he grunted because his name had been mentioned. Rose giggled and reached for another sandwich and Jean caught my eye and blushed.

Slowly the sandwiches were finished and the jar of cider drained. The long evening stretched lazily around us, up into the wood beyond the stack-plat, where the bird song still echoed as each one declared sovereignty over branch and twig for the night; over into the pig meadow, where the sows could be heard making for their sties while their litters squabbled and fought and demanded a nightcap; out beyond the oast where the weary day was red-eyed with sleep and the cows would be blowing and sinking to their knees down by the stream.

It was after such a time that Mother joyfully declared she'd had a brainwave.

I looked at her across the breakfast table. She was sitting leaning on her elbows, clasping a cup of coffee in the palms of her hands. She always warmed her hands on her coffee, winter or summer, because her hands were always cold. So was her nose. 'Cold hands, warm heart,' she often said, and I'd reply, 'Cold nose, good health,' because both were true in her case.

'How sorry I am for people in stuffy old London on a lovely morning like this!' she declared.

I nodded in agreement, wondering what she was leading up to.

'I thought it'd be jolly if we asked some of the old Dulwich friends down for the day.' Her eyes were shining. 'What d'you think?'

'You mean the Crazy Gang, the Mothers' Union?' I ventured.

'Yes. Why not? Let's! I'm sure they'd simply love it. A day in the country and they could all see the farm. I've written and told so many of them about it and all the animals. You could introduce them to the cows. And perhaps the pigs – from a distance. We could have tea on the lawn. It would be a real country tea with clotted cream and jugs of warm milk straight from the cows. It'd be such fun.'

'Hey! Hang on a minute,' I was laughing at her enthusiasm. 'How d'you propose getting that bunch of old biddies *down* here?'

'Oh, we'll think of something.' She wrinkled her nose, frowning as she blew down it. Her face lit up again. 'We could hire a charabanc. An Orange Luxury Coach! I feel sure they've started operating again from Brixton now.'

And in a week she had it all arranged for the following Saturday. Down in the village the grocer and the baker had been alerted and special deliveries were ordered to arrive early on the morning of the visit.

In a weak moment Jean offered to help.

'Oh, would you, my dear? That'd be simply splendid. You *are* a brick.' Which made Jean curl with laughter because she'd never been likened to a house before.

She came early on the Saturday morning and Mother hurried out to meet her. 'I wonder, would you be a dear?' she greeted her, before Jean had a chance to get out of the van. 'I've forgotten all about the extra chairs and crockery. The Vicar said we could borrow them. They're in the village hall.'

Jean settled back behind the steering wheel again with a smile.

'Coo-cee!' Mother's voice came ringing across the yard to me. 'Jean's come. She's going to fetch the chairs and crockery. Can you help?'

So the rat catcher's van was pressed into service and half an hour later we were creaking back along the lonely lane, solid wooden chairs clinging desperately to the slim rope across the open back doors of the van, while I nursed a pile of plates and cups and saucers, slithering and sliding in sympathy with each corner.

I staggered into the kitchen expecting to dump them on the table. But the grocer and baker had got there first, evidently soon after Mother had decided there was just time to give all the brass and copper in the house a good shine and had piled it on the table. Golden loaves tumbled about among pots of jams, boxes of fancy cakes and packets of butter, biscuits, sugar and tea, while Mother slaved with black hands and flying hair, burnishing Swiss cowbells, chubby vases and curling candlesticks, all dotted about among the groceries.

'Ah, *just* finishing,' she greeted us. 'Plonk it down somewhere, there's a good boy. The more the merrier.'

I deposited the crockery with a clatter into the waiting arms of the old velvet chair. 'Hells bells!' I exclaimed, 'you *are* in a turmoil.'

'It's never as bad as it looks,' she assured me, with a glowing smile. She finished polishing a cowbell, held it aloft and shook it so that it gave tongue with a mournful clonking. She raised her head and sniffed. 'Heavens! Jean! The oven! The buns are done. Now *where* did I leave the oven cloth?'

Sadie had it under the table and was chewing it.

'You naughty girl!' Jean knelt down and grabbed one end. Which was just what Sadie was hoping she would do. She sprang into action with an excited bark, and her tail went wild as she growled in the first skirmish of what she hoped was going to be a long tug-of-war.

But I surprised her from behind by grabbing her waving backside. It wasn't really fair, two against one. She gave a yelp, lost the oven cloth and rolled her eyes at me as though I was a rotten spoil-sport.

'Come on, old lady,' I coaxed her. 'We're in the way here. Let's leave them to it. You can come and help me carry the chairs to the garden.'

'And don't forget the pigs, darling!' Mother called after me. 'You *will* make sure they're safely in the meadow, won't you?'

Now it was obvious that Skinny and Fatso had got wind that something out of the ordinary was afoot. I met them both strolling down from the stack-plat, testing the air with raised heads and shining snouts while their month old litters milled around. I guessed the bread van was responsible. Probably the baker had left the doors open while he filled his basket with the special delivery, and great waves of the glorious aroma that always surrounded country bread vans had wafted out on the hot morning air.

They stopped dead when they saw me. The litters moved in to attack the now stationary milk bars with mounting excitement.

'Now then, you two old sods,' I greeted them, 'where d'you think you're off to?'

They grunted and stared at me, unsure of the kindly tone in my voice. It could mean there was food about. It could mean I was after grabbing one of the piglets. It could also mean I was positioning myself to drive them back to the meadow. And they weren't too sure about Sadie either, although she was keeping well out of the way.

There was a hurried consultation of short grunts, increasing pandemonium from the piglets and the sows decided I couldn't be trusted. Best to push off while they still held the initiative. So they both ploughed through the piglets and made off in the direction of the pond, while their young flew after them screaming insults.

During this hot weather they spent most of their time round the pond, flopping about in the wallows they had dug for themselves in the shallows by the orchard. I walked after them and Sadie followed at a distance. She liked a quick romp among the piglets if she happened to find them on their own. It was fun making them scatter and then running round in short circles herself trying to decide which one to follow. But the sows – no, as always some instinct warned her to leave well alone.

She joined me when I stopped and she sat bolt upright, quivering as we watched the sows settle down to feed their litters at the water's edge. 'They'll be okay now,' I told her. 'It's going to be stinking hot again. They won't stray far from the pond.'

She looked up at me. With a quick movement I ruffled her ears and sprang away from her. 'Come on! Can't hang about! Work to do!' and she jumped up and licked my face and tore off for me to give chase.

Soon after two o'clock the coach came squeezing down the lane with a broad silver grin across its orange face. It scuffed the verge on either side and slim, overhanging branches tapped a welcome on the windows.

I spotted it as it rounded the final bend. I called a warning into the kitchen. As usual with Mother, preparations had been completed in the nick of time, she'd washed and changed into her best flowery, cotton dress and was now chasing the last stray hairs and spiking the final comb into place as she hurried across the yard.

The coach stopped opposite the gate with a sigh and anxious faces in the windows began to crease into hesitant smiles as they prepared to face the unknown.

Mother was waving gaily to the greetings being mouthed from behind the windows. 'Ah! There's Mrs Mabbs, *and* Mrs Dinkle. Hurrah! Hello, Mrs Capers, Mildred, Florrie, Mrs Blogs. Oh, and look! There's my little brown teapot!'

Jean was standing beside her, gazing up with her mouth open. 'Who?'

'That little circular woman, the one at the back, all in brown. I can never remember her name but she always reminds me of a little brown teapot.' Mother was walking forward again, calling out more names as she recognised faces.

Jean turned to me with a laugh. 'This is going to be a riot if they all go wandering round the farm. Can't you just imagine Lotty and Daisy charging up to see what's happening and sending them all flying?'

I could and I laughed. 'But it won't happen,' I said. 'My guess is they won't stir very far from the garden.'

One by one they climbed stiffly from the coach and spilled on to the road, all shapes and sizes, peering, chattering, waving, exclaiming.

'Coo, what a loverly old house!'

'Never thought we was going to get down the lane, did you, Ethel?'

'Real country smell, ain't it?'

'Oh, look! There's an old horse.'

'Ain't no bulls are there, ducks?'

There were handshakes, kisses, greetings and introductions to

Jean and I, and gradually we eased them across the yard and into the garden in a straggling gaggle of squeaking shoes, clasped handbags and sighs of wonder.

And then I spotted the two little boys, peering out from among the skirts, red faces bursting out of Sunday suits and tight collars, two coiled springs poised for release.

I caught Jean's eye and pointed. She spotted the boys and waved with a smile.

It was the merest excuse they needed to break ranks. In a moment they were through the undergrowth of skirts.

'That your 'orse, Mister?'

'Ain't 'e big? Like the coalman's horse.'

Colonel had been surveying the arrival from over the hedge, a benign expression on his old face as he nodded greetings. He was behaving as though this was a perfectly normal occurrence and now and then he gave a little blow which quivered his lips, because that was the nearest he could get to making polite conversation.

'What's 'is name, Mister?'

'Colonel.'

'That's a funny name for an 'orse. Can we have a ride?'

'C'mon, Tommy, race yer.'

And they were off up the lane to the gate like a couple of startled bantams, jackets undone and flying behind as little elbows pumped. There were two screams from among the women.

'Horace! Come back here this instant.'

'Tommy! Just you wait 'til I get me hands on yer.'

I laughed. 'Oh, let them run. They'll be all right. I'll give them a ride on the old horse. He won't hurt them.'

I ran after them through the gate, scooped them up and placed them, half protesting now, one behind the other along Colonel's protruding backbone.

The old horse was well aware that it was Saturday afternoon and had planned a quiet weekend to himself, after the bustle of haymaking and the persistent attentions of Dolly. He shook his head and blew hard as I reached for his forelock.

'Come on,' I urged him, 'just a short stroll, that won't hurt you.'

'Don't make 'im run, Mister,' came an anxious voice from above as soon as the rolling movement began.

'Go on, gee-up, gee-up,' called the other one, bouncing and jabbing with his little heels, 'let's have a gallop!' But he was up front and with a double handful of mane for security.

We went at a slow walk, stopping frequently at first for Colonel to complain that this really was asking too much. But when we turned back for home he increased his pace, nodding his head faster at the excited squeals behind him until, finally, he condescended to break into a trot for the last twenty yards or so.

The women were all safely corralled in the garden by the time we returned. Some were enthusing along the herbaceous border, which was now reaching its zenith with the flowers taking deep breaths of sunshine, gently linking arms and swirling with each other now that Mother had freed them from restriction. Some were grouped beneath the cherry tree, gazing up at the ripening fruit, unconsciously scaring off the thieving blackbirds and thrushes lurking in the hedgerows. Some had already collapsed on the chairs, comfortably overflowing them as they settled down to a good natter free from the cares of home, with thoughts of a tasty tea to come and a Talk thrown in for good measure.

Once through the gate I released Horace and Tommy. They flew off among the women like lambs looking for dams, bubbling to tell of their experience. But all they got for their enthusiasm was: 'Lor luv us, look at the state of yer, and 'ere we are only just got 'ere,' as both were unceremoniously upended while their mothers vainly brushed at Colonel's hairs, firmly embedded in the seats of their little Sunday suits.

I thought I had better make myself scarce. So I nipped round the back and found Jean in the kitchen. She was pulling the big, black village hall kettle over the stove with both hands. 'I hope this thing boils before tomorrow,' she laughed, when she saw me.

Order had been restored in the kitchen and now the table was neatly loaded with piles of shining crockery, plates of bread and butter, sandwiches, cakes and buns. There were several pots of strawberry jam and two large dishes of cream, scalded and set from a bucket of milk which Mother had commandeered early on the day before.

'They'll never eat all that,' I said.

'I expect they will.' Jean smiled. 'One of them's already told me they only had a snack on the way down.'

Her cheeks were flushed and she was looking happy. She had thrown herself into the spirit of things and I wanted to kiss her.

Just as I did so the little circular woman rolled into the kitchen. She smiled like a split orange and clasped her chubby hands. 'Oh, lovely. That's sweet, my dears. Don't let me interrupt. Now I just came in to see if there's anything I can do to help. My word! You have been busy. Doesn't it all look nice?'

Jean blushed and moved away from me. 'Everything's under control,' she said. 'It's really all ready except for boiling the kettle.'

The circular woman bustled round the table. I could see why Mother called her 'the little brown teapot'. Apart from her shape she was homely and oozed comfort. 'We don't want Mother doing any more, now do we? She's done quite enough already. She must spend the time talking to all her old friends. And I expect she'll give us one of her Talks too. We're all looking forward to that. Lovely they are. We've missed them since she's been down here. Now all we've got to do is make sure the kettle's bubbling so's we can start tea as soon as she's finished her Talk. After Mrs Capers has said a prayer or two, like. That's the way we run our meetings and I expect Mrs Mabbs and Mrs Dingle will come and help hand round. They usually do.'

So, I thought, she's going to take charge. The meeting had to run its proper course even though the members had been carted bodily into deepest Kent.

'Good,' I said. 'Well, a mothers' meeting is no place for me so I'll wish you luck and leave you to it. Perhaps Horace and Tommy would like to see the pigs.'

'Don't go far away,' Jean warned me. 'You know you're expected to produce that big jug filled with milk warm from the cows at the crucial moment, don't you?'

It was nearly two hours later when I did so. I was worn out and so was Sadie. So were the calves. So were the sheep. So were the pigs. But there was still plenty of life left in Horace and Tommy as they raced to and fro, brandishing sticks taller than themselves, helping Pete to drive the cows in for milking, urging them on as they shied at the big orange coach, with its snoring driver stretched across the back seat. I had removed their jackets and choking ties and done my best to keep them out of cow-pats and pig sties. But, alas, their shoes and legs were plastered because they had joined Sadie in chasing the piglets round the pond while the sows slumbered in their wallows. It wouldn't have been so bad if they'd left it at that. But when Skinny, and then reluctantly Fatso, roused up, shook the mud from their ears and took off after their young, the boys made straight for the wallows and squelched through them with shrieks of delight.

Jean came out to meet us and relieved me of the jug of milk. 'What on earth have you been up to?' she asked.

'We bin farmin', Miss,' Tommy said, proudly.

'It certainly looks like it. Whatever are your mothers going to say?'

'We can clean them up a bit,' I suggested, 'get the worst of it off. Can't really expect anything else, bringing them down to a farm in their best clothes.'

Sadie dragged past us into the kitchen and flopped down on the cool bricks with her tongue hanging out.

Little Brown Teapot bundled over, swept Horace into her arms and perched him on the side of the sink. 'Leave 'em with me,' she laughed, 'I'll clean 'em up and take 'em back to their mums. Little horrors. Still, what can you expect?'

Tea was under way and several volunteers were carting food and drink out to the garden. One stopped when she saw me: 'Are you going to show us the cows after tea?'

'Of course, if you want to see them. I thought we could all take a walk up to the cowshed before you have to leave.' I guessed that was as far as any of them would want to venture. And with the cows tied up it would be safer.

'Yes,' agreed another, 'we all want to see Popsi.' She hurried off with her tray of cups.

I raised my eyebrows at Jean, putting the finishing touches to Tommy's toilet. 'The Animal Talk had its premier today,' she explained. 'Jolly good it was too. Very moving.'

'Yes, *wasn't* it lovely?' Little Brown Teapot was guiding Horace into his jacket. 'What a time dear Popsi had with her calf. Oh, your mother does give such beautiful Talks, we all had a good cry.'

I laughed. 'Good. I'm glad. She spends hours trundling up and down the lawn with the roller rehearsing them.' I looked down at Horace and Tommy, now reasonably presentable and smelling less vile. 'We had a good time too, didn't we, boys?'

But they only grinned as I grabbed each one by the hand. They were both beginning to look decidedly drowsy. 'Come on, let's find your mums. And there's some strawberry jam and cream for tea, how about that?'

By the time tea was finished, and cleared away and washed up by a gang hand picked and directed by Little Brown Teapot, and the women were drifting through the gate into the yard, Horace and Tommy were sound asleep over their mothers' shoulders. Which was a pity because they would have enjoyed the impromptu send-off.

Mother stood in the middle of the yard, marshalling her friends, clapping her hands for attention. 'Now, before you all go, those of you who'd like to come and see the cows, follow me.' And she marched off out into the road to lead them past the coach and up to the cowshed.

When she rounded the back of the coach, to walk the narrow strip of road between it and the hedge, she stopped abruptly. 'Oh, dearie me!' Her eager followers cannoned into her with a variety of exclamations.

As I went to join them to find the trouble, I noticed that the coach was gently swaying. And then I saw Fatso, a filthy, mud-caked Fatso, grunting pleasantly as she used the front bumper as a back scratcher. Her litter had congregated round the front wheels, busy with their own little rubbing sessions and even as we looked, Skinny barged into view and flopped down in the shade of the coach, offering a revolting line of bespattered teats for the delectation of her clamouring young.

Well, it seemed a pity to disturb her. Even more so when Fatso's mob cottoned on and managed to floor her as well. And gradually all the women ventured forward, thronging with 'Ooh's' and 'Aah's' and 'Ain't they sweet'.

It would have been an anti-climax to have taken them to the cowshed after that. So when the sows strolled off with their satisfied litters, and the women started to climb sighing into the bus, I helped Pete drive the cows into the meadow beside them. And I singled out Popsi for them to see through the windows, while the other cows grouped round and solemnly stared back.

Mother waved until the coach had crawled out of sight. Then she turned and smiled. 'I'm so glad they came. They all told me how much they enjoyed it. What fun it's been.' And her eyes were brimming with tears.

20

SOON AFTER HAYMAKING was finished, after several of the matey, after-work get-togethers in the stack-plat, Pete and Bert began referring to Jean as 'your missus'.

During the idle conversation that accompanied milking on the hot afternoons throughout the harvest, one would ask: 'Your missus comin' tonight, is 'er?' Or, by way of casual information: 'Down the pub last night Charlie Miller said as how your missus has been out to 'is place seein' to the rats.'

One day I was feeling fractious. 'Why do you keep calling her my missus?' I asked.

There was a long silence, broken only by the pinging of the milk against the pails and the shifting of the cows, the sort of silence that goes with a sultry afternoon when it's too much effort to talk as well as work and think.

Eventually, Bert said: 'Well, 'er is, ain't 'er?'

'Not my missus. She's just a girl friend.'

Silence again. Then Pete insisted: 'Same thing. You be goin' steady so 'ers your missus. I be goin' steady with Rose, so 'ers my missus. Same thing.'

'But she's only your *missus* once you're *married*.'

The cows' heads stretched forward, their ears back, their eyes half closed as they chewed the cud. Now and then a tail curled up to flick a fly, draping over a back and stopping there, as though it was too much trouble to bring it down again. They weren't interested in anything but relaxing. The boys continued milking, keeping their thoughts to themselves. I knew perfectly well that it was customary for a teenage boy to refer to his girl friend as his 'missus'. It made him feel important among his pals, especially those without a girl friend. Obviously Pete and Bert were wondering why I'd disputed the term, and done so with a show of bad temper I didn't understand myself.

Pete finished the cow he was milking and stood up, banging his stool down against the wall. 'You goin' to *marry* her, then?'

Now it was my turn to be silent. Jean and I had never actually talked about marriage, although we'd got close to mentioning it at times. I liked to believe there was a sort of unspoken agreement between us that we'd be married one day. When the time was right. When the farm was paying. It was an event that would happen some time in the future. Meanwhile there was always so much work looming ahead and marriage was somewhere at the end of it, the light at the end of the tunnel, but with love all the way along through the darkness.

Eventually, I replied: 'Maybe.' And I buried my head in Popsi's flank and milked furiously.

The seed of the idea of marrying Jean had been sown during the snows of winter. In the dark comfort of the cowshed, with the hay wrapping us in a whispering warm couch, and the cows a belching background to our sighs, I began to believe that here was the girl I wanted for always. But I never got around to mentioning it to her. I'd often meant to, but it was always later than it should have been when we rose to go, still clinging in a long, last kiss, which continued as I tried to rub the strands of hay and piercing seeds from her coat.

She would break away and rummage in her pockets for her torch. 'Make sure you get it all off,' she'd say.

I'd shine the torch on her back, a harvest of hay clinging there, woven into the material so that every strand required individual extraction.

'Hurry up! Hell, look at the time! I'll be locked out.'

An ear peeping from her tousled hair would catch the light and look inviting. I'd take it in my lips and whisper: 'You ought to see your hair. I think a blackbird's started nesting in it.'

There would be a frantic search for a comb. Then sighs and squeals as it tore through the tangles. '*Why* do we always leave it so late? And this blesssed hay! After an evening with you I cart enough home in my clothes to keep a calf. It's all very well for you to laugh, but I spend hours picking up all the bits off the floor when I've got undressed so's Mrs Wilkes won't see.'

246

'Sod Ma Wilkes.'

'You don't have to face her.'

Often it would have been easy enough to have said: 'Marry me and then you won't have to face her any longer.'

But the words always remained unspoken in the rush to her van and the hurried, last tongue-peeping kiss through the window as she let out the clutch.

So the seed never managed to grow. And through the busy days of spring and summer, when the work seemed never ending, spilling into the lengthening evenings and swamping the time for loving, it had seemed there was always so much to be done before I'd be in a position to get married.

During the long twilights, when the hay, and then the corn had been gathered for the day, when the cider and the sandwiches were finished and the others had gone home, Bert whistling on his bike, Jack an unsteady shambles, Pete and Rose side by side, not touching but exchanging obvious glances, we would take a last walk across the farm before she had to leave. We wandered wrapped in arms and each gateway was a kissing stop, the place for a hungry, hugging hors d'oeuvre after the starving hours of being so close and yet unable to touch for more than a moment. Most times I opened the gates and we squeezed through; but sometimes she turned in my arms to search for the latch, her body squirming, her lips still clinging and her tongue darting with impatience. And our steps quickened into the far meadow where the cows were lazy lumps in the gloom, turning slowly chewing faces towards us, recognising us and returning to their ruminations.

We would make for the bank above the stream, always the farthest point in our walk, where an oak tree clawed deep and the tip of a gnarled toe sprouted from the soil and dragged at the busy water. We always went to the same spot with silent consent, pressing close together against the strong trunk with the feeling of joining an old friend who shared our secrets. And then the caresses and the unspoken promises of the walk, the preliminaries which only intensified our hunger, drew us down to the soft turf and she was buoyant and yielding, for a moment full-lipped and then fierce-toothed, savage and then sighing as we were lost together in the clinging darkness. Without speaking we knew that we wanted to stay with each other for ever. When we did speak, of parting only until the next evening, the thought of it was unbearable. Yet even in those whispering moments I never managed to mention marriage and then it was too late again in the helter-skelter dash back across the dark and stumbling meadows.

But Pete's direct question in the cowshed was like a dollop of water on the seed. The idea of actually getting married started to grow and assume great importance in my mind. I found myself marshalling all the reasons as to why I should get married now, instead of listing all the obstacles in the way as excuses for my funk.

The hay and corn were harvested and secure in the towering ricks. The hops had been picked and the chattering, squabbling pickers had been paid off and departed with their broken-down prams and ragged-arsed children, leaving the trim green hop garden a Passchendaele of lolling poles, broken bins and tangled bines. That sight alone was daunting enough. But I found I could shrug each time I saw it and tell myself that we had the whole winter ahead to tackle it. Besides, the smell of the dried and pressed hops clung like a halo round the oast house, to remind me that the first cheque from the factors had already arrived. I had gone hot-foot to the bank with it, like a runner with a forked stick, to pay it in and claw the creeping overdraft back towards the black.

The cows were all in calf. Now they were almost dry and the scant strippings from each udder meant that milking was soon done. Pete and Bert could easily manage on their own, if I happened to be away for a few days honeymooning. But in a couple of months we should be floundering in the full flood of winter milk, with the cows in the shed at night, needing indoor feeding and mucking out in the morning. And in November, too, Skinny and Fatso were due with their third litters and there was all the racing and chasing that that would involve. So, if I really was going to get married it was a case of now, or goodness knows when.

So I thought it wise to have a word or two with Mother by way of a start. After all, I would be carting a bride over the threshold to share her kitchen, which was not the easiest of ways to foster harmony among in-laws. When Mother had thrown in her lot with me and decided to come to Maywood, she'd said it would only be until I got married one fine day. But we'd been at the farm long enough for her to feel thoroughly at home, with all her furniture and knick-knacks around her, time for her to have put down some roots—something she always insisted she was engaged upon during her busy bicycle trips. And when I began to think deeply about it I realised I'd been too busy considering all the problems on the farm and had taken the domestic arrangements for granted. And the last thing I wanted to do was to upset Mother's way of life. Yet she and Jean got on fine together. There wouldn't be any difficulty. All the same, it was something I hadn't thought about and it had to be sorted out.

It was late one night when I decided to tackle Mother about it. Now I was determined to get married I couldn't wait any longer to sound her out and I was rehearsing what I would say as I walked towards the house. Jean had left half an hour before. All evening I'd been bursting to ask her. Once she'd asked me what was on my mind. 'A penny for your thoughts', she'd said, but I'd just shrugged and replied darkly that they were worth far more than that. And even when she had increased her offer by kissing stages to a million pounds, I never put into so many words that I wanted to marry her. Somehow I felt Mother had the right to know first.

After I'd waved Jean on her way up the dark lane, it seemed a good idea to take a walk around the stock to collect my thoughts. The moon was high and I smiled to myself as I looked up at it, remembering how Jean had laughed when I'd called it the Parish Lantern because she'd never heard that name for it before. Now it was brighter than ever as I sauntered up the lane, and when I walked in amongst the sheep they were like ghosts floating in a nest of mist with their hot breath drifting above them. They paused in their chewing to watch me and I counted them by habit, halfway through before I realised what I was doing and the mounting numbers took over from my thoughts.

Back in the farmyard I called on Skinny and Fatso. Now that they were again free of their demanding litters, they liked to keep each other company by sharing the same sty at night. They were like a couple of black logs in a sea of straw and I talked to them softly as I leant over the wall. Skinny was alert in a moment, propping herself up on her front legs, glaring up at me and wanting to know why the devil I'd disturbed her at this time of night. Obviously it was no good trying to have a quiet word with her. Fatso would be much more understanding. She'd just shuffled comfortably and grunted deeply at the sound of my voice. So I picked up the flat stick that always leant against the wall and started to scratch her back with long sweeping strokes. She began to roll over on to her side.

'I'm thinking of getting married,' I informed her.

She squeaked with pleasure and wriggled farther over so that the stick could scratch her belly.

'Will you marry me?' I asked aloud. It sounded much too formal.

'How about getting married?' No, that was too off-hand.

'*Say* you'll marry me!' Too dramatic.

'Let's get married!' Ah, that sounded better.

Each time I spoke Fatso answered with a contented grunt. She'd agree to anything to have her tits rubbed.

The light from the kitchen window seemed dim as I walked towards it. Surely Mother hadn't gone to bed already and turned the Aladdin down low? She was a night owl, never in bed before midnight and I'd been quite sure she'd still be up so that I could talk to her quietly of my plans before she went to bed. But as I reached the door there was a strong smell of paraffin fumes. When I opened it, a black cloud wafted slowly out into the night.

Mother was sitting at the table, engrossed in a book open in front of her, pushed close beneath the shining bowl of the lamp. Or had she dozed off? But the bright mantle was charred with black, yellow flames were licking from the top of it and billowing in quiet blackness from the lamp glass.

'Good grief!' I called, 'look at the lamp!'

She looked up and smiled. 'Hello, darling.'

'Can't you see the lamp's smoking?' I was leaning over the table turning down the wick.

'Dearie me, so it is. I *thought* it was getting rather dark in here.'

'You were asleep,' I accused her.

'Rubbish. Of course I wasn't!' She took off her glasses and gazed up at the beams, watched the dark cloud being sucked out of the door and saw the missed cobwebs now clearly visible, fluttering like black lace. She clasped her hand to the side of her face. 'Oh, I *am* vexed,' she moaned. 'Now it'll all have to be spring cleaned again. Oh, bother these old lamps.'

I'd lit another lamp and as the new light pierced the gloom I could see that everything was edged in mourning. From the saucepans along the shelf to the washing up bowl in the sink, from the shining copper preserving pan over the kitchener to the plates lining the dresser, a greasy black film smeared wherever it was touched. It had happened before and was enough to make you weep black tears.

'Oh, not again,' I sighed, 'I wonder just when they'll get around to bringing the electricity this way.'

Mother scraped her chair back and Sadie stretched from her

basket with a loud yawn. Even her golden coat was flecked with black and she looked up sleepily, slowly stretching and swishing her tail as she expected to be turned out for piddle time. I looked at Mother's white hair and I could see black specks there too. There was already a black smudge on her cheek where her hand had rubbed a smut against it.

'Oh well,' she said, with resignation, 'it's no good crying over spilt milk. It'll just have to be cleaned up, that's all. As old Checky says: "These things be sent to try us".' Then she added with a laugh: 'Only I wish it was spilt milk. That's so much easier to clean than this horrid stuff.'

So bang went my plans of a cosy chat about getting married. And during the next two hours the opportune moment didn't seem to present itself as we swept and sloshed and scrubbed until the job was done and we were both as black as chimney sweeps.

It was after breakfast the following morning that I finally tackled her. She was preparing to go out, standing in front of her mirror, holding her hat with both hands behind her head, endeavouring to capture as many strands of hair as possible under it as she brought it forward and jammed it firmly in position.

'And what model is Modom wearing today, may I ask?'

It was an old joke and Mother gave a little laugh as she tucked away at the waving wisps to bury them under her hat. 'Our old friend, the Breton Sailor,' she replied.

She was fond of her hats and had gathered a collection that had become firm family favourite over the years. The Breton Sailor was a blue felt job with a wide brim turned up all round. It had been bought before the war in a dash to the sales, a bargain from the Army and Navy which she'd carried home in triumph, laughing as she told us that the sales assistant had opined: 'Modom looks very jolly in it'. It was designed to be worn on the back of the head and for a while Mother had dared to wear it that way, while her wild white hair clawed like breaking waves round the brim. But gradually she pulled it farther forward, and when we objected, telling her how becoming she looked before, she declared that it never felt safe on the back of her head and anyway, how could she tuck up her hair properly to keep it from her eyes?

The Breton Sailor had come into its own again since we'd been at Maywood. It was eminently suitable for the country because it was as waterproof as a sou'wester and therefore ideal if she was caught out in the rain with maybe a long mile to the nearest

251

shelter. The rain pattered off the crown and gathered in the wide brim, where it swirled round like water in a gutter. Every so often Mother would shake her head, in a habit that she had, and empty the hat as though sluicing out a basin.

As I watched her in front of the mirror, tucking in the stray ends of hair and settling the hat comfortably on her head, while I waited until I had all her attention, I smiled as I remembered the christening of the Breton Sailor. I was fourteen and we were caught in a summer shower on a visit to London, hurrying along Whitehall, racing a bus to a stop as the rain beat down, darkening the fluffy blue felt of the Breton Sailor and gathering in the brim. We climbed into the shelter of the bus with sighs of relief and Mother made her way forward to a spare seat near the front while I found one farther back. And as soon as she sat down, she tossed her head back and sent a cold cascade on to the tightly packed belly and thighs of a portly man in the seat behind. I shall always admire the self control of that unknown gentleman as he pulled a large handkerchief with a flourish from his breast pocket, and dabbed himself thoughtfully without a single murmur of protest. Mother was rummaging in her handbag for the fare, blissfully unaware of the cold shower she'd just administered. And afterwards, when I blurted out what had happened, she laughed and jabbed me with her elbow. 'Such rubbish! You're telling me one of your stories again.' But she believed me in the end when she saw how the next shower of rain collected in the hat and sloshed out at the first nod of her head. 'Oh, I say! How awful! What must that poor man have thought?'

She finished adjusting the hat and banged her hands against her sides. 'Now my bag. Where's my bag? Have you seen it? It must be somewhere.'

'Before you go I've got something to tell you.' I had started at last.

'Yes, darling?' She was still searching the room. 'I must have left it in the kitchen.'

'I'm thinking of getting married.'

She stopped and turned to face me, her cheeks glowing and the unruly white hairs already creeping out from under the hat. She just said: 'Oh.'

'You don't seem very pleased about it.' Now I was feeling belligerent because she'd reacted in just the way I had feared. Mother couldn't hide her feelings, and joy and sadness flowed over her face like sunshine and shadows crossing a field. I knew it wasn't that she disliked Jean. It was just the stabbing thought of losing part of a son to her.

In a moment the cloud had gone and she was hurrying towards me. 'Of course I'm pleased for you! If you're sure you're doing the right thing, then I'm happy. I only want the best for you.' She flung her arms around me and kissed me.

'It won't make any difference to you,' I said, quickly. 'Actually you'll be much freer. You'll be able to pop off and visit everybody whenever you want to without having to worry about me. That'll be a relief for you because I know I'm an awkward cuss and it has been hard going for you sometimes in this old place.'

She patted me on the shoulder. 'But I love looking after you. And it's such fun here with all the animals and everything.' There were tears glistening in her eyes.

'This'll still be your home. You and Jean get on fine. I'm sure we'll all manage okay.'

'Gracious me, yes!' She was smiling again and gave me a playful push. 'I just hope Jean can put up with funny old me. What does she think about that, I wonder?'

'You know she thinks the world of you. But I haven't asked her yet.'

'Not asked her to marry you?'

'Not yet.'

She laughed: 'She may turn you down, my son.'

'I wonder. D'you really think she will?'

But she just gave her gay little laugh and hurried from the room.

Now I couldn't wait to see Jean again. It would be today, tonight and all day tomorrow before she came again. I had to find her now. I knew more or less where she was working and it was only an hour's cycle ride away.

Half an hour later I had changed my clothes and was leaning my bike against the cowshed wall. I had to find Pete and Bert to let them know I wouldn't be around for a while.

I walked through the cowshed and looked out across the yard. They were busy with Colonel, backing him into the cart, getting ready to shift dung out to the hop garden.

As I didn't want to get my shoes dirty, I called across from the doorway: 'I'm just going out. Shan't be long. I'll be back after dinner. You be okay?'

They looked round. Pete scratched his head through his beret. 'Suppose so.'

I turned away out of sight. No point in getting involved in explanations. And I knew just what they would be saying.

'What's 'e got 'is best suit on for?' Bert would be asking.

Pete would shrug. 'Buggered if I know. It ain't market day today.'

'P'raps 'ees orf courtin',' Bert would snigger.

'Not in the daytime, yer silly sod.' Pete would spit and turn to the horse. 'Whoa there, Colonel, let's get on with it then. Us'll find out from him when 'e gets back after dinner, I dare say.'

And Colonel would blow down his nostrils and rattle his bit, as though he knew all about it but wasn't saying.

As I prepared to mount my bike, Skinny and Fatso strolled into the stack-plat. They looked at me for a moment, grunted and started rooting beneath the corn stack, just in case there was anything worth finding. The cows were in the meadow opposite, pausing in their grazing and staring when they spotted me. And Lotty walked up to the gate and looked over it with her surprised expression. She bellowed after me as I rode off up the lane.